London Bus & Allocati

2014

PAUL JORDAN & PAUL SMITH

Metroline Bus No.**VW1391** stopping outside of **Alperton Bus Garage** (AN) on November 2nd, 2013 with the No.245 service to Golders Green.

NOSTALGIA ROAD

THIS BOOK IS DEDICATED TO
HEATHER WALKER-JORDAN

Arriva London No.**ENL9** departing from **Croydon Bus Garage** (TC) on September 21st, 2013 to join Route No.312 to Norwood Junction

First published by Crécy Publishing 2014

© Paul Jordan & Paul Smith 2014

A CIP record for this book is available from the British Library

ISBN 9781908347220

Printed in Malta by Melita Press

Crécy Publishing Limited
1a Ringway Trading Estate
Shadowmoss Road
Manchester M22 5LH

www.crecy.co.uk

Front Cover: Go-Ahead London No.**WVL25** outside **Putney Bus Garage** (AF) on August 31st, 2013.

Back Cover Top: Metroline No.**VW1562** outside of **Uxbridge Garage** (UX) on July 20th, 2013.

Back Cover Bottom Left: London United No.**DE36** at **Shepherds Bush Bus Garage** (S) on August 17th, 2013.

Back Cover Bottom Right: Stagecoach London Routemaster No.**RM1941** at **West Ham Garage** (WH) on September 7th, 2013.

CONTENTS

LIST OF GARAGES
IN ALPHABETICAL ORDER

INTRODUCTION

Arriva London's **Brixton Depot** (BN) on September 21st, 2013

This volume is specifically dedicated to those 76 garages that supplied buses for Transport for London routes as at January 1st, 2014 and the information includes a photograph of the depot, location map, address with postcode, operator, nearest station and some of the bus routes that either pass it or are reasonably adjacent.

There are also NG and OS co-ordinates as well as a list of the routes that are supplied by the garage. In all instances we have endeavoured to be as up to date and accurate as we are able, and none more so than in the allocation lists for each garage. These are correct to December 24th, 2013 and any last minute amendments or new buses supplied following this date and prior to going to press may be found on Page 112.

Commencing on Page 107 is a short section dealing with the four bus garages that currently are not supplying buses to routes but are active in maintenance or storing vehicles. Also, although technically not within our remit, the three garages that maintain and supply the tour buses are covered.

All the garages were visited between June and November 2013 and all the photographs were taken by Paul Jordan. With the exception of Orpington (MB) and Croydon (C) where advantage was taken of open days, the photographs were taken from public places.

Needless to say, using this book does not give any authority to enter any of the establishments and permission to do so must be sought from the appropriate bus operator.

One of the striking things we found was the disparity between different locations; from the classic pre-war garages such as Bow and Camberwell to the portacabin and yard-style of Waterside Way and Kings Cross - all vastly different but having the same objective; keeping London's bus fleet fully operational and able to meet the needs of its citizens. We hope that you find this book useful.

Paul Jordan, **Walsall** and Paul Smith, Kings Heath, **Birmingham** 2014

The Bridgewater Road entrance to **Alperton Bus Garage** on November 2nd, 2013 with Metroline No. **VW1397** pausing on the 245 Route. The exit from the depot is on Ealing Road.

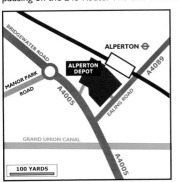

ALPERTON (ON)

Ealing Road, Alperton, Wembley, Middlesex HA0 4EL
Operated by: Metroline
Location: TQ17988375 [51.540372, -0.300206]
Nearest Tube Station: Alperton (100 yards)
Nearest Bus Routes: 245 & 487 - Alperton, Alperton (Stop C)
Bus Routes Serviced: 83/223/224/245 & 487

The garage was built by the London Passenger Transport Board and opened in June 1939. It was one of three depots built by the LPTB and the only modern-day survivor. The garage was extended on the north west side during the period 1976 to 1978 when part of a London Transport railway site was taken over.

VEHICLE ALLOCATION

DE1612	YX58 DWM	DE1966	YX12 DKO	VW1368	LK62 DLO	VW1752	LK59 CWN	VW1768	LK59 CXF
DE1613	YX58 DWN	DE1967	YX12 DKU	VW1369	LK62 DLV	VW1753	LK59 CWO	VW1769	LK59 CXG
DE1614	YX58 DWO	DE1968	YX12 DKV	VW1370	LK62 DLX	VW1754	LK59 CWP	VW1770	LK59 CXH
DE1615	YX58 DWP	DE1969	YX12 DKY	VW1371	LK62 DMV	VW1755	LK59 CWR	VW1771	LK59 CXJ
DE1616	YX58 DWU	DEM1912	YX61 EKR	VW1372	LK62 DND	VW1756	LK59 CWT	VW1772	LK59 CXL
DE1617	YX58 DWV	DEM1913	YX61 EKT	VW1373	LK62 DNE	VW1757	LK59 CWU	VW1773	LK59 CXM
DE1618	YX58 DWY	DEM1914	YX61 EKU	VW1374	LK62 DNU	VW1758	LK59 CWV	VW1774	LK59 CXN
DE1619	YX58 DWZ	DEM1915	YX61 EKV	VW1375	LK62 DNO	VW1759	LK59 CWW	VW1775	LK59 CXO
DE1958	YX12 DKA	DEM1916	YX61 EKW	VW1376	LK62 DNX	VW1760	LK59 CWX	VW1776	LK59 CXP
DE1959	YX12 DKD	DEM1917	YX61 EKY	VW1377	LK62 DOH	VW1761	LK59 CWY	VW1777	LK59 FCO
DE1960	YX12 DKE	DEM1918	YX61 EKZ	VW1389	LK62 DTZ	VW1762	LK59 CWZ	VW1778	LK59 FCP
DE1961	YX12 DKF	VW1249	LK12 ABX	VW1390	LK62 DUA	VW1763	LK59 CXA	VW1779	LK59 FCU
DE1962	YX12 DKJ	VW1251	LK12 ACO	VW1391	LK62 DUH	VW1764	LK59 CXB	VW1780	LK59 FCV
DE1963	YX12 DKK	VW1365	LK62 DKN	VW1392	LK62 DUJ	VW1765	LK59 CXC	VW1781	LK59 FCX
DE1964	YX12 DKL	VW1366	LK62 DKV	VW1393	LK62 DUU	VW1766	LK59 CXD	VW1782	LK59 FCY
DE1965	YX12 DKN	VW1367	LK62 DLJ	VW1394	LK62 DVB	VW1767	LK59 CXE	VW1841	BK10 MFO

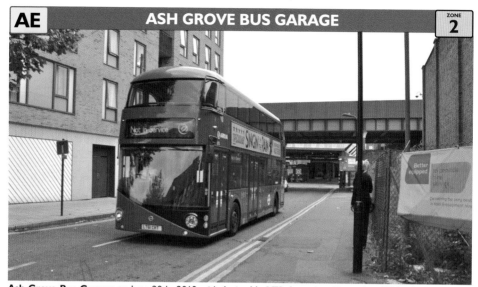

Ash Grove Bus Garage on June 20th, 2013 with Arriva No.**LT3** departing. Opened in 1991 it had spaces for some 140 buses under cover and another 30 in the yard. The roof is supported by ten triangular trusses on reinforced concrete columns.

ASH GROVE (AE)
Mare Street, South Hackney, London E8 4RH
Operated by: Arriva London
Location: TQ34718363 [51.536072, -0.059181]
Nearest Station: Cambridge Heath (0.3 miles)
Nearest Bus Routes: 26/48/55/106/254/D6/N26/ N55 & N253 - St Josephs Hospice (Stop LH)
Bus Routes Serviced: 38/78/106/168 & 254

For historical notes regarding this depot see Page 7.

NB This depot is also used by CT Plus and is coded as HK Ash Grove (See Page 7)

VEHICLE ALLOCATION

DW516	LJ13 CCX	LT3	LT61 CHT	T 80	LJ59 ABZ	VLW131	LJ03 MHA	VLW151	LJ03 MBY
DW517	LJ13 CCY	LT4	LT12 DHT	T 81	LJ59 ACF	VLW132	LJ03 MHE	VLW152	LJ03 MDE
DW518	LJ13 CCZ	LT5	LT12 EHT	T 82	LJ59 ACO	VLW133	LJ03 MHF	VLW153	LJ03 MDF
DW519	LJ13 CLZ	LT6	LT12 FHT	T 83	LJ59 AAE	VLW134	LJ03 MHK	VLW154	LJ03 MDK
DW520	LJ13 CME	LT7	LT12 GHT	T169	LJ60 AUU	VLW135	LJ03 MHL	VLW155	LJ03 MDN
DW521	LJ13 CMF	LT8	LT12 HHT	T170	LJ60 AUV	VLW136	LJ03 MHM	VLW156	LJ03 MDU
DW522	LJ13 CMK	T 66	LJ59 ACY	T171	LJ60 AUW	VLW137	LJ03 MHN	VLW157	LJ03 MPX
DW523	LJ13 CDE	T 67	LJ59 ACZ	T172	LJ60 AUX	VLW138	LJ03 MFN	VLW158	LJ03 MPY
DW524	LJ13 CDF	T 68	LJ59 ADO	T173	LJ60 AUY	VLW139	LJ03 MFP	VLW159	LJ03 MPZ
DW525	LJ13 CDK	T 69	LJ59 ADV	T174	LJ60 AVB	VLW140	LJ03 MFU	VLW160	LJ03 MRU
DW526	LJ13 CDN	T 70	70 CLT	T175	LJ60 ATZ	VLW141	LJ03 MFV	VLW161	LJ03 MRV
DW527	LJ13 CDO	T 71	LJ59 ADZ	T176	LJ60 AUA	VLW142	LJ03 MEV	VLW162	LJ03 MRX
DW528	LJ13 CDU	T 72	LJ59 AEA	T177	LJ60 AUC	VLW143	LJ03 MFA	VLW163	LJ03 MRY
DW529	LJ13 CKU	T 73	LJ59 ABF	T178	LJ60 AUE	VLW144	LJ03 MFE	VLW165	LJ03 MSU
DW530	LJ13 CKV	T 74	LJ59 ABK	T179	LJ60 AUF	VLW145	LJ03 MFF	VLW166	LJ03 MSV
DW531	LJ13 CKX	T 75	LJ59 ABN	VLW126	LF52 UPA	VLW146	LJ03 MFK	VLW167	LJ03 MSX
DW532	LJ13 CKY	T 76	LJ59 ABO	VLW127	LF52 UPB	VLW147	LJ03 MBF	VLW168	LJ03 MMU
DW533	LJ13 CLF	T 77	LJ59 ABU	VLW128	LF52 UPC	VLW148	LJ03 MBU	VLW169	LJ03 MMV
LT1	LT61 AHT	T 78	LJ59 ABV	VLW129	LG52 DAA	VLW149	LJ03 MBV		LJ03 MMX
LT2	LT61 BHT	T 79	LJ59 ABX	VLW130	LJ03 MGZ	VLW150	LJ03 MBX		

ASH GROVE BUS GARAGE

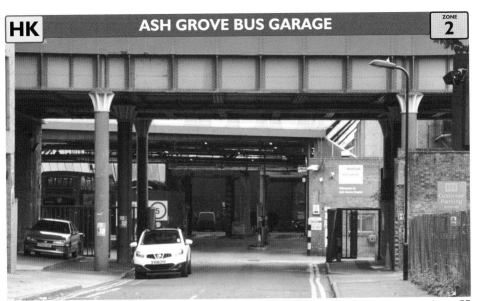

Ash Grove Bus Garage on June 20th, 2013. The piers in the foreground straddling the entrance carry the ex-GE Hackney Fields to London Liverpool Street line. Visible through the bridge is the entrance to the depot.

NB This depot is also used by Arriva London and is coded as AE Ash Grove (See Page 6)

ASH GROVE (HK)
Mare Street, South Hackney, London E8 4RH
Operated by: CT Plus
Location: TQ34718363 [51.536072, -0.059181]
Nearest Station: Cambridge Heath (0.3 miles)
Nearest Bus Routes: 26/48/55/106/254/D6/N26/
N55/N253 - St Josephs Hospice (Stop LH)
Bus Routes Serviced: 153/212/309/385/388/394/
675/W5/W12 & W13

Ash Grove was opened by London Buses in 1991 and, following the split of the company into eleven separate entities, was used by London Forest until it was wound up in 1991.

The depot was re-opened in 1994 by Kentish Bus, but this itself became defunct in 1997 and Ash Grove was not re-opened again until 2000 when East Thames Buses took it over. On October 13th, 2005 the company moved out to Mandela Way (See Page 57) but was subsequently replaced by CT Plus, part of the HCT Group, supporting community transport.

VEHICLE ALLOCATION

DA 2	YX62 DHC	DCS5	HX03 MGV	HTL 2	LR52 LTN	OS 3	YJ59 NRO	OS22	YJ12 GVU
DA 3	YX62 DHD	DCS6	HX03 MGU	HTL 3	LR52 LTJ	OS 4	YJ10 EYF	OS23	YJ12 GVV
DA 4	YX62 DHY	DCS7	HX03 MGJ	HTL 4	LR52 LTF	OS 5	YJ10 EYG	OS24	YJ12 GVW
DA 5	YX62 DKD	DCS8	HX03 MGY	HTL 5	LR52 LWE	OS 6	YJ10 EYH	OS25	YJ12 GVX
DA 6	YX62 DKE	DCS9	HX03 MGZ	HTL 6	LR52 LTK	OS 7	YJ10 EYG	OS26	YJ12 GVY
DA 7	YX62 DKL	DE1	PN07 KPY	HTL 7	LR52 LWF	OS 8	YJ10 EYL	OS27	YJ12 GVZ
DA 8	YX62 DMU	DE2	PN07 KPZ	HTL 8	LR52 LWH	OS 9	YJ60 PFA	SD 1	YR59 NPA
DA 9	YX62 DPF	DE3	PN07 KRD	HTL 9	LR52 LWJ	OS10	YJ60 PFD	SD 2	YR59 NPC
DA10	YX62 DSZ	DE4	PN07 KRE	HTL10	PF52 TFX	OS11	YJ60 PFE	SD 3	YR59 NPD
DA11	YX62 DTV	DE5	PN07 KRF	HTL11	PF52 TGZ	OS12	YJ60 PFF	SD 4	YR59 NPF
DA12	YX62 DTY	DE6	PN07 KRG	HTL12	LR52 LYC	OS13	YJ60 PFG	SD 5	YR59 NPG
DAS1	SN57 DWE	DP1	SN53 EUD	HTL13	LR52 LYJ	OS14	YJ60 PFK	SD 6	YR59 NPJ
DAS2	SN57 DWF	DPS2	BU05 HFG	HTP3	PN03 UMB	OS15	YJ60 PFN	SD 7	YR59 NPN
DCS1	E8 NJB	DPS4	BX54 DLK	HTP4	PN03 UMK	OS16	YJ60 PFO	SD 8	YR59 NPE
DCS2	KV03 ZFF	EO1	PN08 SWJ	HTP5	LR52 KWG	OS19	YJ61 MKA	SD 9	YR59 NPK
DCS3	KV03 ZFG	HEA1	SN62 DND	HTP6	PN03 ULY	OS20	YJ12 GVR	SD10	YR59 NPO
DCS4	KV03 ZFH	HTL 1	LR52 LTO	OS 2	YJ59 NRN	OS21	YJ12 GVT		

Atlas Road Bus Garage on June 22nd, 2013. It was opened on October 1st, 2011 when part of Westbourne Park Depot (See Page 100) was closed to accommodate construction work on the Crossrail project.

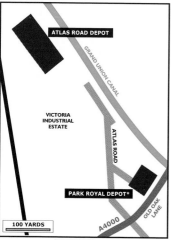

*SEE PAGE 69

ATLAS ROAD (AS)
Atlas Road, Harlesden, London NW10 6DN
Operated by: Tower Transit
Location: TQ21418261 [51.531674, -0.254199]
Nearest Station: Willesden Junction (0.5 miles)
Nearest Bus Routes: 228 & 266 - Old Oak Common, Old Oak Common Lane (Stop J)
Bus Routes Serviced: 28/31/266/328/N28 & N31

The notice at the entrance to **Atlas Road Bus Garage** on June 22nd, 2013, some time after Tower Transit had taken it over from First!

VEHICLE ALLOCATION

TN33197	LT52 XAH	VN37976	BN61 MYA	VNW32375	LK04 HZE	VNW32398	LK54 FNP	VNW32421	LK04 JCX
TN33198	LT52 XAJ	VN37977	BN61 MYB	VNW32376	LK04 HZF	VNW32399	LK04 HXH	VNW32422	LK04 HYZ
TN33199	LT52 XAK	VN37978	BG61 SXJ	VNW32377	LK04 HZG	VNW32400	LK04 HXJ	VNW32423	LK04 JCZ
VN36291	BX12 CVO	VN37979	BG61 SXM	VNW32378	LK04 HZH	VNW32401	LK04 HXL	VNW32424	LK04 HYB
VN36292	BX12 CVM	VN37980	BG61 SXL	VNW32379	LK04 HZJ	VNW32402	LK04 HXM	VNW32425	LK04 HYC
VN36293	BX12 CVK	VN37981	BG61 SXN	VNW32380	LK04 HZL	VNW32403	LK04 HXN	VNW32426	LK04 HYF
VN36294	BX12 CVL	VN37982	BG61 SXO	VNW32381	LK04 HZM	VNW32404	LK04 HXP	VNW32427	LK04 HYG
VN36295	BX12 CVP	VN37983	BG61 SXP	VNW32382	LK04 HZN	VNW32405	LK04 HXR	VNW32428	LK04 HYH
VN37960	BN61 MXG	VN37984	BG61 SXR	VNW32383	LK04 JBU	VNW32406	LK04 HXS	VNW32429	LK04 HYJ
VN37962	BN61 MXK	VNW32361	LK04 HYN	VNW32384	LK04 HZS	VNW32407	LK04 HXT	VNW32430	LK04 HYL
VN37963	BN61 MXJ	VNW32362	LK04 HYM	VNW32385	LK04 HZT	VNW32408	LK04 HXU	VNZ32495	LK54 FLA
VN37964	BN61 MXP	VNW32363	LK04 HYW	VNW32386	LK04 HZU	VNW32409	LK04 HXV	VNZ32496	LK54 FLB
VN37965	BN61 MXM	VNW32364	LK04 HYT	VNW32387	LK04 HZV	VNW32410	LK04 HXW	VNZ32497	LK54 FLC
VN37966	BN61 MXO	VNW32365	LK04 HYX	VNW32388	LK04 HZW	VNW32411	LK04 HXX	VNZ32498	LK54 FLD
VN37967	BN61 MXR	VNW32366	LK04 HYY	VNW32389	LK04 HZX	VNW32412	LK04 JBE	VNZ32499	LK54 FLE
VN37968	BN61 MXS	VNW32367	LK04 HYA	VNW32390	LK04 HZY	VNW32413	LK04 HZP	VNZ32500	LK54 FLF
VN37969	BN61 MXT	VNW32368	LK04 HYS	VNW32391	LK04 HZZ	VNW32414	LK04 JBV	VNZ32501	LK54 FLG
VN37970	BN61 MXU	VNW32369	LK04 HYU	VNW32392	LK04 HXA	VNW32415	LK04 JBX	VNZ32502	LK54 FLH
VN37971	BN61 MXY	VNW32370	LK04 HYV	VNW32393	LK04 HXB	VNW32416	LK04 JBY	WN35001	LK58 EDO
VN37972	BN61 MXX	VNW32371	LK04 HZA	VNW32394	LK04 HXC	VNW32417	LK04 JBZ	WN35002	LK58 EDP
VN37973	BN61 MXW	VNW32372	LK04 HZB	VNW32395	LK04 HXD	VNW32418	LK04 JCJ	WN35003	LK58 EDR
VN37974	BN61 MXV	VNW32373	LK04 HZC	VNW32396	LK04 HXE	VNW32419	LK04 JCU	WN35004	LK09 CZS
VN37975	BG61 SYK	VNW32374	LK04 HZD	VNW32397	LK54 FNO	VNW32420	LK04 JCV		

The entrance to **Barking Bus Garage** on September 18th, 2013, with Arriva London No.**ENL49** standing in the access road.

The depot was opened by Grey-Green in 1992 and consists simply of a main yard and a few ancillary buildings within Ripple Road Industrial Area. Grey-Green was subsumed into the Cowie Group in the mid-1990s and, subsequently, Arriva London.

BARKING (DX)
Ripple Road, Barking IG11 0SL
Operated by: Arriva London
Location: TQ46678358 [51.532288, 0.113521]
Nearest Tube Station: Upney (1.3 miles)
Nearest Bus Routes: 173/287/673 & 687 - Lodge Avenue (Stop P)
Bus Routes Serviced: 128/135/150/173/325/647 & 678

Arriva London No.**ENL74** changing crews outside of **Barking Bus Garage** on September 18th, 2013.

VEHICLE ALLOCATION

ENL49	LJ10 CSF	ENL65	LJ60 AYH	T 18	LJ08 CVO	T187	LJ60 ATF	VLA132	LJ05 GPX
ENL50	LJ10 CSO	ENL66	LJ60 AYK	T 19	519 CLT	T188	LJ60 ATK	VLA133	LJ05 GPY
ENL51	LJ10 CSU	ENL67	LJ60 AYL	T 20	LJ08 CVR	T189	LJ60 ATN	VLA134	LJ05 GPZ
ENL52	LJ59 LVL	ENL68	LJ60 AYM	T 21	LJ08 CUU	T190	LJ60 ATO	VLA135	LJ05 GRF
ENL53	LJ59 LVM	ENL69	LJ60 AYN	T 22	LJ08 CUV	T191	LJ60 ATU	VLA136	LJ05 GRK
ENL54	LJ59 LVN	ENL70	LJ60 AYO	T 23	LJ08 CUW	T192	LJ60 ATV	VLA137	LJ05 GRU
ENL55	LJ10 CSV	ENL71	LJ60 AYP	T 24	324 CLT	T193	LJ60 ATX	VLA138	LJ05 GRX
ENL56	LJ10 CSX	ENL72	LJ60 AYS	T 25	LJ08 CUY	VLA103	LJ54 BCV	VLA139	LJ05 GRZ
ENL57	LJ10 CSY	ENL73	LJ60 AXV	T 26	LJ08 CVA	VLA124	LJ05 BJE	VLA140	LJ05 GSO
ENL58	LJ10 CSZ	ENL74	LJ60 AXW	T180	LJ60 AUH	VLA125	LJ05 BJF	VLA141	LJ05 GSU
ENL59	LJ10 CTE	T 12	LJ08 CVG	T181	LJ60 AUK	VLA126	LJ05 BJK	VLA142	LJ55 BTE
ENL60	LJ10 CTF	T 13	LJ08 CVH	T182	LJ60 AUL	VLA127	LJ05 BJO	VLA143	LJ55 BTF
ENL61	LJ10 CTK	T 14	LJ08 CVK	T183	LJ60 AUM	VLA128	LJ05 BJU		
ENL62	LJ60 ATY	T 15	LJ08 CVL	T184	LJ60 AUN	VLA129	LJ05 GLZ		
ENL63	LJ60 AYF	T 16	LJ08 CVM	T185	LJ60 ASX	VLA130	LJ05 GME		
ENL64	LJ60 AYG	T 17	217 CLT	T186	LJ60 ASZ	VLA131	LJ05 GMF		

Barking Bus Garage on September 18th, 2013 with Stagecoach London No.19795 passing on a Route No.145 service to Dagenham.

BARKING (BK)

205 Longbridge Road, Barking IG11 8UE
Operated by: Stagecoach London
Location: TQ45288516 [51.518865, 0.143123]
Nearest Tube Station: Upney (0.7 miles)
Nearest Bus Routes: 5/145/387 & N15 - Barking Bus Garage, Faircross (Stop BC)
Bus Routes Serviced: 5/15/62/101/145/169/366/387/396/687 & N15

When the garage was opened by the London General Omnibus Company in January 1924 the entrance was on the corner of South Park Drive and Longbridge Road. The depot was extended eastwards in 1931 and again more recently when two adjoining dwellings were purchased and demolished to create more parking for vehicles.

Looking northeast towards **Barking Bus Garage** on September 18th, 2013, showing the original entrance on the corner of South Park Road and Longbridge Road, now filled-in and used as offices.

Barking Bus Garage on September 18th, 2013 with Stagecoach London Buses, including Nos **25312**, **17884**, **17888** and **19781**, parked at the east end of the site on the additional space created when the dwellings were demolished.

VEHICLE ALLOCATION

17485	LX51 FMD	17894	LX03 ORG	19772	LX11 BFN	19847	LX12 CZA	36276	LX11 AWO
17526	LX51 FOJ	17895	LX03 ORH	19773	LX11 BFO	19848	LX12 CZB	36277	LX11 AWP
17581	LV52 HFO	17896	LX03 ORJ	19774	LX11 BFP	19849	LX12 CZC	36278	LX11 AWR
17582	LV52 HFP	17897	LX03 ORK	19775	LX11 BFU	19850	LX12 CZD	36279	LX11 AWU
17583	LV52 HFR	17898	LX03 ORN	19776	LX11 BFV	19851	LX12 CZE	36280	LX11 AWV
17585	LV52 HFT	17899	LX03 ORP	19777	LX11 BFY	19852	LX12 CZF	36281	LX11 AWW
17587	LV52 HFW	17900	LX03 ORS	19778	LX11 BFZ	19853	LX12 CZG	36282	LX11 AWY
17856	LX03 NEY	17901	LX03 ORT	19779	LX11 BGE	19854	LX12 CZH	36283	LX11 AWZ
17857	LX03 NFA	17902	LX03 ORU	19780	LX11 BGF	19855	LX12 CZJ	36284	LX11 AXA
17858	LX03 NFC	17904	LX03 ORW	19781	LX11 BGK	19856	LX12 CZK	36285	LX11 AXB
17859	LX03 NFD	19756	LX11 BDF	19782	LX11 BGO	19857	LX12 CZL	36286	LX11 AXC
17860	LX03 NFE	19757	LX11 BDO	19783	LX11 BGU	19858	LX12 CZM	36287	LX11 AXD
17861	LX03 NFF	19758	LX11 BDU	19784	LX11 BGV	25301	LX58 CHF	36288	LX11 AXF
17862	LX03 NFG	19759	LX11 BDV	19785	LX11 BGY	25302	LX58 CHG	36289	LX11 AXG
17863	LX03 NFH	19760	LX11 BDY	19794	LX11 BHN	25303	LX58 CHH	36290	LX11 AXH
17878	LX03 NGJ	19761	LX11 BDZ	19795	LX11 BHO	25304	LX58 CHJ	36291	LX11 AXJ
17880	LX03 NGU	19762	LX11 BEJ	19796	LX11 BHP	25305	LX58 CHK	36292	LX11 AXK
17881	LX03 NGV	19763	LX11 BEO	19797	LX11 BHU	25306	LX58 CHL	36293	LX11 AXM
17882	LX03 NGY	19764	LX11 BEU	19798	LX11 BHV	25307	LX58 CHN	36294	LX11 AXN
17883	LX03 NGZ	19765	LX11 BEY	19799	LX11 BHW	25308	LX58 CHO	36295	LX11 AXO
17884	LX03 NHA	19766	LX11 BFA	19800	LX11 BHY	25309	LX58 CHV	36296	LX11 AXP
17885	LX03 OPT	19767	LX11 BFF	19801	LX11 BHZ	25310	LX09 AAE	36297	LX11 AXR
17886	LX03 OPU	19768	LX11 BFJ	19802	LX11 BJE	25311	LX09 AAK	36298	LX11 AXS
17887	LX03 OPV	19769	LX11 BFK	19803	LX11 BJF	25312	LX09 AAJ	36299	LX11 AXT
17888	LX03 OPW	19770	LX11 BFL	19804	LX11 BJJ	25313	LX09 AAF		
17893	LX03 ORF	19771	LX11 BFM	19805	LX11 BJK	25314	LX09 AAN		

The exit from **Battersea Bus Garage** on August 31st, 2013 with Abellio No.2427 awaiting to depart.

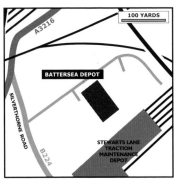

BATTERSEA (QB)
Silverthorne Road, Battersea, London SW8 3HE
Operated by: Abellio
Location: TQ28877644 [51.473148, -0.145334]
Nearest Station: Queenstown Road (0.4 miles)
Nearest Bus Routes: 137/156/452 & N137 -
Battersea, Silverthorne Road (Stop T)
Bus Routes Serviced: 3/156/211/344/414/452/C2/
C3/C10 & N3

Opened on May 17th, 2010 by the Mayor of London, Boris Johnson, Battersea Depot occupies part of the site of the former Longhedge Works which were built by the London Chatham & Dover Railway in 1862 and closed by BR in the mid-50s. Most of the works was demolished in 1957 but part of it still remains at the rear of Stewarts Lane Depot.

Abellio No.9406 leaving **Battersea Bus Garage** along the service road on August 31st, 2013. The depot and offices can be seen on the right.

The entrance to **Battersea Bus Garage**, at the north east end of the site, on August 31st, 2013. Abellio No.9531 is visible in the foreground with the wash plant in view in the centre of the picture.

VEHICLE ALLOCATION

2414	SN61 DGX	8557	YX11 AEF	9467	LJ09 OJZ	9504	LF59 XDZ	9541	SN12 ACY
2415	SN61 DGY	8558	YX11 AEG	9468	LJ09 OKA	9505	SN59 AVR	9542	SN12 ACZ
2416	SN61 DGZ	8559	YX11 AEJ	9469	LJ09 OKB	9506	SN59 AVT	9543	SN12 ADO
2417	SN61 DHA	8560	YX11 AEK	9470	LJ09 OKC	9507	SN59 AVU	9544	SN12 AUO
2418	SN61 CXX	8561	YX11 AEL	9471	LJ09 OKD	9508	SN59 AVV	9545	SN12 AOS
2419	SN61 CXY	8562	YX11 AEM	9472	LJ09 OKE	9509	SN59 AVW	9546	SN12 AOT
2420	SN61 CXZ	8563	YX11 AEN	9473	LJ09 OKF	9510	SN59 AVX	9547	SN12 AOU
2421	SN61 CYA	8564	YX11 AEO	9474	LJ09 OKG	9511	SN59 AVY	9548	SN12 AOV
2422	SN61 CYC	8565	YX11 AEP	9475	LJ09 OKH	9512	SN59 AVZ	9549	SN12 AOW
2423	SN61 CYE	8566	YX11 AET	9476	LJ09 OKK	9513	SN59 AWA	9550	SN12 AOX
2424	SN61 CYF	9401	LJ56 VSZ	9477	LJ09 OKL	9514	SN59 AWC	9551	SN12 AOY
2425	SN61 CYG	9402	LJ56 VTA	9478	LJ09 OKM	9515	SN59 AWF	9552	SN12 AOZ
2426	SN61 CYH	9403	LJ56 VTC	9479	LJ09 OKN	9516	SN59 AWG	9553	SN12 APF
2427	SN61 CYJ	9404	LJ56 VTD	9480	LJ09 OKO	9517	SN59 AWH	9554	SN12 APK
2428	SN61 CYK	9405	LJ56 VTE	9481	LJ09 OKP	9518	SN59 AWJ	9555	SN12 APO
2429	SN61 CYL	9406	LJ56 VTF	9482	LJ09 OKR	9519	SN59 AWM	9556	SN12 APU
2430	SN61 CYO	9407	LJ56 VTG	9483	LJ09 OKS	9520	SN59 AWO	9557	SN12 APV
2431	SN61 CYP	9408	LJ56 VTK	9484	LJ09 OKT	9521	SN59 AWP	9558	SN12 APX
2432	SN61 CYS	9409	LJ56 VTL	9485	LJ09 OKU	9522	SN59 AWR	9751	YN51 KVH
2433	SN61 CYT	9410	LJ56 VTM	9486	LJ09 OKV	9523	SN59 AWU	9757	YN51 KVP
2434	SN61 CYU	9411	LJ56 VTN	9487	LJ09 OKW	9524	SN12 AAV	9759	YN51 KVS
2435	SN61 CYV	9412	LJ56 VTO	9488	LJ09 OKX	9525	SN12 AAX	9812	LG52 HWN
2436	SN61 CYW	9413	LJ56 VTP	9489	LJ09 OKY	9526	SN12 AAY	9813	LG52 ZXB
2437	SN61 CYX	9414	LJ56 VTT	9490	LJ09 OLA	9527	SN12 AAZ	9814	LG52 URZ
2438	SN12 AUE	9415	LJ56 VTU	9491	LJ09 OLB	9528	SN12 ABF	9815	LG52 XWE
2439	SN12 AUF	9416	LJ56 VTV	9492	LJ09 OLC	9529	SN12 ABK	9816	LG52 XYK
2440	SN12 AUH	9417	LJ56 VTW	9493	LJ09 OLE	9530	SN12 ABO	9817	LG52 XYM
2441	SN12 AUJ	9418	LJ07 OPE	9494	LJ09 OLG	9531	SN12 ABU	9818	LG52 XYP
2442	SN12 AUK	9419	LJ56 VTY	9495	LJ09 OLH	9532	SN12 ABV	9819	LG52 XYO
2443	SN12 AUL	9420	LJ07 OPF	9496	LJ09 OLK	9533	SN12 ABX	9820	LG52 XYN
8437	RX51 FGM	9421	LJ07 OPG	9497	LJ09 OLM	9534	SN12 ABZ	9821	LG52 XYY
8440	RX51 FGP	9422	LJ07 OPH	9499	LJ09 OLN	9535	SN12 ACF	9822	LG52 XYZ
8552	YX11 AEA	9423	LJ07 OPK	9499	LJ09 OLO	9536	SN12 ACJ	9823	LG52 XZA
8553	YX11 AEB	9424	LJ56 VUD	9500	LJ09 OLP	9537	SN12 ACO	9824	LG52 XZS
8554	YX11 AEC	9425	LJ07 OPL	9501	LJ09 OLR	9538	SN12 ACU	9825	LG52 XZR
8555	YX11 AED	9426	LJ56 VUF	9502	LJ09 OLT	9539	SN12 ACV	9826	LG52 XYL
8556	YX11 AEE	9427	LJ07 OPM	9503	LJ09 OLU	9540	SN12 ACX	9827	LG52 XZT

Abellio No.**9073** standing outside of **Beddington Bus Garage** on September 21st, 2013.

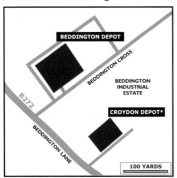

*SEE PAGE 30

BEDDINGTON (BC)
Unit 10, Beddington Cross, Beddington Farm Road, Croydon CR0 4XH
Operated by: Abellio
Location: TQ29826653 [51.383058, -0.135957]
Nearest Tram Station: Therapia Lane (0.5 miles)
Nearest Bus Route: 455 - Beddington, Beddington Cross (Southbound)
Bus Routes Serviced: 152/157/322/407/455/931/ P13 & T33

The west end of **Beddington Bus Garage** on September 21st, 2013. The depot was opened by Connex in 2000.

VEHICLE ALLOCATION

8013	BX54 DLZ	8062	Y38 YVV	8497	KX04 HRF	8527	YX59 BYV	9025	BX55 XLW
8014	BX54 DME	8107	YX58 DTV	8498	KX04 HRG	8528	YX59 BYW	9026	BX55 XLY
8015	BX54 DMF	8108	YX58 DTY	8501	LJ56 ONN	8775	YX61 ELC	9027	BX55 XLZ
8016	BX54 DMO	8109	YX58 DTZ	8502	LJ56 ONO	8776	YX61 ELH	9028	BX55 XMA
8017	BX54 DMU	8434	RX51 FGG	8503	LJ56 ONP	8777	YX12 DLD	9029	BX55 XMB
8018	BX54 DMV	8471	HX04 HTY	8504	LJ56 ONR	8778	YX12 DLE	9030	BX55 XMC
8019	BX54 DMY	8472	HX04 HTZ	8505	LJ56 ONS	8779	YX12 DLF	9031	BX55 XMD
8020	BX54 DMZ	8473	LF06 YRJ	8506	LJ56 ONT	8780	YX12 DLJ	9032	BX55 XME
8024	BU05 HDY	8474	LF06 YRK	8516	YX59 BYJ	8781	YX12 DLK	9033	BX55 XMG
8025	BU05 HEJ	8475	LF06 YRL	8517	YX59 BYK	8782	YX12 DLN	9066	BX55 XNV
8026	BU05 HFA	8476	LF06 YRM	8518	YX59 BYL	8783	YX12 DLO	9067	BX55 XNW
8027	BU05 HFB	8477	LF06 YRN	8519	YX59 BYM	8784	YX12 DLU	9068	BX55 XNY
8028	BU05 HFC	8488	KX03 HZF	8520	YX59 BYN	8785	YX12 DLV	9071	LF06 YRD
8029	BU05 HFD	8491	KX03 HZT	8521	YX59 BYO	8786	YX12 DLY	9072	LF06 YRE
8031	BU05 HFK	8492	KX03 HZV	8522	YX59 BYP	8787	YX12 DLZ	9073	LF06 YRG
8035	BU05 HFV	8493	KX03 HZY	8523	YX59 BYR	9021	BX55 XLS	9739	YN51 KUU
8036	BU05 HFW	8494	KX03 HZZ	8524	YX59 BYS	9022	BX55 XLT		
8037	BU05 HFX	8495	KX04 HRD	8525	YX59 BYT	9023	BX55 XLU		
8044	V304 MDP	8496	KX04 HRE	8526	YX59 BYU	9024	BX55 XLV		

Go-Ahead London No.**VWL13** exiting from the service road between the two sections of **Belvedere Bus Garage** on September 7th, 2013. The vehicle is operating on Route No.180 which terminates at Crabtree Manorway North and turns around in the depot.

BELVEDERE (BV)
Burts Wharf, Crabtree Manor Way, Kent DA17 6LJ
Operated by: Go-Ahead London
Location: TQ50208043 [51.502829, 0.162525]
Nearest Station: Belvedere (1.3 miles)
Nearest Bus Routes: 180 - Crabtree Manorway North (Alighting Stop)
Bus Routes Serviced: 180/244/669 & N1

The garage was purchased by Harris Buses in 1998 and used by that company until it folded in 2000. It was then taken over by East London Buses (an operating name for London Buses) and subsequently sold to Go-Ahead London in October 2009.

The office and amenities block at **Belvedere Bus Garage** on September 7th, 2013.

The **Belvedere Bus Garage** compound on the west side of the service road on September 7th, 2013 with Go-Ahead London single-decker No.**SE61** to the fore.

VEHICLE ALLOCATION

SE55	YX60 DXT	SE62	YX60 EPO	VWL11	LB02 YXJ	VWL18	LF52 TGU	VWL25	LF52 THN
SE56	YX60 FSN	SE63	YX60 FSU	VWL12	LB02 YXK	VWL19	LF52 TGV	VWL26	LF52 THU
SE57	YX60 DXU	SE64	YX60 EPP	VWL13	LB02 YXL	VWL20	LF52 TGX	PVL362	PJ53 SOE
SE58	YX60 FSO	SE65	YX60 EPU	VWL14	LB02 YXM	VWL21	LF52 TGY		
SE59	YX60 FSP	SE66	YX60 EOP	VWL15	LB02 YXN	VWL22	LF52 TGZ		
SE60	YX60 FSS	SE67	YX60 FCZ	VWL16	LF52 TGN	VWL23	LF52 THG		
SE61	YX60 DXW	SE68	YX60 FDA	VWL17	LF52 TGO	VWL24	LF52 THK		

BX | BEXLEYHEATH BUS GARAGE | ZONE 6

Bexleyheath Bus Garage on September 7th, 2013 with Go-Ahead London Nos **WVL365** & **SE73** parked on the forecourt.

PELHAM ROAD

LONG LANE

BEXLEYHEATH DEPOT

ERITH ROAD A220

MAYPLACE ROAD EAST

A221

100 YARDS

BEXLEYHEATH (BX)
Erith Road, Bexleyheath, Kent DA7 6BX
Operated by: Go-Ahead London
Location: TQ49727566 [51.460206, 0.153714]
Nearest Station: Barnehurst (0.6 miles)
Nearest Bus Routes: 89/229/422/602/B11/B16 & N89 - Bexleyheath, Bexleyheath Bus Garage (Stop NW)
Bus Routes Serviced: 89/132/229/401/422/486/625/658/661/669/B11/B16/N21 & N89

Bexleyheath was unique in that it was the only depot specifically built for trolleybuses by the London Passenger Transport Board. It suffered from bomb damage during WWII and, following conversion to an omnibus garage, closed in 1986 but reopened in 1988.

VEHICLE ALLOCATION

DWL15	BX04 BXN	E203	SN61 BKK	PVL154	X554 EGK	SE76	YX60 FCF	WVL357	LX60 DWG
E 39	LX06 FKO	E204	SN61 BKL	PVL155	X615 EGK	SE77	YX60 FCG	WVL358	LX60 DWJ
E 40	LX56 ETD	E205	SN61 DCV	PVL160	X616 EGK	SE78	YX60 FCL	WVL359	LX60 DWK
E 41	LX56 ETE	E206	SN61 DCX	PVL161	X561 EGK	SE79	YX60 FCM	WVL360	LX60 DWL
E 42	LX56 ETF	E207	SN61 DCY	PVL162	X562 EGK	SE80	YX60 FCO	WVL361	LX60 DWM
E 43	LX56 ETJ	E229	YX61 DSE	PVL163	X563 EGK	SE81	YX60 FCP	WVL362	LX60 DWN
E 44	LX56 ETK	E230	YX61 DSO	PVL164	X564 EGK	SE82	YX60 FCU	WVL363	LX60 DWO
E 45	LX56 ETL	E231	YX61 DSU	PVL165	X656 EGK	SE83	YX60 FCV	WVL364	LX60 DWP
E 46	LX56 ETO	E232	YX61 DSV	PVL166	X566 EGK	SE84	YX60 FCY	WVL365	LX60 DWU
E 47	LX56 ETR	E233	YX61 DSY	PVL167	X567 EGK	VWL 1	LB02 YWX	WVL366	LX60 DWV
E 48	LX56 ETT	E234	YX61 DSZ	PVL229	Y729 TGH	VWL 2	LB02 YWY	WVL367	LX60 DWW
E 49	LX56 ETU	E235	YX61 DTF	PVL363	PJ53 SOH	VWL 3	LB02 YWZ	WVL368	LX60 DWZ
E 50	LX56 ETV	E236	YX61 DTK	PVL364	PJ53 SOU	VWL 4	LB02 YXA	WVL369	LX60 DWZ
E 51	LX56 ETY	E237	YX61 DTN	PVL365	PJ53 SPU	VWL 6	LB02 YXB	WVL370	LX60 DXA
E 52	LX56 ETZ	E238	YX61 DPF	PVL366	PJ53 SPV	VWL 7	LB02 YXE	WVL371	LX60 DXB
E 53	LX56 EUA	E239	YX61 DPK	PVL367	PJ53 SPX	VWL 8	LB02 YXF	WVL372	LX60 DXC
E 54	LX56 EUB	E240	YX61 DPN	PVL368	PJ53 SPZ	VWL 9	LB02 YXG	WVL373	LX60 DXD
E 55	LX56 EUC	E241	YX61 DPO	PVL369	PJ53 SRO	WVL272	LX06 ECF	WVL374	LX60 DXE
E 56	LX56 EUD	E242	YX61 DPU	PVL370	PJ53 SRU	WVL273	LX06 ECJ	WVL375	LX60 DXF
E 62	LX57 CHV	E243	YX61 DPV	SE69	YX60 FBU	WVL350	LX60 DVY	WVL376	LX60 DXG
E 63	LX57 CHY	E244	YX61 DPY	SE70	YX60 FBY	WVL351	LX60 DVZ	WVL377	LX60 DXH
E 64	LX57 CHZ	E245	YX61 DPZ	SE71	YX60 FBZ	WVL352	LX60 DWA	WVL378	LX60 DXJ
E 65	LX57 CJE	LDP202	SN51 UAR	SE72	YX60 FCA	WVL353	LX60 DWC	WVL379	LX60 DXK
E 66	LX57 CJF	LDP205	SN51 UAU	SE73	YX60 FCC	WVL354	LX60 DWD	WVL455	LJ61 GVP
E 67	LX57 CJJ	PVL152	X552 EGK	SE74	YX60 FCD	WVL355	LX60 DWE	WVL456	LJ61 GVT
E202	SN61 BKJ	PVL153	X553 EGK	SE75	YX60 FCE	WVL356	LX60 DWF		

Bow Bus Garage on September 17th, 2013 with Stagecoach No.18213 leaving to take up duties on Route No.8 to Tottenham Court Road. The depot was built on the site of a mental asylum and was opened as an electric tram shed by London County Council between 1908 and 1910. It was closed to trams by London Transport on November 5th, 1939 and used as a trolleybus garage until 1959, at which point it was utilized solely for omnibuses.

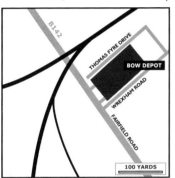

BOW (BW)
Fairfield Road, Bow, London E3 2ZH
Operated by: Stagecoach London
Location: TQ37418311 [51.530099, -0.020788]
Nearest DLR Station: Bow Church (0.3 miles)
Nearest Bus Routes: 8/205/276 & 488 - Bow Bus Garage (C)
Bus Routes Serviced: 5/8/15/205/277/N8 & N15

VEHICLE ALLOCATION

12128	LX61 DFD	12151	LX61 DCY	15117	LX09 FZO	17782	LX03 BVU	18212	LX04 FWZ
12129	LX61 DFE	12152	LX61 DCZ	15118	LX09 FZP	17783	LX03 BVV	18213	LX04 FXA
12130	LX61 DFF	12153	LX61 DDA	15119	LX09 FZR	17784	LX03 BVW	18214	LX04 FXB
12131	LX61 DFG	15097	LX09 FYS	15120	LX09 FZS	17785	LX03 BVY	18215	LX04 FXC
12132	LX61 DFJ	15098	LX09 FYT	15121	LX09 FZT	17786	LX03 BVZ	18216	LX04 FXD
12133	LX61 DFK	15099	LX09 FYU	15122	LX09 FZU	17787	LX03 BWA	18217	LX04 FXE
12134	LX61 DFL	15100	527 CLT	15123	LX09 FZV	17818	LX03 BXN	18218	LX04 FXF
12135	LX61 DFN	15101	LX09 FYW	15124	LX09 FZW	17819	LX03 BXP	18219	LX04 FXG
12136	LX61 DFO	15102	LX09 FYY	17451	LX51 FKR	17846	LX03 BYZ	18220	LX04 FXH
12137	LX61 DFP	15103	LX09 FYZ	17740	LY52 ZDX	17855	LX03 NEU	18221	LX04 FXJ
12138	LX61 DDL	15104	LX09 FZA	17741	LY52 ZDZ	17879	LX03 NGN	18222	LX04 FXK
12139	LX61 DDN	15105	LX09 FZB	17742	LY52 ZFA	17903	LX03 ORV	18223	LX04 FXL
12140	LX61 DDO	15106	LX09 FZC	17743	LY52 ZFB	18201	LX04 FWL	18224	LX04 FXM
12141	LX61 DDU	15107	LX09 FZD	17744	LY52 ZFC	18202	LX04 FWM	18225	LX04 FXP
12142	LX61 DDV	15108	LX09 FZE	17750	LX03 BTE	18203	LX04 FWN	18226	LX04 FXR
12143	LX61 DDY	15109	LX09 FZF	17751	LX03 BTF	18204	LX04 FWP	18227	LX04 FXS
12144	LX61 DDZ	15110	LX09 FZG	17752	LX03 BTU	18205	LX04 FWR	18228	LX04 FXT
12145	LX61 DEU	15111	LX09 FZH	17753	LX03 BTV	18206	LX04 FWS	18229	LX04 FXU
12146	LX61 DFA	15112	LX09 FZJ	17754	LX03 BTY	18207	LX04 FWT	18230	LX04 FXV
12147	LX61 DFC	15113	LX09 FZK	17755	LX03 BTZ	18208	LX04 FWU	18231	LX04 FXW
12148	LX61 DCO	15114	LX09 FZL	17756	LX03 BUA	18209	LX04 FWV	18234	LX04 FYA
12149	LX61 DCU	15115	LX09 FZM	17757	LX03 BUE	18210	LX04 FWW	18235	LX04 FYB
12150	LX61 DCV	15116	LX09 FZN	17781	LX03 BVT	18211	LX04 FWY		

Brentford Bus Garage on August 17th, 2013 with Metroline No.**VW1052** leaving the depot. It was originally the coach depot for Armchair Transport and became a bus garage in 1998 when the company won the franchise to operate Route No.260.

COMMERCE ROAD
BUSINESS PARK

BRENTFORD DEPOT

COMMERCE ROAD

DISUSED RAILWAY LINE TRACK BED

A315

BRENT

100 YARDS

BRENTFORD (AH)
Armchair House, Commerce Road, Brentford TW8 8LZ
Operated by: Metroline
Location: TQ17037755 [51.484694, -0.315841]
Nearest Station: Syon Lane (0.8 miles)
Nearest Bus Routes: 235/237/267/635/E2/E8 & N9 (Brent Lea)
Bus Routes Serviced: 190/209/237/609/E2 & E8

Metroline Nos **DE0192** & **VW1052** in the yard at **Brentford Bus Garage** on August 17th, 2013.

The Metroline office block and bus stop at **Brentford Bus Garage** on August 17th, 2013.

VEHICLE ALLOCATION

DE 993	LK09 ENC	DE1009	LK09 ENY	TP 413	LK03 CFG	VW1047	LK10 BXR	VW1062	LK60 AEG
DE 994	LK09 ENE	DE1010	LK09 ENM	TP 415	LK03 CFL	VW1048	LK10 BXS	VW1063	LK60 AEJ
DE 995	LK09 ENF	DE1011	LK09 ENN	VW1034	LK59 JJU	VW1049	LK10 BXU	VW1064	LK60 AEL
DE 996	LK09 ENH	DE1012	LK09 ENO	VW1035	LK10 BXC	VW1050	LK10 BXV	VW1065	LK60 AEM
DE 997	LK09 ENJ	DE1013	LK09 ENP	VW1036	LK10 BXD	VW1051	LK10 BXW	VW1066	LK60 AEN
DE 998	LK09 ENL	DE1014	LK09 ENR	VW1037	LK10 BXE	VW1052	LK10 BXX	VW1067	LK60 AEO
DE1000	LK09 EOB	DP 37	W137 WGT	VW1038	LK10 BXF	VW1053	LK10 BXY	VW1068	LK60 AEP
DE1001	LK09 EOC	OTH971	LK58 CTY	VW1039	LK10 BXG	VW1054	LK10 BXZ	VW1069	LK60 AET
DE1002	LK09 EOD	OTH972	LK58 CTZ	VW1040	LK10 BXH	VW1055	LK10 BYA	VW1070	LK60 AEU
DE1003	LK09 EOE	OTH973	LK58 CUA	VW1041	LK10 BXJ	VW1056	LK60 AEA	VW1071	LK60 AEV
DE1004	LK09 ENT	OTH974	LK09 EKG	VW1042	LK10 BXL	VW1057	LK60 AEB	VW1072	LK60 AEW
DE1005	LK09 ENU	OTH975	LK09 EKH	VW1043	LK10 BXM	VW1058	LK60 AEC	VW1244	LK12 AAJ
DE1006	LK09 ENV	TP 406	LK03 CEV	VW1044	LK10 BXN	VW1059	LK60 AED	VW1245	LK12 AAN
DE1007	LK09 ENW	TP 411	LK03 CFE	VW1045	LK10 BXO	VW1060	LK60 AEE	VW1247	LK12 ABF
DE1008	LK09 ENX	TP 412	LK03 CFF	VW1046	LK10 BXP	VW1061	LK60 AEF	VW1248	LK12 ABO

Metroline Nos **VW1070** and **DE998** passing on Commerce Road, just east of **Brentford Bus Garage** on August 17th, 2013.

The north end of the yard at **Brentford Bus Garage** on August 17th, 2013, showing the additional bus parking available and the wash plant.

Brixton Bus Garage on September 21st, 2013 with Arriva London No.**DW86** parked in the entrance road, in the foreground, Arriva London Nos **DW66** & **DW121** in the exit road and Go-Ahead No.**WVL119**, pausing outside of the depot, on Route No.333. Brixton Bus Garage was originally known as Telford Avenue and re-named in 1950

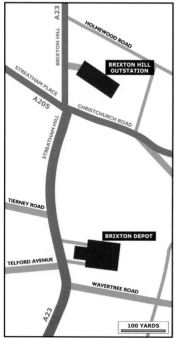

BRIXTON (BN)
39 Streatham Hill, London, SW2 4TB
Operated by: Arriva London
Location: TQ30547317 [51.442471, -0.123635]
Nearest Station: Streatham Hill (0.5 miles)
Nearest Bus Routes: 57/133/137/333/417/N133 & N137 - Streatham Hill/Telford Avenue (Stop TA)

Opened as a tram depot by the London Tramways Company Ltd on December 7th, 1892, closed to trams by London Transport on April 7th, 1951 and subsequently utilized as an omnibus garage. (Buses had first operated from January 7th, 1951.) It was extended in 1993.

BRIXTON HILL (OUTSTATION)
219 Brixton Hill, SW2 1NR
Operated by: Arriva London
Location: TQ30507352 [51.445957, -0.123727]
Nearest Station: Streatham Hill (0.6 miles)
Nearest Bus Routes: 45/59/109/118/133/159/250/ 333/N109 & N133 - Holmewood Road (Stop BT)

Opened as a tram depot by London County Council on March 6th, 1924 and closed by London Transport on April 7th, 1951. It was sold for commercial use but subsequently reinstated as an omnibus depot to cater for increased bus services introduced by Ken Livingstone when he was Mayor of London.

Bus Routes Serviced: 50/59/109/137/159/319 & N109

The former tram depot at Brixton in use as the **Brixton Bus Garage (Outstation)** on September 21st, 2013.

VEHICLE ALLOCATION

DLA181	W381 VGJ	DLA332	LG52 DCU	DW 59	LJ04 LFE	DW124	LJ05 BNE	HV136	LT63 UJS		
DLA182	W382 VGJ	DLA333	LG52 DCV	DW 60	LJ04 LFF	DW125	LJ05 BNF	HV137	LT63 UJU		
DLA183	W383 VGJ	DLA334	LG52 DCX	DW 61	LJ04 LDA	DW126	LJ05 BNK	HV138	LT63 UJV		
DLA184	W384 VGJ	DLA335	LG52 DCY	DW 62	LJ04 LDC	DW127	LJ05 BNL	HV139	LT63 UJW		
DLA185	W385 VGJ	DLA336	LG52 DCZ	DW 63	LJ04 LDD	DW128	LJ05 GKX	HV140	LT63 UJX		
DLA186	W386 VGJ	DLA337	LJ03 MFX	DW 64	WLT 664	DW129	LJ05 GKY	HV141	LT63 UJY		
DLA187	W387 VGJ	DLA338	LJ03 MFY	DW 65	LJ04 LDF	DW130	LJ05 GKZ	HV142	LT63 UJZ		
DLA188	W388 VGJ	DLA339	LJ03 MFZ	DW 66	LJ04 LDK	DW131	LJ05 GLF	HV143	LT63 UJD		
DLA205	W436 WGJ	DLA340	LJ03 MGE	DW 68	LJ04 LDN	DW132	LJ05 GLK	HV144	LT63 UJE		
DLA206	W437 WGJ	DLA341	LJ03 MGU	DW 69	LJ04 LDU	DW133	LJ05 GLV	HV145	LT63 UJF		
DLA207	W407 VGJ	DLA342	LJ03 MGV	DW 70	WLT 970	DW271	LJ59 LWU	HV146	LT63 UJG		
DLA208	W408 VGJ	DLA343	LJ03 MDV	DW 71	LJ04 LGF	DW272	LJ59 LWV	HV147	LT63 UJH		
DLA209	W409 VGJ	DLA344	LJ03 MDX	DW 72	LJ04 LGG	DW274	LJ59 LWX	HV148	LT63 UJJ		
DLA210	W438 WGJ	DLA345	LJ03 MDY	DW 73	LJ04 LGK	DW275	LJ59 LWY	HV149	LT63 UJK		
DLA211	W411 VGJ	DLA346	LJ03 MDZ	DW 74	LJ04 LGL	DW276	LJ59 LWZ	HV150	LT63 UJL		
DLA212	W412 VGJ	DLA347	LJ03 MEU	DW 75	LJ04 LGN	DW277	LJ59 LXA	HV151	LT63 UJM		
DLA213	W413 VGJ	DLA371	LJ03 MVC	DW 76	WLT 676	DW278	LJ59 LXB	HV152	LT63 UJN		
DLA256	X508 GGO	DLA372	LJ03 MVD	DW 77	LJ04 LGV	DW279	LJ59 LWF	VLA102	LJ54 BCU		
DLA270	Y452 UGC	DW 37	LJ53 NJN	DW 78	LJ04 LGW	DW280	LJ59 LWG	VLA144	LJ55 BTO		
DLA271	Y471 UGC	DW 38	LJ53 NHE	DW 79	LJ04 LGX	DW281	LJ59 LWH	VLA145	LJ55 BTU		
DLA298	Y498 UGC	DW 39	LJ53 NHF	DW 80	LJ04 LGY	DW282	LJ59 LWK	VLA146	LJ55 BTV		
DLA311	Y511 UGC	DW 40	LJ53 NHG	DW 81	LJ04 LFU	DW283	LJ59 LWL	VLA147	LJ55 BTX		
DLA312	Y512 UGC	DW 41	LJ53 NHH	DW 82	LJ04 LFV	DW284	LJ59 LWM	VLA148	LJ55 BTY		
DLA313	Y513 UGC	DW 42	LJ53 NHK	DW 83	LJ04 LFW	DW285	LJ59 LWN	VLA149	LJ55 BTZ		
DLA314	Y514 UGC	DW 43	LJ53 NHL	DW 84	LJ04 LFX	DW286	LJ59 LWO	VLA150	LJ55 BUA		
DLA315	Y529 UGC	DW 44	LJ53 NHM	DW 85	WLT 385	DW287	LJ59 LWP	VLA151	LJ55 BUE		
DLA316	Y516 UGC	DW 45	LJ53 NHN	DW 86	LJ04 LFZ	DW288	LJ59 LWR	VLA152	LJ55 BPZ		
DLA317	Y517 UGC	DW 46	LJ53 NHO	DW 87	LJ04 LGA	DW289	LJ59 LVU	VLA153	LJ55 BRV		
DLA318	Y518 UGC	DW 47	WLT 348	DW 88	LJ04 LGC	DW290	LJ59 LVV	VLA154	LJ55 BRX		
DLA319	Y519 UGC	DW 48	WLT 348	DW 89	LJ04 LGD	DW291	LJ59 LVW	VLA155	LJ55 BRZ		
DLA322	LG52 DAO	DW 49	LJ53 NGU	DW 90	LJ04 LGE	DW292	LJ59 LVX	VLA156	LJ55 BSO		
DLA323	LG52 DAU	DW 50	LJ53 NGV	DW 91	LJ04 LFG	DW293	LJ59 LVY	VLA157	LJ55 BSU		
DLA324	LG52 DBO	DW 51	LJ04 LDX	DW 92	LJ04 LFH	DW294	LJ59 LVZ	VLA158	LJ55 BSV		
DLA325	LG52 DBU	DW 52	LJ04 LDY	DW 93	LJ04 LFK	DW295	LJ59 LWA	VLA159	LJ55 BSX		
DLA326	LG52 DBV	DW 53	LJ04 LDZ	DW118	LJ05 BMV	DW296	LJ10 CUH	VLA160	LJ55 BSY		
DLA327	LG52 DBY	DW 54	LJ04 LEF	DW119	319 CLT	DW297	LJ10 CUK	VLA161	LJ55 BSZ		
DLA328	LG52 DBZ	DW 55	LJ04 LEU	DW120	LJ05 BMZ	HV132	LT63 UHR	VLA162	LJ55 BVP		
DLA329	LG52 DCE	DW 56	656 DYE	DW121	LJ05 BNA	HV133	LT63 UJO	VLA163	LJ55 BVR		
DLA330	LG52 DCF	DW 57	LJ04 LFB	DW122	LJ05 BNB	HV134	LT63 UJP				
DLA331	LG52 DCO	DW 58	LJ04 LFD	DW123	LJ05 BND	HV135	LT63 UJR				

Bromley Bus Garage on September 21st, 2013 with all three exits and entrances in view.

BROMLEY (TB)
111 Hastings Road, Bromley, Kent BR2 8NH
Operated by: Stagecoach London
Location: TQ42416611 [51.375785, 0.044762]
Nearest Station: Bromley South (2.7 miles)
Nearest Bus Routes: 261/261/336/358 & 402 -
Bromley Common, Bromley Bus Garage (Stop BN)
Bus Routes Serviced: 61/208/227/246/261/269/
314/636/637/638/664/R5/R7 & R10

Stagecoach London No.36313 receiving attention on Lower Gravel Road alongside of **Bromley Bus Garage** on September 21st, 2013.

Stagecoach London Buses allocated to **Bromley Bus Garage** are also accommodated in a compound on the north side of Lower Gravel Road and on September 21st, 2013 Nos 17779, 23105, 17970, 17973, 17845, 19132, 10144 & 17842 were amongst those parked here.

VEHICLE ALLOCATION

10139	LX12 DFU	10188	SN63 NBJ	17843	LX03 BYV	19137	LX56 EAP	36311	LX58 CAA
10140	LX12 DFV	10189	SN63 NBK	17844	LX03 BYW	19138	LX56 EAW	36312	LX58 CAE
10141	LX12 DFY	10190	SN63 NBL	17845	LX03 BYY	19139	LX56 EAY	36313	LX58 CAO
10142	LX12 DFZ	10191	SN63 NBM	17864	LX03 NFJ	19140	LX56 EBA	36541	LX12 DJE
10143	LX12 DGE	10192	SN63 NBO	17965	LX53 JZH	19835	LX61 DDE	36542	LX12 DJF
10144	LX12 DGF	10193	SN63 NBX	17966	LX53 JZJ	23101	LX12 DKK	36543	LX12 DJJ
10145	LX12 DGO	10194	SN63 NBY	17967	LX53 JZK	23102	LX12 DKL	36544	LX12 DJK
10146	LX12 DGU	10195	SN63 NBZ	17968	LX53 JZL	23103	LX12 DKN	36545	LX12 DJO
10147	LX12 DGV	17448	Y448 NHK	17969	LX53 JZM	23104	LX12 DKO	36546	LX12 DJU
10148	LX12 DGY	17449	Y449 NHK	17970	LX53 JZN	23105	LX12 DKU	36547	LX12 DJV
10149	LX12 DGZ	17531	LX51 FOT	17971	LX53 JZO	23106	LX12 DKV	36548	LX12 DJY
10150	LX12 DHA	17779	LX03 BVR	17972	LX53 JZP	23107	LX12 DKY	36549	LX12 DJZ
10151	LX12 DHC	17780	LX03 BVS	17973	LX53 JZR	23108	LX12 DLD	36550	LX12 DKA
10152	LX12 DHD	17788	LX03 BWB	17974	LX53 JZT	23109	LX12 DLE	36551	LX12 DKD
10153	LX12 DHE	17794	LX03 BWH	17975	LX53 JZU	23110	LX12 DLF	36552	LX12 DKE
10154	LX12 DHF	17795	LX03 BWJ	19131	LX56 EAF	23111	LX12 DLJ	36553	LX12 DKF
10164	SN63 JVM	17831	LX03 BYF	19132	LX56 EAG	23112	LX12 DLK	36581	YX63 LGA
10184	SN63 NBD	17832	LX03 BYG	19133	LX56 EAJ	23113	LX12 DLN	36582	YX63 LGC
10185	SN63 NBE	17833	LX03 BYH	19134	LX56 EAK	34362	LV52 HKO	36583	YX63 LGD
10186	SN63 NBF	17841	LX03 BYT	19135	LX56 EAM	36309	LX58 BZW		
10187	SN63 NBG	17842	LX03 BYU	19136	LX56 EAO	36310	LX58 BZY		

The Hastings Road entrance to **Bromley Bus Garage** viewed on September 21st, 2013.

An interior view of **Bromley Bus Garage** on September 21st, 2013 with Stagecoach No. **17968** receiving some attention.

The Camberwell New Road entrance to **Camberwell Bus Garage** on August 31st, 2013. The depot was built in 1914 but did not come into commercial use until 1919 due to requisitioning for the war effort.

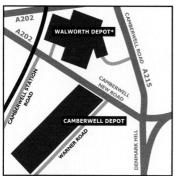

*SEE PAGE 94

CAMBERWELL (Q)
Warner Road, London SE5 9LU
Operated by: Go-Ahead London
Location: TQ32317666 [51.474136, -0.095157]
Nearest Station: Denmark Hill (0.7 miles)
Nearest Bus Routes: 36/185/436 & N136 - Warner Road (Stop H)
Bus Routes Serviced:12/45/68/185/345/355/360/468/N68/P5 & X68

The entrance at the south end **Camberwell Bus Garage** on August 31st, 2013. The garage suffered from some bomb damage during WWII and was modernized during the 1950s.

The south end of **Camberwell Bus Garage** on August 31st, 2013.

VEHICLE ALLOCATION

DWL13	BX04 BXL	LDP261	SN53 KKW	WHV 6	LJ61 GWC	WVL147	LX53 AYY	WVL252	LX06 EAY
E100	LX09 EZU	LDP262	SN53 KKX	WHV 7	LJ61 GXE	WVL148	LX53 AYZ	WVL253	LX06 EBA
E101	LX09 EZV	PVL233	Y733 TGH	WHV 8	LJ61 GXF	WVL149	LX53 BJK	WVL254	LX06 EBC
E102	LX09 EZW	PVL272	PN02 XBW	WHV 9	LJ61 GXG	WVL151	LX53 BJU	WVL255	LX06 EBD
E103	LX09 EZZ	PVL298	PJ02 RFK	WHV10	LJ61 GXH	WVL212	LX06 DYS	WVL256	LX06 EBF
E104	LX09 FAF	PVL299	PJ02 RFL	WHV11	LJ61 GXK	WVL213	LX06 DYT	WVL257	LX06 EBG
E105	LX09 FAJ	PVL300	PJ02 RFN	WHV12	LJ61 GXL	WVL214	LX06 DYU	WVL258	LX06 EBJ
E106	LX09 FAK	PVL301	PJ02 RFO	WHV13	LJ61 GXM	WVL215	LX06 DYV	WVL259	LX06 EBK
E107	LX09 FAM	PVL302	PJ02 RFX	WHV14	LJ61 GXN	WVL216	LX06 DYW	WVL260	LX06 EBL
E108	LX09 FAO	PVL303	PJ02 RFY	WHV15	LJ61 GXO	WVL217	LX06 DYY	WVL261	LX06 EBM
E109	LX09 FAU	PVL304	PJ02 RFZ	WHV16	LJ61 GXP	WVL218	LX06 DZA	WVL262	LX06 EBN
E110	LX09 FBA	PVL305	PJ02 RGO	WHY 1	LX06 ECN	WVL219	LX06 DZB	WVL263	LX06 EBO
E111	LX09 FBB	PVL306	PJ02 RGU	WHY 2	LX55 EAC	WVL220	LX06 DZC	WVL264	LX06 EBP
E112	LX09 FBC	PVL307	PJ02 RGV	WHY 3	LX55 EAE	WVL222	LX06 DZE	WVL265	LX06 EBU
E113	LX09 FBD	PVL308	PJ02 TVN	WHY 4	LX55 EAF	WVL223	LX06 DZF	WVL266	LX06 EBV
E114	LX09 FBE	PVL309	PJ02 TVO	WHY 5	LX55 EAG	WVL224	LX06 DZG	WVL267	LX06 EBZ
E115	LX09 FBF	PVL310	PJ02 TVP	WHY 6	LX55 EAJ	WVL225	LX06 DZH	WVL268	LX06 ECA
E116	LX09 FBG	PVL311	PJ02 TVT	WHY 7	LX57 CLZ	WVL226	LX06 DZJ	WVL269	LX06 ECC
E117	LX09 FBJ	PVL312	PJ02 TVU	WHY 8	LX11 DVA	WVL227	LX06 DZK	WVL270	LX06 ECD
E118	LX09 FBK	PVL313	PJ52 LVP	WHY 9	LX11 DVB	WVL228	LX06 DZL	WVL380	LX60 DXM
E119	LX09 FBN	PVL314	PJ52 LVR	WHY10	LX11 DVC	WVL229	LX06 DZM	WVL381	LX60 DXO
E120	LX09 FBO	PVL315	PJ52 LVS	WHY11	LX11 DVF	WVL230	LX06 DZN	WVL382	LX60 DXP
E121	LX09 FBU	PVL316	PJ52 LVT	WHY12	LX11 DVG	WVL231	LX06 DZO	WVL383	LX60 DXR
E122	LX09 FBV	PVL317	PJ52 LVU	WHY13	LX11 DVH	WVL232	LX06 DZP	WVL384	LX60 DXS
E123	LX09 FBY	PVL318	PJ52 LVV	WVL 87	LF52 ZNV	WVL233	LX06 DZR	WVL385	LX60 DXT
E124	LX09 FBZ	PVL326	PJ52 LWE	WVL129	LX53 AZA	WVL234	LX06 DZS	WVL435	LJ61 GWU
E125	LX09 FCA	PVL327	PJ52 LWF	WVL130	LX53 AZB	WVL235	LX06 DZT	WVL436	LJ61 GWV
E126	LX09 FCC	PVL328	PJ52 LWG	WVL131	LX53 AZC	WVL236	LX06 DZU	WVL437	LJ61 GWW
E127	LX09 FCD	SE85	YX11 CPE	WVL132	LX53 AZD	WVL237	LX06 DZV	WVL438	LJ61 GWX
E128	LX09 FCE	SE86	YX11 CPF	WVL133	LX53 AZF	WVL238	LX06 DZW	WVL439	LJ61 GWY
LDP206	SN51 UAV	SE87	YX11 CPK	WVL134	LX53 AZG	WVL239	LX06 DZY	WVL440	LJ61 GWZ
LDP249	SN53 KKF	SE88	YX11 CPN	WVL135	LX53 AZJ	WVL240	LX06 DZZ	WVL441	LJ61 GXA
LDP250	SN53 KKG	SE89	YX11 CPO	WVL136	LX53 AZL	WVL241	LX06 EAA	WVL442	LJ61 GXB
LDP251	SN53 KKH	SE90	YX11 CPU	WVL137	LX53 AZN	WVL242	LX06 EAC	WVL443	LJ61 GXC
LDP252	SN53 KKJ	SE91	YX11 CPY	WVL138	LX53 AZO	WVL243	LX06 EAE	WVL444	LJ61 GXD
LDP253	SN53 KKL	SE92	YX11 CPZ	WVL139	LX53 AYM	WVL244	LX06 EAF	WVL445	LJ61 GWD
LDP254	SN53 KKM	SE93	YX11 CPZ	WVL140	LX53 AYN	WVL245	LX06 EAG	WVL446	LJ61 GWE
LDP255	SN53 KKO	VWL10	LB02 YXH	WVL141	LX53 AYO	WVL246	LX06 EAJ	WVL447	LJ61 GWF
LDP256	SN53 KKP	WHV 1	LJ61 GVW	WVL142	LX53 AYP	WVL247	LX06 EAK	WVL448	LJ61 GWG
LDP257	SN53 KKR	WHV 2	LJ61 GVX	WVL143	LX53 AYT	WVL248	LX06 EAM	WVL449	LJ61 GWK
LDP258	SN53 KKT	WHV 3	LJ61 GVY	WVL144	LX53 AYU	WVL249	LX06 EAO		
LDP259	SN53 KKU	WHV 4	LJ61 GVZ	WVL145	LX53 AYV	WVL250	LX06 EAP		
LDP260	SN53 KKV	WHV 5	LJ61 GWA	WVL146	LX53 AYW	WVL251	LX06 EAW		

Catford Bus Garage on September 21st, 2013 with Go-Ahead No.WVL411 mingling amongst Stagecoach London Nos 34389, 19839, 10137, 18455 & 36536 on the garage forecourt.

CATFORD (TL)
180 Bromley Road, Catford, London SE6 2XA
Operated by: Stagecoach London
Location: TQ37827249 [51.434474, -0.018465]
Nearest Station: Bellingham (0.3 miles)
Nearest Bus Routes: 47/54/136/171/199/208/320/ N47 & N136 - Catford Bus Garage (Stop)
Bus Routes Serviced: 47/124/136/178/199/273/ 354/356/380/621/660/N47/N136 & P4

The garage was originally opened by the London General Omnibus Company in 1914 but was immediately requisitioned for war use. It re-opened in 1920 as a garage for Thomas Tilling and was doubled in size three years later. It has since undergone modifications to accommodate double-decker buses and was last modernized in 1970.

VEHICLE ALLOCATION

10124	LX12 DDY	18487	LX55 BFF	25112	WLT 461	34395	LX03 CBU	36319	LX58 CBV
10125	LX12 DDZ	18488	LX55 BEJ	25113	LX09 BGK	34396	LX03 CBV	36320	LX58 CBY
10126	LX12 DEU	18489	LX06 AFZ	25114	LX09 BGU	34397	LX03 CBY	36321	LX58 CCA
10127	LX12 DFA	18490	LX06 AGO	25115	LX09 BGV	34551	LX53 LGF	36322	LX58 CCD
10128	LX12 DFC	18491	LX06 AGU	34353	LV52 HKE	34552	LX53 LGG	36323	LX58 CCE
10129	LX12 DFD	18492	LX06 AGV	34355	LV52 HKG	34553	LX53 LGJ	36324	LX58 CCF
10130	LX12 DFE	18493	LX06 AGY	34357	LV52 HKJ	34554	LX53 LGK	36325	LX58 CCJ
10131	LX12 DFF	18494	LX06 AGZ	34358	LV52 HKK	34556	LX53 LGN	36326	LX58 CCK
10132	LX12 DFG	18495	LX06 AHA	34359	LV52 HKL	34557	LX53 LGO	36343	LX09 ADU
10133	LX12 DFJ	18496	LX06 AHC	34360	LV52 HKM	34558	LX53 LGU	36528	LX12 DHG
10134	LX12 DFK	18497	LX06 AHD	34361	LV52 HKN	34559	LX53 LGV	36529	LX12 DHJ
10135	LX12 DFL	18498	LX06 AHE	34363	LV52 HKP	34560	LX53 LGW	36530	LX12 DHK
10136	LX12 DFN	18499	LX06 AHF	34364	LV52 HKT	36301	LX56 DZU	36531	LX12 DHL
10137	LX12 DFO	19836	LX61 DDF	34365	LV52 HKU	36302	LX56 DZV	36532	LX12 DHM
10138	LX12 DFP	19837	LX61 DDJ	34370	LV52 HGG	36303	LX56 DZW	36533	LX12 DHN
17478	LX51 FLP	19838	LX61 DDK	34372	LV52 HGK	36304	LX56 DZY	36534	LX12 DHO
18455	LX55 EPA	19839	LX61 DAA	34376	LV52 HGO	36305	LX56 DZZ	36535	LX12 DHP
18463	LX55 EPN	19840	LX61 DAO	34387	LX03 BZV	36306	LX56 EAA	36536	LX12 DHU
18464	LX55 EPO	19841	LX61 DAU	34388	LX03 BZW	36307	LX56 EAC	36537	LX12 DHV
18481	LX55 BDY	19842	LX61 DBO	34389	LX03 BZY	36308	LX56 EAE	36538	LX12 DHY
18482	LX55 BDZ	19843	LX61 DBU	34390	LX03 CAA	36314	LX58 CAV	36539	LX12 DHZ
18483	LX55 BEO	19844	LX61 DBV	34391	LX03 CAE	36315	LX58 CAU	36540	LX12 DJD
18484	LX55 BEY	19845	LX61 DBY	34392	LX03 CAU	36316	LX58 CBF		
18485	LX55 BFA	19846	LX61 DBZ	34393	LX03 CAV	36317	LX58 CBO		
18486	LX55 BFE	25111	YJ08 PGO	34394	LX03 CBF	36318	LX58 CBU		

Clapton Bus Garage on June 22nd, 2013 with Arriva London No.**VLW197** in view.

CLAPTON (CT)
15 Bohemia Place, Mare Street, London E8 1DU
Operated by: Arriva London
Location: TQ35128499 [51.547676, -0.053296]
Nearest Station: Hackney Central (200 yards)
Nearest Bus Routes: 30/38/242/276/394 & N38 - Hackney Central (Stop T)
Bus Routes Serviced: 38/242/393 & N38

This garage was originally a horse tram depot, opened by the North Metropolitan Tramways in 1883 and taken over by London County Council on July 1st, 1903. It was rebuilt and enlarged in 1909 and closed to trams by London Transport on September 10th, 1939. It later had a spell of use as a Go-Kart circuit, before re-opening as a bus garage.

VEHICLE ALLOCATION

DW201	LJ09 KRO	DW226	LJ59 AEV	DW251	LJ59 AAX	DW407	LJ11 AEX	ENS 5	LJ07 EDR
DW202	LJ09 SUO	DW227	LJ59 AEW	DW252	LJ59 AAY	DW408	LJ11 AEY	ENS 6	LJ07 EDU
DW203	LJ09 SUU	DW228	LJ59 AEX	DW253	LJ59 AAZ	DW409	LJ11 AEZ	ENS 7	LJ07 EDV
DW204	LJ09 SUV	DW229	LJ59 AEY	DW254	LJ59 GVC	DW410	LJ11 AFA	ENS 8	LJ07 EDX
DW205	LJ09 SUX	DW230	LJ59 AEZ	DW255	LJ59 GVE	DW412	LJ11 AEC	ENS 9	LJ07 EEA
DW206	LJ09 SUY	DW231	LJ59 AFA	DW256	LJ59 GVF	DW413	LJ11 AED	ENS10	LJ07 EEB
DW207	LJ09 SVA	DW232	LJ59 AEB	DW257	LJ59 GVG	DW414	LJ11 AEE	ENS11	LJ07 ECF
DW208	LJ09 SVC	DW233	LJ59 AEC	DW258	LJ59 GVK	DW415	LJ11 AEF	ENS12	LJ07 ECN
DW209	LJ09 SVD	DW234	LJ59 AED	DW259	LJ59 GTF	DW416	LJ11 AEG	ENS13	LJ07 ECT
DW210	LJ09 SVE	DW235	LJ59 AEE	DW260	LJ59 GTU	DW417	LJ11 AEK	ENS14	LJ07 ECV
DW211	LJ09 SVF	DW236	LJ59 AEF	DW261	361 CLT	DW418	LJ11 AEL	PDL115	LJ54 LHR
DW212	LJ09 SSO	DW237	LJ59 AEG	DW262	LJ59 GUA	DW419	LJ11 AEM	PDL116	LJ54 LGV
DW213	LJ09 SSU	DW238	LJ59 AEK	DW263	LJ59 LXU	DW420	LJ11 AEN	VLW 86	LF52 UPW
DW214	LJ09 SSV	DW239	LJ59 AEL	DW264	LJ59 LXV	DW421	LJ11 ACV	VLW 87	LF52 UPX
DW215	LJ09 SSX	DW240	LJ59 AEM	DW265	LJ59 LXW	DW422	LJ11 ACX	VLW 88	WLT 888
DW216	LJ09 SSZ	DW241	LJ59 AEN	DW266	LJ59 LXX	DW423	LJ11 ACY	VLW 89	LF52 UPZ
DW217	LJ09 STX	DW242	LJ59 ACU	DW267	LJ59 LXY	DW424	LJ11 ACZ	VLW 90	LF52 URA
DW218	LJ09 STZ	DW243	LJ59 ACV	DW268	LJ59 LXZ	DW425	LJ61 CEN	VLW 91	LF52 UPD
DW219	LJ09 SUA	DW244	LJ59 ACX	DW269	LJ59 GVK	DW426	LJ61 CEO	VLW 92	WLT 892
DW220	LJ09 SUF	DW245	LJ59 AAF	DW270	LJ59 LWT	DW427	LJ61 CEU	VLW 93	LF52 UPG
DW221	LJ09 SUH	DW246	LJ59 AAK	DW273	LJ59 LWW	ENL18	LJ58 AWF	VLW 94	LF52 UPH
DW222	LJ59 AEO	DW247	LJ59 AAN	DW403	LJ11 AET	ENS 1	LJ07 EDK	VLW 95	LF52 UPJ
DW223	LJ59 AEP	DW248	LJ59 AAO	DW404	LJ11 AEU	ENS 2	LJ07 EDL	VLW 96	LF52 UPK
DW224	LJ59 AET	DW249	LJ59 AAU	DW405	LJ11 AEV	ENS 3	LJ07 EDO		
DW225	LJ59 AEU	DW250	LJ59 AAV	DW406	LJ11 AEW	ENS 4	LJ07 EDP		

The entrance to **Cricklewood Bus Garage** on November 2nd, 2013 with the modern maintenance facility visible on the right.

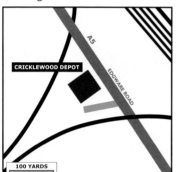

CRICKLEWOOD (W)
329 Edgware Road, Dollis Hill, London NW2 6JP
Operated by: Metroline
Location: TQ23348632 [51.558423, -0.214375]
Nearest Station: Cricklewood (0.6 miles)
Nearest Bus Routes: 32/245/266/332 & N16 -
Dollis Hill, Cricklewood Bus Garage (Stop BA)
Bus Routes Serviced: 16/32/139/189/210/232/
316/326/332/632/643/C11 & N16

The first garage on this site opened for service in May 1905. Originally known as Dollis Hill, it was the first depot to be used by the London General Omnibus Company for motor vehicles. It closed temporarily in 2007 to allow for the complete rebuilding of the depot with its buses parking on a site on the opposite side of Edgware Road. The rebuilt depot opened again in January 2009.

Metroline No.**TEH1229** departing from **Cricklewood Bus Garage** on November 2nd, 2013.

Metroline No.**DE1127** leaving **Cricklewood Bus Garage** on November 2nd, 2013 to take up duties on Route No.143 to Archway.

VEHICLE ALLOCATION

DE 859	LK08 DWO	DE1031	LK59 AVV	TA644	LK05 GGE	TE1094	LK60 AHA	TEH1223	LK61 BKA
DE 860	LK08 DWP	DE1032	LK59 AVW	TA645	LK05 GGF	TE1095	LK60 AHC	TEH1224	LK61 BKD
DE 861	LK08 DWU	DE1033	LK59 AVX	TA646	LK05 GGJ	TE1096	LK60 AHD	TEH1225	LK61 BKE
DE 862	LK08 DWV	DE1115	LK10 BYB	TA647	LK05 GGO	TE1097	LK60 AHE	TEH1226	LK61 BKF
DE 863	LK08 DWW	DE1116	LK10 BYC	TA648	LK05 GGP	TE1098	LK60 AHG	TEH1227	LK61 BKG
DE 864	LK08 DWX	DE1117	LK10 BYD	TA649	LK05 GGU	TE1099	LK60 AHJ	TEH1228	LK61 BKJ
DE 865	LK08 DWY	DE1118	LK10 BYG	TA650	LK05 GGV	TE1100	LK60 AHL	TEH1229	LK61 BKL
DE 866	LK08 DWZ	DE1119	LK10 BYJ	TA651	LK05 GGX	TE1101	LK60 AHN	TEH1230	LK61 BKN
DE 867	LK08 DXA	DE1120	LK10 BYL	TA652	LK05 GGY	TE1102	LK60 AHO	TEH1231	LK61 BKO
DE 868	LK08 DXB	DE1121	LK10 BYM	TA653	LK05 GGZ	TE1103	LK60 AHP	TEH1232	LK61 BKU
DE 869	LK08 DXC	DE1122	LK10 BYN	TA654	LK05 GHA	TE1104	LK60 AHU	TEH1233	LK61 BKV
DE 870	LK08 DXD	DE1123	LK10 BYO	TA655	LK05 GHB	TE1307	LK12 AVD	TEH1234	LK61 BKY
DE 871	LK58 CPX	DE1124	LK10 BYP	TA656	LK05 GHD	TE1308	LK12 AVJ	TEH1235	LK61 BKZ
DE 872	LK58 CPY	DE1125	LK10 BYR	TA657	LK05 GHF	TE1309	LK12 AVN	TEH1236	LK61 BLF
DE 873	LK58 CPZ	DE1126	LK10 BYS	TA658	LK05 GHG	TE1310	LK12 AVT	TEH1237	LK61 BLJ
DE 874	LK58 CMY	DE1127	LK10 BYT	TA659	LK05 GHH	TE1311	LK12 AVU	TEH1238	LK61 BLN
DE 875	LK58 CMZ	DE1128	LK10 BYU	TE 889	LK08 NVD	TE1312	LK12 AWA	TEH1239	LK61 BLV
DE 876	LK58 CNA	DE1129	LK10 BYV	TE 890	LK08 NVE	TE1313	LK12 AWC	TEH1240	LK61 BLX
DE 877	LK58 CNC	DE1130	LK10 BYW	TE 891	LK08 NVF	TE1314	LK12 AWJ	TEH1241	LK61 BLZ
DE 952	LK58 CSX	DE1131	LK10 BYX	TE 892	LK08 NVG	TE1315	LK12 AWN	TEH1242	LK61 BMO
DE 953	LK58 CSY	DE1132	LK10 BYY	TE 893	LK08 NVH	TE1316	LK12 AWO	TEH1449	LK13 BGE
DE 954	LK58 CSZ	DE1133	LK10 BYZ	TE 894	LK08 NVJ	TE1317	LK12 AWP	TEH1450	LK13 BGF
DE 955	LK58 CTE	DE1134	LK10 BZA	TE 895	LK08 NVL	TE1448	LK13 BFZ	TEH1451	LK13 BGO
DE 956	LK58 CTF	DE1135	LK10 BZB	TE1073	LK10 BZV	TEH 915	SN08 AAO	TEH1452	LK13 BGU
DE 957	LK58 CTO	DE1136	LK10 BZC	TE1074	LK10 BZX	TEH 916	LK58 CPN	TEH1453	LK13 BGV
DE 958	LK58 CTU	DE1137	LK10 BZD	TE1075	LK10 BZY	TEH 917	LK58 CPO	TEH1454	LK13 BGX
DE 959	LK58 CTV	DE1138	LK10 BZE	TE1076	LK60 AEX	TEH 918	LK58 CPU	TEH1455	LK13 BGY
DE 960	LK58 CTX	DE1139	LK10 BZF	TE1077	LK60 AEY	TEH 919	LK58 CPV	TEH1456	LK13 BGZ
DE1015	LK59 AUW	DE1140	LK10 BZG	TE1078	LK60 AEZ	TEH1105	LK60 AHV	TEH1457	LK13 BHA
DE1016	LK59 AUY	DE1141	LK10 BZH	TE1079	LK60 AFA	TEH1106	LK60 AHX	TEH1458	LK13 BHD
DE1017	LK59 AVB	DE1142	LK10 BZJ	TE1080	LK60 AFE	TEH1107	LK60 AHZ	TEH1459	LK13 BHE
DE1018	LK59 AVC	DE1143	LK10 BZL	TE1081	LK60 AFF	TEH1108	LK60 AJO	TEH1460	LK13 BHF
DE1019	LK59 AVD	DE1144	LK10 BZM	TE1082	LK60 AFN	TEH1109	LK60 AJU	TEH1461	LK13 BHJ
DE1020	LK59 AVF	DE1145	LK10 BZN	TE1083	LK60 AFO	TEH1110	LK60 AJV	TEH1462	LK13 BHL
DE1021	LK59 AVG	DE1146	LK10 BZO	TE1084	LK60 AFU	TEH1111	LK60 AJV	TEH1463	LK13 BHN
DE1022	LK59 AVJ	DE1147	LK10 BZP	TE1085	LK60 AFV	TEH1112	LK60 AJX	TEH1464	LK13 BHO
DE1023	LK59 AVL	DE1148	LK10 BZR	TE1086	LK60 AFX	TEH1113	LK60 AJY	TEH1465	LK13 BHP
DE1024	LK59 AVM	DE1149	LK10 BZS	TE1087	LK60 AFY	TEH1114	LK60 AKF	TEH1466	LK13 BHU
DE1025	LK59 AVN	TA638	LK05 GFO	TE1088	LK60 AFZ	TEH1217	LK61 BJO	TEH1467	LK13 BHV
DE1026	LK59 AVO	TA639	LK05 GFV	TE1089	LK60 AGO	TEH1218	LK61 BJU	TP 430	LK03 GFV
DE1027	LK59 AVP	TA640	LK05 GFX	TE1090	LK60 AGU	TEH1219	LK61 BJV		
DE1028	LK59 AVR	TA641	LK05 GFY	TE1091	LK60 AGV	TEH1220	LK61 BJX		
DE1029	LK59 AVT	TA642	LK05 GFZ	TE1092	LK60 AGY	TEH1221	LK61 BJY		
DE1030	LK59 AVU	TA643	LK05 GGA	TE1093	LK60 AGZ	TEH1222	LK61 BJZ		

CROYDON BUS GARAGE

ZONE **4**

Croydon Bus Garage on the occasion of an open day on September 21st, 2013 celebrating the 30th Anniversary of Metrobus. The depot was opened by the company in December 2005 and Metrobus No.872 is viewed operating a shuttle service for visitors.

*SEE PAGE 14 †SEE PAGE 107

CROYDON (C)
134 Beddington Lane, Croydon, Surrey CR9 4ND
Operated by: Metrobus
Location: TQ30116625 [51.381692, -0.134208]
Nearest Tram Station: Therapia Lane (0.6 miles)
Nearest Bus Routes: 455 - Beddington, Beddington Cross (Southbound)
Bus Routes Serviced: 54/64/75/119/127/130/202/293/359/405/434/N64 & T32

VEHICLE ALLOCATION

189	YY13 VKO	444	YV03 RCZ	717	AJ58 WBG	890	PN09 ENK	949	YN07 EXH
190	YY13 VKP	445	YV03 RAU	718	AE09 DHU	891	PN09 ENL	950	YN07 EXK
191	YY13 VKR	446	YV03 RAX	719	AE09 DHN	892	PN09 ENM	951	YN07 EXM
192	YY13 VKS	447	YV03 RBF	720	AE09 DHL	893	PN09 ENO	952	YN07 EXO
210	SN03 WLX	451	YU52 XVK	721	AJ58 WBK	894	PO59 KFW	955	YR58 SNY
211	SN03 WLZ	455	YN03 DFA	722	AJ58 WBF	895	PO59 KFX	956	YR58 SNZ
212	SN03 WMC	480	YN53 RYP	723	AE09 DHV	896	PO59 KFY	957	YP58 UFV
213	SN03 WMF	481	YN53 RYR	870	PN09 EKR	897	PO59 KFZ	958	YT59 DYA
214	SN03 WMG	561	YN08 OAS	871	PN09 EKT	898	PO59 KGA	959	YT59 DYB
215	SN03 WMK	562	YN58 BNA	872	PN09 EKU	899	PO59 KGE	960	YT59 DYC
216	SN03 WMP	563	YN08 OAV	873	PN09 EKV	917	YN06 JYB	961	YT59 DYD
219	SN03 WMY	564	YN08 OAW	874	PN09 EKW	918	YN06 JYC	962	YT59 DYF
286	SN03 YCK	565	YN08 OAX	875	PN09 EKX	919	YN06 JYD	963	YT59 DYG
334	W334VGX	566	YN08 OAY	876	PN09 EKY	920	YN06 JYE	964	YT59 DYH
431	YV03 PZW	567	YN08 OAZ	877	PN09 ELO	921	YN06 JYF	965	YT59 DYN
432	YV03 PZX	615	YN06 JXU	878	PN09 ELU	922	YN06 JYG	966	YT59 DYJ
433	YV03 PZY	706	YX58 DXB	879	PN09 ELV	923	YN06 JYH	967	YT59 DYM
434	YV03 PZZ	707	YX58 DXC	880	PN09 ELW	924	YN06 JYJ	968	YT59 DYO
435	YV03 PZE	708	YX58 DXD	881	PN09 ELX	925	YN06 JYK	969	YT59 DYP
436	YV03 PZF	709	AE09 DHG	882	PN09 EMF	926	YN06 JYL	970	YT59 DYS
437	YV03 PZG	710	AE09 DHK	883	PN09 EMK	927	YN06 JYO	971	YT59 DYU
438	YV03 PZH	711	AJ58 WBD	884	PN09 EMV	928	YN56 FDA	972	YT59 DYV
439	YV03 PZJ	712	AE09 DHM	885	PN09 EMX	929	YN56 FDC	973	YT59 DYW
440	YV03 PZK	713	AE09 DHP	886	PN09 ENC	935	YN56 FDK		
441	YV03 PZL	714	AJ58 WBE	887	PN09 ENE	936	YN56 FDL		
442	YV03 PZM	715	AE09 DHJ	888	PN09 ENF	947	YN07 EXF		
443	YV03 RCY	716	AE09 DHO	889	PN09 ENH	948	YN07 EXG		

Croydon Bus Garage on September 21st, 2013 with Arriva London No.**T283** passing on a Route No.466 service. The depot was opened by the London General Omnibus Company in 1915 but was totally destroyed by bombing during WWII and reconstructed during the mid-1950s.

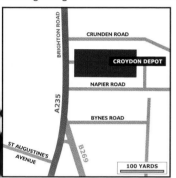

CROYDON (TC)
Brighton Road, Croydon, Surrey CR2 6EL
Operated by: Arriva London
Location: TQ32626343 [51.354497, -0.097483]
Nearest Station: South Croydon (0.8 miles)
Nearest Bus Routes: 60/166/312/407/466 & N68
- South Croydon Bus Garage (Stop)
Bus Routes Serviced: 60/166/194/197/264/312/
403/405/412/466/612/627/685/N133 & T31

VEHICLE ALLOCATION

DLA239	X439 FGP	DW 22	822 DYE	DW105	LJ05 BJY	ENL24	LJ58 AUY	T 57	LJ08 CYL
DLA242	X442 FGP	DW 23	LJ53 BFX	DW106	LJ05 BJZ	ENL25	LJ58 AVB	T 58	LJ08 CYO
DLA252	X452 FGP	DW 24	LJ53 BFY	DW107	LJ05 BKA	ENL26	LJ58 AVC	T 59	LJ08 CYP
DLA287	Y487 UGC	DW 25	725 DYE	DW108	LJ05 BHL	ENL27	LJ58 AVD	T 60	LJ08 CYS
DLA296	Y496 UGC	DW 26	LJ53 BGF	DW109	LJ05 BHN	ENL28	LJ58 AUC	T 61	LJ08 CXR
DW 1	801 DYE	DW 27	LJ53 BGK	DW110	LJ05 BHO	ENL29	LJ58 AUE	T 62	LJ08 CXS
DW 2	LJ03 MWN	DW 28	LJ53 BGO	DW111	LJ05 BHP	PDL117	LJ05 GOP	T 63	LJ08 CXT
DW 3	LJ03 MWP	DW 29	LJ53 BGU	DW112	LJ05 BHU	PDL118	LJ05 GOU	T 64	LJ08 CXU
DW 4	LJ03 MWU	DW 30	LJ53 NHV	DW113	LJ05 BHV	PDL119	LJ05 GOX	T 65	LJ08 CXV
DW 5	LJ03 MWV	DW 31	LJ53 NHX	DW114	LJ05 BHW	PDL120	LJ05 GPF	T118	LJ10 HVO
DW 6	LJ03 MVT	DW 32	LJ53 NHY	DW115	LJ05 BHX	PDL123	LJ05 GPU	T119	LJ10 HVP
DW 7	WLT 807	DW 33	LJ53 NHZ	DW116	LJ05 BHY	T 42	LJ08 CSU	T120	LJ10 HVR
DW 8	LJ03 MVV	DW 34	734 DYE	DW117	LJ05 BHZ	T 43	LJ08 CSV	T121	LJ10 HVA
DW 9	LJ03 MVW	DW 35	LJ53 NJF	ENL 1	LJ07 ECW	T 44	LJ08 CSX	T279	LJ13 CHL
DW 10	LJ03 MVX	DW 36	LJ53 NJK	ENL 2	LJ07 ECX	T 45	LJ08 CSY	T280	LJ13 CHN
DW 11	LJ03 MVY	DW 94	LJ54 BFP	ENL 3	LJ07 ECY	T 46	LJ08 CSZ	T281	LJ13 CHO
DW 12	LJ03 MVZ	DW 95	VLT 295	ENL 4	LJ07 ECZ	T 47	LJ08 CTE	T282	LJ13 CHV
DW 13	LJ03 MWA	DW 96	LJ54 BFV	ENL 5	LJ07 EDC	T 48	LJ08 CTF	T283	LJ13 CIIX
DW 14	LJ03 MWC	DW 97	LJ54 BFX	ENL 6	LJ07 EDF	T 49	LJ08 CTK	T284	LJ13 CHY
DW 15	LJ03 MWD	DW 98	LJ54 BFY	ENL 7	LJ07 EBO	T 50	LJ08 CTO	T285	LJ13 CGG
DW 16	LJ03 MVF	DW 99	LJ54 BFZ	ENL 8	LJ07 EBP	T 51	LJ08 CYC	T286	LJ13 CGK
DW 17	LJ03 MVG	DW100	LJ54 BGE	ENL 9	LJ07 EBU	T 52	LJ08 CYE	T287	LJ13 CGO
DW 18	LJ53 NHT	DW101	LJ54 BGF	ENL10	LJ58 AVT	T 53	LJ08 CYF		
DW 19	WLT 719	DW102	LJ54 BGK	ENL21	LJ58 AUV	T 54	LJ08 CYG		
DW 20	LJ53 BFP	DW103	LJ05 BJV	ENL22	LJ58 AUW	T 55	LJ08 CYH		
DW 21	LJ53 BFU	DW104	LJ05 BJX	ENL23	LJ58 AUX	T 56	LJ08 CYK		

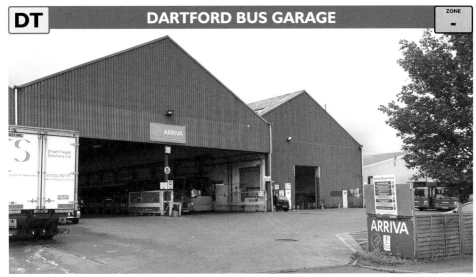

Dartford Bus Garage on September 7th, 2013 with an interesting ensemble of vans, taxis and a Polish Coach Reg No.**854 9435**.

DARTFORD (DT)
Central Road, Dartford, Kent, DA1 5BG
Operated by: Arriva Southern
Location: TQ54427468 [51.450276, 0.221242]
Nearest Station: Dartford (0.3 miles)
Nearest Bus Routes: 96/428 & 492 - Dartford,
Home Gardens (Stop D)
Bus Routes Serviced: 160/286/428/492/B12/B13
& B15

Arriva London single-deckers Nos **3294**, **3292**, **3293**, **3302** & **3295** parked in the yard at **Dartford Bus Garage** on September 7th, 2013.

VEHICLE ALLOCATION

3502	KE51 PUA	3957	GK53 AOY	3995	GN07 DMU	4032	GN09 AVZ	6461	GN61 JRX
3514	LJ03 MZE	3982	GN07 DLE	3996	GN07 DMV	4033	GN09 AWA	6462	GN61 JRO
3945	GK53 AOH	3983	GN07 DLF	4005	GN08 CGZ	4034	GN09 AWC	6463	GN61 JRZ
3946	GK53 AOJ	3984	GN07 DLJ	4006	GN08 CHC	4035	GN09 AWF	6464	GN61 JSU
3947	GK53 AOL	3985	GN07 DLK	4007	GN08 CHD	6213	GK53 AOA	6465	GN61 JRU
3948	GK53 AON	3986	GN07 DLO	4023	GN58 BUP	6214	GK53 AOB	6466	KX61 LDL
3949	GK53 AOO	3987	GN07 DLU	4024	GN58 BUU	6215	GK53 AOC	6467	KX61 LDN
3950	GK53 AOP	3988	GN07 DLV	4025	GN58 BUV	6216	GK53 AOD	6468	KX61 LDO
3951	GK53 AOR	3989	GN07 DLX	4026	GN58 LVA	6217	GK53 AOE	6469	KX61 LDU
3952	GK53 AOT	3990	GN07 DLY	4027	GN58 LVB	6218	GK53 AOF	6470	KX61 LDV
3953	GK53 AOU	3991	GN07 DLZ	4028	GN09 AVV	6219	GK53 AOG		
3954	GK53 AOV	3992	GN07 DME	4029	GN09 AVW	6458	GN61 JPY		
3955	GK53 AOW	3993	GN07 DMF	4030	GN09 AVX	6459	GN61 JSV		
3956	GK53 AOX	3994	GN07 DMO	4031	GN09 AVY	6460	GN61 JRV		

Edgware Bus Garage on October 16th, 2013.

EDGWARE (BT)
Approach Road, Edgware, Middlesex HA8 7AN
Operated by: London Sovereign
Location: TQ19679171 [51.611558, -0.272959]
Nearest Tube Station: Edgware (Adjacent)
Nearest Bus Routes: Edgware Bus Station adjacent
Bus Routes Serviced: 13/114/183/251/292/324/
605 & N13

A depot has been sited at Edgware since the London General Omnibus Company opened one in 1925. It was approximately located where the bus station is today and this garage was built in 1984.

NB This depot is also used by Metroline and is coded as EW Edgware (See Page 34)

VEHICLE ALLOCATION

DE57	YX11 GBE	SLE 3	YN54 OAC	SLE40	YN55 NKJ	VH 1	BD13 OHU	VLE27	PA04 CYK
DE58	YX11 GBF	SLE 4	YN54 OAE	SLE41	YN55 NKK	VH 2	BD13 OHV	VLE28	PA04 CYL
DE59	YX11 GBO	SLE 5	YN54 OAG	SLE42	YN55 NKL	VH 3	BD13 OHW	VLE29	PA04 CYP
DE60	YX11 GBU	SLE 6	YN54 OAH	SP68	YT59 RXR	VH 4	BD13 OHX	VLE30	PA04 CYS
DE61	YX11 GBV	SLE21	YN55 NHT	SP69	YT59 RXS	VH 5	BD13 OHY	VLE31	PA04 CYT
DE62	YX11 GBY	SLE22	YN55 NHU	SP70	YT59 RXU	VH 6	BD13 OHZ	VLE32	PO54 ABZ
DE63	YX11 GBZ	SLE23	YN55 NHV	SP71	YT59 RXV	VH 7	BD13 OJA	VLE33	PO54 ACF
DE64	YX11 GCF	SLE24	YN55 NHX	SP72	YT59 RXW	VH 8	BD13 OJB	VLE34	PO54 ACJ
DE65	YX11 GCK	SLE25	YN55 NHY	SP73	YT59 RXX	VH 9	BD13 OJC	VLE35	PO54 ACU
DE66	YX11 GCO	SLE26	YN55 NHZ	SP74	YT59 RXY	VH10	BD13 OJE	VLE36	PO54 ACV
DE67	YX11 GCU	SLE27	YN55 NJE	SP75	YT59 RXZ	VH11	BD13 OHJ	VLE37	PO54 ACX
DE68	YX11 GCV	SLE28	YN55 NJF	SP76	YT59 RYA	VH12	BT13 YWK	VLE38	PO54 ACY
DE69	YX11 GCY	SLE29	YN55 NJJ	SP77	YT59 RYB	VH13	BT13 YWL	VLE39	PO54 ACZ
DE70	YX11 GCZ	SLE30	YN55 NJK	SP78	YT59 RYC	VH14	BT13 YWN	VLP18	PJ53 OUN
SDE18	YX60 BZA	SLE31	YN55 NJU	SP79	YT59 RYD	VH15	BT13 YWJ	VLP19	PJ53 OUO
SDE19	YX60 BZB	SLE32	YN55 NJV	SP80	YT59 RYF	VH16	BT13 YWM	VLP20	PJ53 OUP
SDE20	YX60 BZC	SLE33	YN55 NKA	SP81	YT59 RYG	VH17	BT13 YWP	VLP21	PJ53 OUU
SDE21	YX60 BZD	SLE34	YN55 NKC	SP82	YT59 RYH	VH18	BT13 YWO	VLP22	PJ53 OUV
SDE22	YX60 BZE	SLE35	YN55 NKD	SP83	YT59 RYJ	VH19	BT13 YWR	VLP23	PJ53 OUW
SDE23	YX60 BZF	SLE36	YN55 NKE	SP84	YT59 RYK	VH20	BT13 YWS	VLP24	PJ53 OUX
SDE24	YX60 BZG	SLE37	YN55 NKF	SP85	YT59 RYM	VH21	BT13 YWW	VLP25	PJ53 OUY
SLE 1	YN54 OAA	SLE38	YN55 NKG	SP86	YT59 RYN	VH22	BT13 YWU	VLP26	PJ53 OVA
SLE 2	YN54 OAB	SLE39	YN55 NKH	SP87	YT59 RYO	VH23	BT13 YWV	VLP27	PJ53 OVB

The main entrance and yard at **Edgware Bus Garage** on October 16th, 2013.

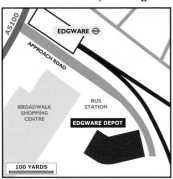

EDGWARE (EW)
Approach Road, Edgware, Middlesex HA8 7AN
Operated by: Metroline
Location: TQ19679171 [51.611558, -0.272959]
Nearest Tube Station: Edgware (Adjacent)
Nearest Bus Routes: Edgware Bus Station adjacent
Bus Routes Serviced: 107/113/186/204/240/606/
N5/N98 & N113

In 1992, as Cricklewood Bus Garage (See Page 28), was due to open with new facilities, Edgware was considered for closure and a year later became a midibus base. In 1999 London Sovereign took over half of the depot and Metroline subsequently moved in to share the facilities in 2000.

**NB This depot is also used by London Sovereign
and is coded as BT Edgware** (See Page 33)

VEHICLE ALLOCATION

TE 712	LK56 FHE	TE 730	LK07 AZG	TE 837	LK57 AXS	TE 885	LK08 DXX	TE 990	LK59 DZP
TE 713	LK56 FHF	TE 731	LK07 AZJ	TE 838	LK57 AXT	TE 886	LK08 DXY	TE 991	LK59 DZR
TE 714	LK56 FHG	TE 732	LK07 AZL	TE 839	LK57 AXU	TE 887	LK08 DXZ	TE 992	LK59 DZT
TE 715	LK56 FHH	TE 733	LK07 AZN	TE 840	LK57 AXV	TE 888	LK08 DYA	VPL141	X641 LLX
TE 716	LK56 FHJ	TE 734	LK07 AZO	TE 841	LK57 AXW	TE 976	LK59 DYY	VPL147	X647 LLX
TE 717	LK56 FHM	TE 735	LK07 AZP	TE 842	LK57 AXX	TE 977	LK59 DZA	VPL151	X651 LLX
TE 718	LK56 FHN	TE 736	LK07 AZR	TE 843	LK57 AXY	TE 978	LK59 DZB	VPL162	Y162 NLK
TE 719	LK56 FHO	TE 737	LK07 AZT	TE 844	LK57 AXZ	TE 979	LK59 DZC	VPL200	Y149 NLK
TE 720	LK56 FHP	TE 738	LK07 AZU	TE 845	LK57 AYA	TE 980	LK59 DZD	VPL201	Y201 NLK
TE 721	LK56 FHR	TE 828	LK57 AXF	TE 846	LK57 AYB	TE 981	LK59 DZE	VPL203	Y203 NLK
TE 722	LK56 FHS	TE 829	LK57 AXG	TE 847	LK57 AYC	TE 982	LK59 DZF	VPL205	LK51 XGD
TE 723	LK56 FHT	TE 830	LK57 AXH	TE 878	LK08 DXO	TE 983	LK59 DZG	VPL210	Y143 NLK
TE 724	LK07 AYZ	TE 831	LK57 AXJ	TE 879	LK08 DXP	TE 984	LK59 DZH	VPL213	LK51 XGG
TE 725	LK07 AZA	TE 832	LK57 AXM	TE 880	LK08 DXR	TE 985	LK59 DZJ	VPL216	LK51 XGL
TE 726	LK07 AZB	TE 833	LK57 AXN	TE 881	LK08 DXS	TE 986	LK59 DZL	VPL217	LK51 XGM
TE 727	LK07 AZC	TE 834	LK57 AXO	TE 882	LK08 DXU	TE 987	LK59 DZM	VPL218	LK51 XGN
TE 728	LK07 AZD	TE 835	LK57 AXP	TE 883	LK08 DXV	TE 988	LK59 DZN	VPL219	LK51 XGO
TE 729	LK07 AZF	TE 836	LK57 AXR	TE 884	LK08 DXW	TE 989	LK59 DZO	VPL221	LK51 XGR

A general view of **Enfield Bus Garage** on August 20th, 2013. It was opened in 1927 by the London General Omnibus Company, subsequently expanded and then modernized and refurbished in the 1980s, re-opening in 1984.

ENFIELD (E)
Southbury Road, Ponders End, Middlesex EN3 4HX
Operated by: Arriva London
Location: TQ34989617 [51.606783, -0.041104]
Nearest Station: Southbury (200 yards)
Nearest Bus Routes: 121/191/307/313/349 & 377
Bus Routes Serviced: 121/192/279/307/313/317/349/379 & N279

Arriva Nos **VL50** & **VL84** parked up at **Enfield Bus Garage** on August 20th, 2013 as No.**PDL142** leaves the depot on the No.377 service to Oakwood.

VEHICLE ALLOCATION

DLA126	V326 DGT	DW570	LJ13 CKN	ENX 3	LJ61 CKK	T238	LJ61 LLN	VLW101	LG52 DDF
DLA127	V327 DGT	DW571	LJ13 CKO	ENX 4	LJ61 CKL	T239	LJ61 LLO	VLW102	LG52 DDJ
DLA129	V329 DGT	DW572	LJ13 CKP	ENX 5	LJ61 CKN	T240	LJ61 LLP	VLW103	LG52 DDK
DLA130	V330 DGT	DW573	LJ13 CHZ	ENX 6	LJ61 CKO	T241	LJ61 LKM	VLW104	LG52 DDL
DLA132	V332 DGT	DW574	LJ13 CJE	ENX 7	LJ61 CHY	T242	LJ61 LKN	VLW105	LJ03 MHU
DLP 76	LJ51 OSX	DW575	LJ13 CJF	ENX 8	LJ61 CHZ	T243	LJ61 LKO	VLW106	LJ03 MHV
DLP 77	LJ51 OSY	DW576	LJ13 CJO	PDL140	SN06 BPU	T244	LJ61 LKP	VLW107	LJ03 MHX
DLP 78	LJ51 OSZ	DW577	LJ13 CJU	PDL141	SN06 BPV	T245	LJ61 LKU	VLW108	LJ03 MHY
DLP 79	LJ51 ORA	DW578	LJ13 CJV	PDL142	SN06 BPX	T246	LJ61 LKV	VLW109	LJ03 MHZ
DLP 80	LJ51 ORC	EN 1	LJ57 USS	PDL143	SN06 BPY	T247	LJ61 LKX	VLW110	LJ03 MJE
DLP 81	LJ51 ORF	EN 2	LJ57 UST	PDL144	SN06 BPZ	T248	LJ61 LKY	VLW111	LJ03 MJF
DLP 82	LJ51 ORG	EN 3	LJ57 USU	PDL145	SN06 BRF	T249	LJ61 LKZ	VLW112	LJ03 MJK
DW556	LJ13 CEN	EN 4	LJ57 USV	T224	LJ61 CFP	T250	LJ61 LLA	VLW113	LJ03 MJU
DW557	LJ62 FNF	EN 5	LJ57 USW	T225	LJ61 CFU	T251	LJ61 LJY	VLW117	LF52 UPN
DW558	LJ62 FNG	EN 6	LJ57 USX	T226	LJ61 CFV	T252	LJ61 LJZ	VLW118	LF52 UPO
DW559	LJ62 FNR	EN 7	LJ57 USY	T227	LJ61 CFX	T253	LJ61 LKA	VLW119	LF52 UOS
DW560	LJ62 FOD	EN 8	LJ57 USZ	T228	LJ61 CFY	T254	LJ61 LKC	VLW120	LF52 UOT
DW561	LJ13 CEO	EN 9	LJ57 UTA	T229	LJ61 CFZ	T255	LJ61 LKD	VLW121	LF52 UOU
DW562	LJ13 CEU	EN10	LJ57 UTB	T230	LJ61 CGE	T256	LJ61 LKE	VLW122	LF52 UOV
DW563	LJ13 CKC	EN11	LJ57 UTC	T231	LJ61 LLC	T257	LJ61 LKF	VLW123	LF52 UOW
DW564	LJ13 CKD	EN12	LJ57 UTE	T232	LJ61 LLD	T258	LJ61 LKG	VLW124	LF52 UOX
DW565	LJ13 CKE	EN13	LJ57 UTF	T233	LJ61 LLE	T259	LJ61 LKK	VLW125	LF52 UOY
DW566	LJ13 CKF	EN14	LJ12 BYW	T234	LJ61 LLF	VLW 97	LF52 UPL		
DW567	LJ13 CKG	EN15	LJ12 BYX	T235	LJ61 LLG	VLW 98	LF52 UPM		
DW568	LJ13 CKK	ENX 1	LJ61 CKF	T236	LJ61 LLK	VLW 99	LG52 DDA		
DW569	LJ13 CKL	ENX 2	LJ61 CKG	T237	LJ61 LLM	VLW100	LG52 DDE		

Quality Line No.**MCL1** entering **Epsom Bus Garage** on October 16th, 2013.

100 YARDS

LONGMEAD ROAD

EPSOM DEPOT

ROY RICHMOND WAY

LONGMEAD LIGHT
INDUSTRIAL ESTATE

EPSOM (EB)
3 Roy Richmond Way, Epsom, Surrey KT19 9AF
Operated by: Quality Line
Location: TQ21166208 [51.344875, -0.262117]
Nearest Station: Ewell West (0.7 miles)
Nearest Bus Routes: 418/668/868/E5 & E9 -
Longmead, opposite Blenheim High School
Bus Routes Serviced: 404/406/411/418/463/465/
467/470/641/K5/S1/S3/S4 & X26

VEHICLE ALLOCATION

DD01	SK07 DZA	MCL14	BN12 EOW	OP19	YN53 SVR	OPL06	YJ62 FXA	SD38	PL05 PLN
DD02	SK07 DZB	MCL15	BN12 EOX	OP20	YN53 ZXA	OPL07	YJ62 FXG	SD39	PL05 PLO
DD03	SK07 DZC	MCL16	BN12 EOY	OP21	YN53 ZXB	OPL08	YJ62 FXK	SD40	PL05 PLU
DD04	SK07 DZD	MCL17	BN12 EOZ	OP23	YJ09 MHK	OV01	YJ60 KGA	SD41	PL05 PLV
DD05	SK07 DZE	OP01	YE52 FHH	OP24	YJ09 MHL	OV02	YJ60 KGE	SD42	PL05 PLX
DD06	SK07 DZF	OP02	YE52 FHJ	OP25	YJ09 MHM	OV03	YJ60 KGF	SD43	PE56 UFH
DD07	SK07 DZG	OP03	YE52 FHK	OP26	YJ09 MHN	OV04	YJ60 KGG	SD44	PE56 UFJ
DD08	SK07 DZH	OP04	YE52 FHL	OP27	YJ09 MHO	OV05	YJ60 KGK	SD45	PE56 UFK
DD09	SK07 DZJ	OP05	YE52 FHM	OP28	YJ09 MHU	OV06	YJ60 KGN	SD46	PE56 UFL
DD10	SK07 DZL	OP06	YE52 FHN	OP29	YJ09 MHV	OV07	YJ60 KGO	SD47	PE56 UFM
DD11	SN11 BVG	OP07	YE52 FHO	OP30	YJ09 MHX	OV08	YJ60 KGP	SD48	PE56 UFN
DD12	SN11 BVH	OP08	YE52 FHP	OP31	YJ11 EJA	OV09	YJ12 PKV	SD49	PE56 UFP
DD13	YX61 FYR	OP09	YE52 FHR	OP32	YJ11 EJC	OV10	YJ12 PKX	SD50	PE56 UFR
MCL 1	BW03 ZMZ	OP10	YE52 FHS	OP33	YJ11 EJD	OV11	YJ12 PKY	SD51	PE56 UFS
MCL 8	BN12 EOP	OP11	YE52 FGU	OP34	YJ13 HJN	OV12	YJ12 PKZ	SD52	PN07 KRZ
MCL 9	BN12 EOR	OP14	YN53 SUF	OPL01	YJ62 FUD	OV13	YJ12 PLF	SD53	PN07 KSE
MCL10	BN12 EOS	OP15	YN53 SVK	OPL02	YJ62 FUG	SD26	W874 VGT	SD54	LJ08 RJY
MCL11	BN12 EOT	OP16	YN53 SVL	OPL03	YJ62 FVN	SD27	W875 VGT	SDL01	Y539 XAG
MCL12	BN12 EOU	OP17	YN53 SVO	OPL04	YJ62 FVT	SD28	W876 VGT	SDL02	SN51 TDO
MCL13	BN12 EOV	OP18	YN53 SVP	OPL05	YJ62 FWB	SD33	SN51 UCO	SDL03	SN51 TCU

The parking area at the rear of **Epsom Bus Garage**, viewed on October 16th, 2013.

The rear of the depot buildings at **Epsom Bus Garage**, viewed on October 16th, 2013.

A general view of **Fulwell Bus Garage** on August 17th, 2013.

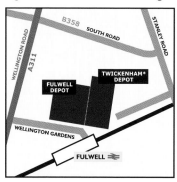

FULWELL (FW)
Wellington Road, Fulwell, Middlesex TW2 5NX
Operated by: London United
Location: TQ14817191 [51.434809, -0.350929]
Nearest Station: Fulwell (Adjacent)
Nearest Bus Routes: 267 & R70 - Fulwell (Stop A)
Bus Routes Serviced: 33/65/71/110/131/216/267/
281/371/671/681 & 691

Fulwell was originally opened as a tramshed by the London United Tramways Company Ltd on April 2nd, 1903. On May 16th, 1931 the ten northernmost roads were taken over for trolleybuses and it was subsequently closed to trams on October 27th, 1935 by London Transport. The depot was then used as a trolleybus garage and works before conversion to an omnibus depot on May 9th, 1962.

NB Both London United and Abellio* utilize this depot with the former occupying the west end and Abellio the east. (*See Page 92)

Fulwell-allocated London United No.DE121 passing its home depot whilst operating Route No.33 on August 17th, 2013.

London United No.**TA129** standing at the entrance to **Fulwell Bus Garage** on August 17th, 2013.

VEHICLE ALLOCATION

DE 23	YX09 HJK	DPS585	SN51 TCX	SLE56	YN55 NLE	SP 98	YT59 SGV	TA316	SN03 DZR
DE 24	YX09 HJN	DPS586	SN51 TDX	SLE57	YN55 NLG	SP 99	YT59 SGX	TA317	SN03 DZS
DE 25	YX09 HJO	DPS587	SN51 TBO	SLE58	YN55 NLJ	SP100	YT59 SGY	TA318	SN03 DZT
DE 26	YX09 HJU	DPS655	LG02 FFZ	SLE59	YN55 NLK	SP101	YT59 SGZ	TA319	SN03 DZV
DE 27	YX09 HJV	DPS659	LG02 FGE	SLE60	YN55 NLL	SP102	YT59 SHJ	TA321	SN03 DZX
DE 28	YX09 HJY	DPS661	LG02 FGJ	SLE61	YN55 NLM	SP103	YT59 SHV	TA322	SN03 EAA
DE 29	YX09 HJZ	DPS663	LG02 FGM	SLE62	YN55 NLO	SP104	YT59 SFF	TA323	SN03 EAC
DE 30	YX09 HKZ	DPS665	LG02 FGO	SLE63	YN55 NLP	SP105	YT59 DXY	TA324	SN03 EAE
DE 31	YX09 HLA	DPS667	LG02 FGU	SLE64	YN55 NLR	SP106	YT59 DXZ	TA325	SN03 EAF
DE 68	SK07 DXT	DPS670	LG02 FGZ	SP 26	YN08 DHM	SP107	YT59 DYX	TA326	SN03 EAG
DE 69	SK07 DXU	DPS681	SN03 LDY	SP 27	YN08 DHO	SP108	YT59 DYY	TA327	SN03 EAJ
DE 71	SK07 DXW	DPS682	SN03 LDZ	SP 28	YN08 DHP	SP163	YP59 OEY	TA328	SN03 EAM
DE 73	SK07 DXY	DPS683	SN03 LEF	SP 52	YT09 BNK	SP164	YP59 OEZ	TA329	SN03 EAP
DE109	YX60 CAA	DPS684	SN03 LEJ	SP 53	YT09 BNL	TA204	SN51 SYA	TA330	SN03 EAW
DE110	YX60 CAE	DPS685	SN03 LEU	SP 54	YT09 BNN	TA205	SN51 SYC	TA331	SN03 EAX
DE111	YX60 CAO	DPS686	SN03 LFA	SP 55	YT09 BJU	TA206	SN51 SYE	TA332	SN03 EBA
DE112	YX60 CAU	DPS687	SN03 LFB	SP 56	YT09 ZCA	TA207	SN51 SYF	TA333	SN03 EBC
DE113	YX60 CAV	DPS689	SN03 LFE	SP 57	YT09 ZCE	TA208	SN51 SYG	TA334	SN03 EBD
DE114	YX60 CBF	DPS690	SN03 LFF	SP 58	YT09 ZCF	TA209	SN51 SYH	TA335	SN03 EBF
DE115	YX60 CBO	DPS694	SN03 LFK	SP 59	YT09 ZCJ	TA210	SN51 SYJ	TA336	SN03 EBG
DE116	YX60 CBU	DPS724	SN55 DVT	SP 60	YT09 ZCK	TA211	SN51 SYO	TA337	SN03 EBJ
DE117	YX60 CBV	DPS725	SN55 DVU	SP 61	YT09 ZCL	TA212	SN51 SYR	TA338	SN03 EBK
DE118	YX60 CBY	DPS726	SN55 DVV	SP 62	YT09 ZCN	TA213	SN51 SYS	TA339	SN03 EBL
DE119	YX60 CCA	DPS727	SN55 DVW	SP 63	YT09 ZCO	TA214	SN51 SYT	TA340	SN03 EBM
DE120	YX60 CCD	HDE1	SN09 CHC	SP 64	YT09 ZCU	TA219	SN51 SYY	TA341	SN03 LFL
DE121	YX60 CCE	HDE2	SN09 CHD	SP 65	YT09 BJV	TA220	SN51 SYZ	TA342	SN03 LFM
DE122	YX60 CCF	HDE3	SN09 CHF	SP 66	YT09 BJX	TA221	SN51 SZC	TA343	SN03 LFP
DE123	YX60 CCJ	HDE4	SN09 CHG	SP 67	YT09 BJY	TA222	SN51 SZD	TA344	SN03 LFR
DE124	YX60 CCK	HDE5	SN09 CHH	SP 88	YT59 SFK	TA223	SN51 SZE	TA345	SN03 LFS
DE125	YX60 CCN	SLE45	YN55 NKP	SP 89	YT59 SFN	TA224	SN51 SZT	TA346	SN03 LFT
DE126	YX60 CCO	SLE46	YN55 NKR	SP 90	YT59 SFO	TA225	SN51 SZU	TLA 3	SN53 EUJ
DE127	YX60 BZH	SLE47	YN55 NKS	SP 91	YT59 SFU	TA229	LG02 FAA	TLA 4	SN53 EUK
DE128	YX60 BZJ	SLE48	YN55 NKT	SP 92	YT59 SFV	TA232	LG02 FAK	VA71	V187 OOE
DPS549	Y549 XAG	SLE50	YN55 NKW	SP 93	YT59 SFX	TA233	LG02 FAM	VA80	V203 OOE
DPS551	Y551 XAG	SLE51	YN55 NKX	SP 94	YT59 SFY	TA237	LG02 FBB	VA86	W116 EON
DPS552	Y552 XAG	SLE53	YN55 NLA	SP 95	YT59 SFZ	TA313	SN03 DZK	VA92	W126 EON
DPS581	SN51 TCV	SLE54	YN55 NLC	SP 96	YT59 SGO	TA314	SN03 DZM		
DPS584	SN51 TBZ	SLE55	YN55 NLD	SP 97	YT59 SGU	TA315	SN03 DZP		

The entrance to **Garston Bus Garage** on August 20th, 2013.

GARSTON (GR)

Marshwood House, 934 St Albans Road, Watford, Hertfordshire WD2 9NN
Operated by: Arriva Shires
Location: TL11760035 [51.690754, -0.384822]
Nearest Station: Garston (0.4 miles)
Nearest Bus Routes: 142/258/268/288/303/305/340/631/640/642/H2/H3/H18 & H19
Bus Routes Serviced: 142/258/268/288/303/305/340/631/640/642/H2/H3/H18 & H19

The exit road at **Garston Bus Garage** on August 20th, 2013.

VEHICLE ALLOCATION

2468	YJ06 YRP	3709	YJ06 LFL	3804	SN56 AXG	6021	KL52 CXO	6123	LJ05 BKX
2469	YJ06 YRR	3710	YJ06 LDK	3805	SN56 AXH	6023	KL52 CXR	6164	LJ55 BVS
2470	YJ06 YRS	3711	YJ06 HRA	3811	LJ58 AVU	6024	KL52 CXS	6165	LJ55 BVT
2471	YJ06 YRT	3712	YJ06 HRC	3812	LJ58 AVV	6025	YJ54 CFG	6166	LJ55 BVU
2472	YJ06 YRU	3713	YJ06 HRD	3813	LJ58 AVX	6026	YJ55 WPO	6167	LJ55 BVV
3218	S315 JUA	3714	YJ06 HRF	3814	LJ58 AVY	6027	YJ55 WOA	6168	LJ55 BVW
3220	S317 JUA	3716	YJ06 HRJ	3815	LJ58 AVZ	6028	YJ55 WOB	6169	LJ55 BVX
3221	S318 JUA	3717	YJ06 HPA	3816	LJ58 AWA	6029	YJ55 WOC	6170	LJ55 BVY
3258	V258 HBH	3718	YJ06 HPC	3817	LJ58 AWC	6030	YJ55 WOD	6171	LJ55 BVZ
3260	V260 HBH	3719	YJ06 HPF	5448	SN08 AAE	6031	YJ55 WOH	6172	LJ55 BVD
3297	Y297 TKJ	3720	YJ06 HPJ	6008	KL52 CWZ	6032	YJ55 WOM	6173	LJ55 BVE
3299	Y299 TKJ	3721	YJ06 HPK	6010	KL52 CXB	6033	YJ55 WOR	6174	LJ55 BVF
3301	Y301 TKJ	3722	YJ06 HPL	6011	KL52 CXC	6034	YJ55 WOU	6175	LJ55 BVG
3515	LJ03 MUW	3723	YJ06 HPN	6015	KL52 CXG	6035	YJ55 WOV	6176	LJ55 BVH
3704	YJ06 LFE	3724	YJ06 HPO	6016	KL52 CXH	6036	YJ55 WOX	6177	LJ55 BVK
3705	YJ06 LFF	3725	YJ06 HPP	6017	KL52 CXJ	6041	LJ05 GLY	6178	LJ55 BVL
3706	YJ06 LFG	3726	YJ06 HPU	6018	KL52 CXK	6100	KX59 AEE	6179	LJ55 BVM
3707	YJ06 LFH	3727	YJ06 HNT	6019	KL52 CXM	6101	KX59 AEF		
3708	YJ06 LFK	3728	YJ06 HNU	6020	KL52 CXN	6109	LJ05 BLV		

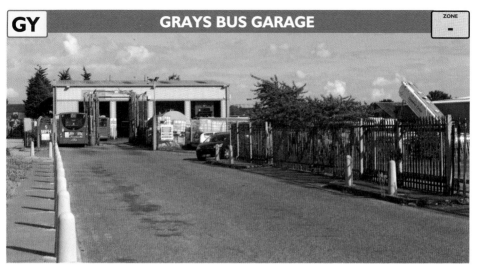

Grays Bus Garage viewed on September 18th, 2013.

MAGNET INDUSTRIAL ESTATE

MILL LANE

GRAYS DEPOT

EUROPA PARK

MAGNET ROAD

LONDON ROAD

THE CHASE

A126

100 YARDS

GRAYS (GY)
Unit 7, Europa Park, London Road, Grays, Essex RM20 4DB
Operated by: Arriva Southern
Location: TQ59567800 [51.478434, 0.296224]
Nearest Station: Grays (1.7 miles)
Nearest Bus Routes: 22/22A/25/44/73/73A/83/100 & 201 - South Stifford, The Shant (Eastbound)
Bus Routes Serviced: 66/346/370/375 & 499

Arriva Southern No.DWL13 leaving **Grays Bus Garage** on September 18th, 2013.

The entrance and wash plant at **Grays Bus Garage** on September 18th, 2013, with Arriva Southern No.3997 on the left and No.3973 on the right.

VEHICLE ALLOCATION

3309	LJ54 BCX	3999	GN57 BPE	4068	GN10 KWE	4077	YX10 EBU	6116	LJ05 BKG
3310	LJ54 BAA	4000	GN08 CGO	4069	GN10 KWF	4078	YX10 EBV	6117	LJ05 BKK
3524	LJ51 DDX	4001	GN08 CGU	4070	GN10 KWG	4079	YX10 EBZ	6118	LJ05 BKL
3525	LJ51 DDV	4002	GN08 CGV	4071	GN10 KWH	6110	LJ05 BLX	6119	LJ05 BKN
3971	YE06 HPX	4003	GN08 CGX	4072	GN10 KWJ	6111	LJ05 BLZ	6120	LJ05 BKO
3972	YE06 HPY	4004	GN08 CGY	4073	GN10 KWK	6112	LJ05 BMO	6121	LJ05 BKU
3973	YE06 HPZ	4008	GN08 CHF	4074	YX10 EBN	6113	LJ05 BMU	6122	LJ05 BKV
3997	GN57 BOU	4009	GN08 CHG	4075	YX10 EBO	6114	LJ05 BKD		
3998	GN57 BOV	4010	GN08 CHH	4076	YX10 EBP	6115	LJ05 BKF		

The office block at **Greenford Bus Garage** on July 20th, 2013. The garage, sited on part of a Council Depot, opened in 1993 as a base for the operation of midibuses. Metroline subsequently took the depot over from Ealing Community Transport and the buses are accommodated in a compound at the east end of the site.

GREENFORD (G)
Council Depot, Greenford Road, Greenford, Middlesex UB6 9AP
Operated by: Metroline
Location: TQ14438187 (Office), TQ14538186 (Compound) [51.524035, -0.350297]
Nearest Station: Greenford (1.6 miles)
Nearest Bus Routes: 92/282 & E5 - Greenford Depot (Stop U)
Bus Routes Serviced: 92/95/282/E1/E3/E5/E7/E9 & E10

The depot consists of an office on the approach road and a compound sited to the east of it.

VEHICLE ALLOCATION

DE1675	YX09 FLA	DE1686	YX09 FNJ	DE1899	YX11 AEW	DE1910	YX11 CNV	TP1516	LK03 NKT
DE1676	YX09 FLB	DE1687	YX09 FNK	DE1900	YX11 AEY	DE1911	YX11 CNY	TP1517	LK03 NKU
DE1677	YX09 FLC	DE1688	YX09 FKS	DE1901	YX11 AEZ	TP1507	LT52 XAD	TP1518	LK03 NKW
DE1678	YX09 FLD	DE1689	YX09 FKT	DE1902	YX11 AFA	TP1508	LK03 NKC	TP1519	LK03 NKX
DE1679	YX09 FLE	DE1690	YX09 FKU	DE1903	YX11 AFE	TP1509	LK03 NKD	TP1520	LK03 NKZ
DE1680	YX09 FLF	DE1691	YX09 FKV	DE1904	YX11 AFF	TP1510	LK03 NKE	TP1521	LK03 NLA
DE1681	YX09 FLG	DE1692	YX09 FKW	DE1905	YX11 AFJ	TP1511	LK03 NKF	TP1522	LK03 NLC
DE1682	YX09 FLH	DE1693	YX09 FKY	DE1906	YX11 CNK	TP1512	LK03 NKG	TP1523	LK03 NLP
DE1683	YX09 FLJ	DE1694	YX09 FLM	DE1907	YX11 CNN	TP1513	LK03 NKP	TP1524	LK03 NLR
DE1684	YX09 FLK	DE1897	YX11 AEU	DE1908	YX11 CNO	TP1514	LK03 NKR		
DE1685	YX09 FLL	DE1898	YX11 AEV	DE1909	YX11 CNU	TP1515	LK03 NKS		

Harrow Bus Garage on July 20th, 2013 with London Sovereign No.**DPS629** parked on the drive before operating on the No.H9 service.

HARROW (SO)
331 Pinner Road, Harrow HA1 4HJ
Operated by: London Sovereign
Location: TQ14028843 [51.582973, -0.355871]
Nearest Tube Station: North Harrow (400 yards)
Nearest Bus Routes: 183 & H18/183 & H19 - The Gardens (Stop WK)
Bus Routes Serviced: 398/H9/H10/H11/H13/H14 & H17

London Sovereign Nos **DE96**, **DE92** & **DPS630** on the exit road at **Harrow Bus Garage** on July 20th, 2013. The depot opened in 1994 but due to a low roof beam across the centre of the site it can only accommodate single-deck vehicles.

South Mimms (SM)-allocated Sullivan Buses No.**ELV2** passing **Harrow Bus Garage** on a rail-replacement service on July 20th, 2013.

VEHICLE ALLOCATION

DE50	YX59 BYA	DE74	YX11 FZA	DE84	YX11 FZL	DE94	YX11 FZW	DPS633	SK02 XHH
DE51	YX59 BYB	DE75	YX11 FZB	DE85	YX11 FZM	DE95	YX11 FZY	DPS634	SK02 XHJ
DE52	YX59 BYC	DE76	YX11 FZC	DE86	YX11 FZN	DE96	YX11 FZZ	DPS635	SK02 XHL
DE53	YX59 BYD	DE77	YX11 FZD	DE87	YX11 FZO	DE97	YX11 COH	DPS636	SK02 XHM
DE54	YX59 BYF	DE78	YX11 FZE	DE88	YX11 FZP	DE98	YX11 COJ	DPS637	SK02 XHN
DE55	YX59 BYG	DE79	YX11 FZF	DE89	YX11 FZR	DE99	YX11 CNJ	DPS638	SK02 XHO
DE56	YX59 BYH	DE80	YX11 FZG	DE90	YX11 FZS	DPS628	SK02 XGX	DPS639	SK02 XHP
DE71	YX11 GDA	DE81	YX11 FZH	DE91	YX11 FZT	DPS629	SK02 XHD	DPS640	SK02 XHR
DE72	YX11 GDE	DE82	YX11 FZJ	DE92	YX11 FZU	DPS630	SK02 XHE		
DE73	YX11 GDF	DE83	YX11 FZK	DE93	YX11 FZV	DPS632	SK02 XHG		

Harrow Weald Bus Garage on July 20th, 2013 with Metroline Nos **VP616**, **VP336** & **VP615** parked in the entrance. It was opened in 1930 by the London General Omnibus Company and within two years extended over the forecourt to provide extra covered space.

HARROW WEALD (HD)
467 High Road, Harrow Weald, Middlesex HA3 6EJ
Operated by: Metroline
Location: TQ14999104 [51.606461, -0.340454]
Nearest Station: Headstone Lane (0.9 miles)
Nearest Bus Routes: 182/258/340/640/H12 & H18
- Harrow Weald Bus Garage (Stop WT)
Bus Routes Serviced: 140/182/H12 & N16

Harrow Weald Bus Garage viewed from the north on July 20th, 2013.

VEHICLE ALLOCATION

VP317	LR52 BLK	VP333	LR52 BNK	VP467	LK03 GKF	VP488	LK03 GMX	VP619	LK04 UXB
VP318	LR52 BLN	VP334	LR52 BNL	VP468	LK03 GKG	VP604	LK04 UWJ	VP620	LK04 UXC
VP319	LR52 BLV	VP335	LR52 BNN	VP469	LK03 GKJ	VP605	LK04 UWL	VP621	LK04 UXD
VP320	LR52 BLX	VP336	LR52 BNO	VP470	LK03 GKL	VP606	LK04 UWM	VP622	LK04 UXE
VP321	LR52 BLZ	VP337	LR52 BNU	VP471	LK03 GKN	VP607	LK04 UWN	VP623	LK04 UXF
VP322	LR52 BMO	VP338	LR52 BNV	VP472	LK03 GKP	VP608	LK04 UWP	VP624	LK04 UXG
VP323	LR52 BMU	VP339	LR52 BNX	VP474	LK03 GKV	VP609	LK04 UWR	VP625	LK04 UXH
VP324	LR52 BMV	VP340	LR52 BNY	VP476	LK03 GKY	VP610	LK04 UWS	VP626	LK54 FWE
VP325	LR52 BMY	VP341	LR52 BNZ	VP477	LK03 GKZ	VP611	LK04 UWT	VP627	LK54 FWF
VP326	LR52 BMZ	VP342	LR52 BOF	VP479	LK03 GLJ	VP612	LK04 UWU	VP628	LK54 FWG
VP327	LR52 BNA	VP343	LR52 BOH	VP480	LK03 GLV	VP613	LK04 UWV	VPL207	Y207 NLK
VP328	LR52 BNB	VP344	LR52 BOJ	VP481	LK03 GLY	VP614	LK04 UWW	VPL222	LK51 XGS
VP329	LR52 BND	VP345	LR52 BOU	VP484	LK03 GMF	VP615	LK04 UWX		
VP330	LR52 BNE	VP346	LR52 BOV	VP485	LK03 GMG	VP616	LK04 UWY		
VP331	LR52 BNF	VP347	LR52 BPE	VP486	LK03 GMU	VP617	LK04 UWZ		
VP332	LR52 BNJ	VP466	LK03 GKE	VP487	LK03 GMV	VP618	LK04 UXA		

HAYES BUS GARAGE

Hayes Bus Garage on November 2nd, 2013.

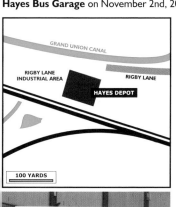

HAYES (HZ)
12 Rigby Lane, Hayes, Middlesex UB3 1ET
Operated by: Metroline
Location: TQ08037980 [51.506779, -0.444692]
Nearest Station: Hayes & Harlington (1.4 miles)
Nearest Bus Routes: 350 – Hayes Town, Swallowfield Way (Northbound)
Bus Routes Serviced: 195/207/427 & N207

Metroline No.**SN1929** exiting from **Hayes Bus Garage** along Rigby Lane on November 2nd, 2013.

VEHICLE ALLOCATION

DE1783	YX10 BCU	SN1920	YR61 RPV	SN1936	YR61 RTO	SN1952	YR61 RVE	VW1827	BK10 MFF
DE1784	YX10 BCV	SN1921	YR61 RPX	SN1937	YR61 RTU	SN1953	YR61 RVF	VW1828	BK10 MFJ
DE1785	YX10 BCY	SN1922	YR61 RPY	SN1938	YR61 RTV	SN1954	YR61 RVJ	VW1829	BK10 LSO
DE1786	YX10 BCZ	SN1923	YR61 RPZ	SN1939	YR61 RTX	SN1955	YR61 RVK	VW1830	BK10 LSU
DE1787	YX10 BDE	SN1924	YR61 RRO	SN1940	YR61 RTZ	SN1956	YR61 RVL	VW1831	BK10 LSV
DE1788	YX10 BDF	SN1925	YR61 RRU	SN1941	YR61 RUA	SN1957	YR61 RVM	VW1832	BK10 LSX
DE1789	YX10 BDO	SN1926	YR61 RRV	SN1942	YR61 RUC	VW1817	BF10 LSZ	VW1833	BK10 LSY
DE1790	YX10 BDU	SN1927	YR61 RRX	SN1943	YR61 RUH	VW1818	BF10 LTA	VW1834	BK10 LTE
DE1791	YX10 BDV	SN1928	YR61 RRY	SN1944	YR61 RUJ	VW1819	BV10 WVP	VW1835	BK10 LTJ
DE1792	YX10 BDY	SN1929	YR61 RRZ	SN1945	YR61 RUO	VW1820	BV10 WVR	VW1836	BV10 WVN
DE1793	YX10 BDZ	SN1930	YR61 RSO	SN1946	YR61 RUU	VW1821	BV10 WVS	VW1837	BV10 WVO
DE1794	YX10 BEJ	SN1931	YR61 RSU	SN1947	YR61 RUV	VW1822	BV10 WVT	VW1838	BV10 WVU
DE1795	YX10 BEO	SN1932	YR61 RSV	SN1948	YR61 RUW	VW1823	BK10 MEV	VW1839	BV10 WVW
DE1796	YX10 BEU	SN1933	YR61 RSX	SN1949	YR61 RUY	VW1824	BK10 MFA	VW1840	BV10 WVX
DE1797	YX10 BEY	SN1934	YR61 RSY	SN1950	YR61 RVA	VW1825	BK10 MFE		
SN1919	YR61 RPU	SN1935	YR61 RSZ	SN1951	YR61 RVC	VW1826	BK10 MFN		

Hayes Bus Garage on November 2nd, 2013 with Abellio London No.**8591** parked in the entrance.

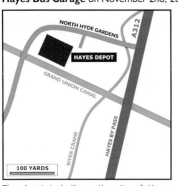

The depot is built on the site of Hayes Creosoting Works which were opened by the Great Western Railway in 1935 for the production of railway sleepers.

HAYES (WS)

West London Coach Centre, North Hyde Gardens, Hayes, Middlesex UB3 4QT
Operated by: Abellio
Location: TQ10627916 [51.501164, -0.410775]
Nearest Station: Hayes & Harlington (1 mile)
Nearest Bus Routes: 195 – Hayes Town, The Crane (Eastbound)
Bus Routes Serviced: 112/350/H28/U7 & U9

VEHICLE ALLOCATION

8041	V301 MDP	8464	RL02 ZTB	8490	KX03 HZS	8589	YX62 DVA	9768	YN51 KWC
8065	SK02 TZN	8465	RL02 ZTC	8499	KX05 KFW	8590	YX62 DVC	9769	YN51 KWD
8113	KX06 LYS	8466	GM03 TGM	8583	YX62 DAU	8591	YX62 DVG	9770	YN51 KWE
8114	KX06 LYT	8467	HX04 HTP	8584	YX62 DBU	9763	YN51 KVW	9771	YN51 KWF
8115	KX56 HCZ	8468	HX04 HTT	8585	YX62 DDE	9764	YN51 KVX	9772	YN51 KWG
8438	RX51 FGN	8469	HX04 HTU	8586	YX62 DDO	9765	YN51 KVZ		
8439	RX51 FGO	8470	HX04 HTV	8587	YX62 DFE	9766	YN51 KWA		
8463	RL02 FVN	8489	KX03 HZR	8588	YX62 DFO	9767	YN51 KWB		

Beddington (BC)-allocated Abellio Dennis Dart SLF Type No.8488 on Beddington Lane, passing Croydon (C) Depot on the 455 Route to Wallington on September 21st, 2013.

ARRIVA LONDON BUS No.VLA36 AT BRIXTON

Norwood (N)-allocated London Arriva Volvo B7TL Type No.VLA36 on Streatham Hill, Brixton on September 21st, 2013.

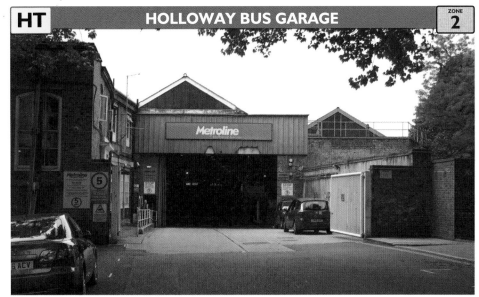

The entrance to **Holloway Bus Garage**, off Pemberton Gardens, on September 17th, 2013.

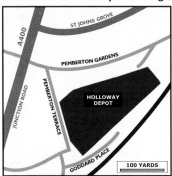

HOLLOWAY (HT)
37A Pemberton Gardens, London N19 5RR
Operated by: Metroline
Location: TQ29458639 [51.561868, -0.133199]
Nearest Station: Upper Holloway (0.3 miles)
Nearest Bus Routes: 17/43/263/271 & N41 – Upper Holloway, Upper Holloway (Stop T)
Bus Routes Serviced: 4/17/43/91/134/143/271/ 390/603/N5/N20/N91 & W7

It was opened between 1907 and 1909 by London County Council as a tram depot, closed to trams and trolleybuses by London Transport on April 6th, 1952 and subsequently utilized as an omnibus garage. Although it was re-named as Highgate in 1950, the original name was reapplied in 1971.

The exit from **Holloway Bus Garage** on September 17th, 2013 with Metroline Nos **VW1298** & **VW1252** visible inside the building.

VEHICLE ALLOCATION

LT 9	LTZ 1009	LT116	LTZ 1116	TE 924	LK58 KGA	VPL233	Y233 NLK	VW1267	LK12 AFU
LT 10	LTZ 1010	LT117	LTZ 1117	TE 925	LK58 KGE	VPL234	Y234 NLK	VW1268	LK12 AFV
LT 11	LTZ 1011	TE 665	LK55 KJV	TE 926	LK58 KGF	VPL235	Y235 NLK	VW1269	LK12 AFX
LT 12	LTZ 1012	TE 666	LK55 KJX	TE 927	LK58 KGG	VPL581	LK04 NLZ	VW1270	LK12 AHA
LT 13	LTZ 1013	TE 667	LK55 KJY	TE 928	LK58 KGJ	VPL582	LK04 NMA	VW1271	LK12 AHC
LT 14	LTZ 1014	TE 668	LK55 KJZ	TE 929	LK58 KGN	VPL583	LK04 NME	VW1272	LK12 AHD
LT 15	LTZ 1015	TE 669	LK55 KKA	TE 930	LK58 KGO	VPL584	LK04 NMF	VW1273	LK12 AHO
LT 16	LTZ 1016	TE 670	LK55 KKB	TE 931	LK09 EKO	VPL585	LK04 NMJ	VW1274	LK12 AHU
LT 17	LTZ 1017	TE 671	LK55 KKC	TE 932	LK58 KGU	VPL586	LK04 NMM	VW1275	LK12 AHZ
LT 18	LTZ 1018	TE 672	LK55 KKD	TE 933	LK58 KGV	VPL587	LK04 NMU	VW1276	LK12 AJX
LT 19	LTZ 1019	TE 673	LK55 KKE	TE 934	LK58 KGY	VPL588	LK04 NMV	VW1277	LK12 AKN
LT 20	LTZ 1020	TE 674	LK55 KKF	TE 935	LK09 EKP	VPL589	LK04 NMX	VW1278	LK12 AKO
LT 21	LTZ 1021	TE 675	LK55 KKG	TP 403	LK03 CEJ	VPL590	LK04 NMY	VW1279	LK12 ALO
LT 22	LTZ 1022	TE 676	LK55 KKH	TP 404	LK03 CEN	VPL591	LK04 NMZ	VW1280	LK12 AMO
LT 23	LTZ 1023	TE 677	LK55 KKJ	TP 408	LK03 CEY	VPL592	LK04 NNA	VW1281	LK12 AMV
LT 24	LTZ 1024	TE 678	LK55 KKL	TP 409	LK03 CFA	VPL593	LK04 NNB	VW1282	LK12 ANF
LT 25	LTZ 1025	TE 679	LK55 KKM	TP 410	LK03 CFD	VPL594	LK04 NNC	VW1283	LK12 AOA
LT 26	LTZ 1026	TE 680	LK55 KKO	TP 414	LK03 CFJ	VPL595	LK04 NND	VW1284	LK12 AOL
LT 27	LTZ 1027	TE 681	LK55 KKP	TP 417	LK03 CFN	VPL596	LK04 NNE	VW1285	LK12 AOO
LT 28	LTZ 1028	TE 682	LK55 KKR	TP 418	LK03 CFP	VPL597	LK04 NNF	VW1286	LK12 AOT
LT 29	LTZ 1029	TE 683	LK55 KKS	TP 419	LK03 CFU	VPL598	LK04 NNG	VW1287	LK12 AOX
LT 30	LTZ 1030	TE 684	LK55 KKT	TP 421	LK03 CFX	VPL599	LK04 NNH	VW1288	LK12 AOY
LT 31	LTZ 1031	TE 685	LK55 KKU	TP 422	LK03 CFY	VPL600	LK04 NNJ	VW1289	LK12 APF
LT 32	LTZ 1032	TE 686	LK55 KKV	TP 423	LK03 CFZ	VPL601	LK04 NNL	VW1290	LK12 APV
LT 33	LTZ 1033	TE 687	LK06 FLA	TP 426	LK03 CGG	VPL602	LK04 NNM	VW1291	LK12 APZ
LT 34	LTZ 1034	TE 688	LK55 KKY	TP 427	LK03 CGU	VPL603	LK04 NNP	VW1292	LK12 ARO
LT 35	LTZ 1035	TE 689	LK55 KKZ	TP 428	LK03 CGV	VPL629	LK54 FWH	VW1293	LK12 ARU
LT 36	LTZ 1036	TE 690	LK55 KLA	TP 432	LK03 GFY	VPL630	LK54 FWJ	VW1294	LK12 ARX
LT 37	LTZ 1037	TE 691	LK55 KLB	TP 451	LK03 GHU	VPL631	LK54 FWL	VW1295	LK12 ARZ
LT 38	LTZ 1038	TE 692	LK55 KLC	TPL257	LN51 KYR	VPL632	LK54 FWM	VW1296	LK12 ASZ
LT 39	LTZ 1039	TE 896	LK08 NVM	TPL258	LN51 KYS	VPL633	LK54 FWN	VW1297	LK12 ATU
LT 40	LTZ 1040	TE 897	LK08 NVN	TPL259	LN51 KYT	VPL634	LK54 FWO	VW1298	LK12 ATV
LT 95	LTZ 1095	TE 898	LK08 NVO	TPL260	LN51 KYU	VPL635	LK54 FWP	VW1299	LK12 AUE
LT 96	LTZ 1096	TE 899	LK08 NVP	TPL261	LN51 KYV	VPL636	LK54 FWR	VW1300	LK12 AUF
LT 97	LTZ 1097	TE 900	LK58 CNE	TPL263	LN51 KYX	VPL637	LK54 FWT	VW1301	LK12 AUM
LT 98	LTZ 1098	TE 901	LK58 CNF	TPL264	LN51 KYY	VW1243	LK12 AAF	VW1302	LK12 AUN
LT 99	LTZ 1099	TE 902	LK58 CNN	TPL265	LN51 KYZ	VW1246	LK12 AAU	VW1303	LK12 AUU
LT100	LTZ 1100	TE 903	LK58 CNO	TPL266	LN51 KZA	VW1250	LK12 ACF	VW1304	LK12 AUV
LT101	LTZ 1101	TE 904	LK58 CNU	TPL267	LN51 KZB	VW1252	LK12 ACZ	VW1305	LK12 AUW
LT102	LTZ 1102	TE 905	LK58 CNV	TPL268	LN51 KZC	VW1253	LK12 ADU	VW1306	LK12 AUY
LT103	LTZ 1103	TE 906	LK58 CNX	TPL269	LN51 KZD	VW1254	LK12 ADV	VW1378	LK62 DPE
LT104	LTZ 1104	TE 907	LK58 CNY	TPL270	LR02 BAA	VW1255	LK12 ADX	VW1379	LK62 DPU
LT105	LTZ 1105	TE 908	LK58 CNZ	VPL155	X665 LLX	VW1256	LK12 AEA	VW1380	LK62 DPY
LT106	LTZ 1106	TE 909	LK58 COA	VPL224	LK51 XGU	VW1257	LK12 AEB	VW1381	LK62 DRV
LT107	LTZ 1107	TE 910	LK58 COH	VPL225	LK51 XGV	VW1258	LK12 AEF	VW1382	LK62 DRZ
LT108	LTZ 1108	TE 911	LK58 COJ	VPL226	LK51 XGW	VW1259	LK12 AEG	VW1383	LK62 DSE
LT109	LTZ 1109	TE 912	LK58 COU	VPL227	LK51 XGX	VW1260	LK12 AET	VW1384	LK62 DSU
LT110	LTZ 1110	TE 913	LK58 CPE	VPL228	LK51 XGY	VW1261	LK12 AEU	VW1385	LK62 DSV
LT111	LTZ 1111	TE 914	LK58 CPF	VPL229	LK51 XGZ	VW1262	LK12 AFO	VW1386	LK62 DTN
LT112	LTZ 1112	TE 920	LK58 KFW	VPL230	LK51 XHA	VW1263	LK12 AEW	VW1387	LK62 DTU
LT113	LTZ 1113	TE 921	LK58 KFX	VPL231	LK51 XHB	VW1264	LK12 AEZ	VW1388	LK62 DTV
LT114	LTZ 1114	TE 922	LK58 KFY	VPL232	Y232 NLK	VW1265	LK12 AFA	VW1468	LK13 BJE
LT115	LTZ 1115	TE 923	LK58 KFZ			VW1266	LK12 AFE		

Hounslow Bus Garage on August 17th, 2013 with London United No.**ADE41** awaiting its next duty.

HOUNSLOW (AV)
Kingsley Road, Hounslow, London TW3 1PA
Operated by: London United
Location: TQ14347607 [51.471623, -0.354852]
Nearest Tube Station: Hounslow East (200 yards)
Nearest Bus Routes: 81/120/222/281/423/681/
H32 & H98 - Hounslow Bus Station
Bus Routes Serviced: 27 (Night Service only)/81/
111/120/203/222/696/697/H32/H37/H98 & N9

The site of the garage and bus station was originally occupied by Hounslow Town District Line station which closed on May 2nd, 1909. The garage was opened by the London General Omnibus Company in 1913 and re-roofed in the 1930s. It was substantially rebuilt in the 1950s with the bus station also being constructed alongside at the same time.

VEHICLE ALLOCATION

ADE 1	YX12 FNG	ADE31	YX12 GHO	DLE24	SN60 ECT	SP 11	YN56 FBU	SP174	YT10 XBX
ADE 2	YX12 FNH	ADE32	YX12 GHU	DLE25	SN60 ECV	SP 12	YN56 FBV	SP175	YT10 XBY
ADE 3	YX12 FNJ	ADE33	YX62 AHE	MCL1	BD11 LWN	SP 13	YN56 FBX	SP176	YT10 XBZ
ADE 4	YX12 FNK	ADE34	YX62 AOE	MCL2	BD11 LWO	SP 14	YN56 FBY	SP177	YT10 XCA
ADE 5	YX12 FNL	ADE35	YX62 ARZ	MCL3	BD11 LWP	SP 15	YN56 FBZ	SP178	YT10 XCB
ADE 6	YX12 FNM	ADE36	YX62 BXF	MCL4	BD11 LWR	SP 23	YN08 DHJ	SP179	YT10 XCC
ADE 7	YX12 FNN	ADE37	YX62 BXR	MCL5	BD11 LWS	SP 24	YN08 DHK	SP180	YT10 XCD
ADE 8	YX12 FNO	ADE38	YX62 BXU	MCL6	BD11 LWT	SP 25	YN08 DHL	SP181	YT10 XCE
ADE 9	YX12 FNP	ADE39	YX62 BXY	MCL7	BD11 LWU	SP 38	YP58 ACF	SP182	YT10 XCF
ADE10	YX12 FNR	ADE40	YX62 BXZ	OT 1	YJ11 EHG	SP 41	YT09 BKA	SP183	YT10 XCG
ADE11	YX12 FNS	ADE41	YX62 BYG	OT 2	YJ11 EHH	SP 42	YT09 BMO	SP184	YT10 XCH
ADE12	YX12 FNT	ADE42	YX62 BYJ	OT 3	YJ11 EHK	SP 43	YT09 BMU	SP185	YT10 XCJ
ADE13	YX12 FNU	ADE43	YX62 BYK	OT 4	YJ11 EHL	SP 44	YT09 BMY	SP186	YT10 XCK
ADE14	YX12 FNV	ADE44	YX62 BZE	OT 5	YJ11 EHM	SP 45	YT09 BMZ	SP187	YT10 XCL
ADE15	YX12 FNW	ADE45	YX62 BZS	OT 6	YJ11 EHN	SP 46	YT09 BNA	SP188	YT10 XCM
ADE16	YX12 FNY	DLE 1	SN60 EAX	OT 7	YJ11 EHO	SP 47	YT09 BNB	SP189	YT10 XCN
ADE17	YX12 FNZ	DLE 2	SN60 EAY	OT 8	YJ11 EHP	SP 48	YT09 BND	SP190	YT10 XCO
ADE18	YX12 FOA	DLE 3	SN60 EBA	OT 9	YJ11 EHR	SP 49	YT09 BNE	VA74	V190 OOE
ADE19	YX12 FOC	DLE 4	SN60 EBC	OT10	YJ11 EHS	SP 50	YT09 BNF	VM1	BF62 UXU
ADE20	YX12 FOD	DLE 5	SN60 EBD	OT11	YJ11 EHT	SP 51	YT09 BNJ	VP105	W448 BCW
ADE21	YX12 FOF	DLE 6	SN60 EBF	OT12	YJ11 EHU	SP136	YP59 ODS	VP106	W449 BCW
ADE22	YX12 FOH	DLE 7	SN60 EBG	OT13	YJ11 EHV	SP165	YT10 UWA	VP107	W451 BCW
ADE23	YX12 FOJ	DLE 8	SN60 EBJ	OT14	YJ11 EHW	SP166	YT10 UWB	VP108	W452 BCW
ADE24	YX62 AEW	DLE 9	SN60 EBK	OT15	YJ11 EHX	SP167	YT10 UWD	VP109	W453 BCW
ADE25	YX62 AGU	DLE11	SN60 EBM	OT16	YJ11 EHZ	SP168	YT10 UWF	VP110	W454 BCW
ADE26	YX12 FON	DLE19	SN60 ECC	SP 6	YN56 FCG	SP169	YT10 UWG	VP111	W457 BCW
ADE27	YX12 FOP	DLE20	SN60 ECD	SP 7	YN56 FCJ	SP170	YT10 UWH		
ADE28	YX12 GHJ	DLE21	SN60 ECE	SP 8	YN56 FBA	SP171	YT10 XBU		
ADE29	YX12 GHK	DLE22	SN60 ECF	SP 9	YN56 FBB	SP172	YT10 XBV		
ADE30	YX12 GHN	DLE23	SN60 ECJ	SP 10	YN56 FBO	SP173	YT10 XBW		

A general view of **Hounslow Heath Bus Garage** on August 17th, 2013.

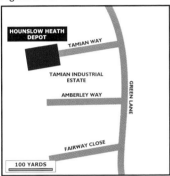

HOUNSLOW HEATH (HH)
Tamian Way, Hounslow, Middlesex TW4 6BL
Operated by: London United
Location: TQ11317505 [51.463274, -0.398773]
Nearest Tube Station: Hounslow West (1.5 miles)
Nearest Bus Routes: 117 & 635 - Green Lane (Stop R)
Bus Routes Serviced: 116/216/285/423/482/635/698/H22 & H91

London United Nos **TLA1**, **TLA8** & **TA218** line up at **Hounslow Heath Bus Garage** on August 17th, 2013.

The north entrance to **Hounslow Heath Bus Garage** on August 17th, 2013.

VEHICLE ALLOCATION

DE 1	YX58 DVA	DE 18	YX58 DVW	DPS677	LG02 FHH	SP 2	YN56 FCC	SP197	YR10 FGD
DE 2	YX58 DVB	DE 19	YX58 DUV	DPS678	LG02 FHJ	SP 3	YN56 FCD	SP198	YR10 FGE
DE 3	YX58 DVC	DE 20	YX58 DUY	DPS679	LG02 FHK	SP 4	YN56 FCE	SP199	YR10 FGF
DE 4	YX58 DVF	DE 21	YX58 DWK	DPS680	LG02 FHL	SP 5	YN56 FCF	SP200	YR10 FGG
DE 5	YX58 DVG	DE 22	YX09 HJJ	DPS707	SN55 HKK	SP 16	YN08 DEU	SP201	YR10 FGJ
DE 6	YX58 DVH	DLE10	SN60 EBL	DPS708	SN55 HKL	SP 17	YN08 DHA	SP202	YR10 FGK
DE 7	YX58 DVJ	DLE12	SN60 EBO	DPS709	SN55 HKM	SP 18	YN08 DHC	SP203	YR10 FGM
DE 8	YX58 DVK	DLE13	SN60 EBP	DPS710	SN55 HKO	SP 19	YN08 DHD	SP204	YR10 FGN
DE 9	YX58 DVL	DLE14	SN60 EBU	DPS711	SN55 HKP	SP 20	YN08 DHE	SP205	YR10 FGO
DE 10	YX58 DVM	DLE15	SN60 EBV	DPS712	SN55 HKT	SP 21	YN08 DHF	SP206	YR10 FGP
DE 11	YX58 DVN	DLE16	SN60 EBX	DPS713	SN55 HKU	SP 22	YN08 DHG	TA215	SN51 SYU
DE 12	YX58 DVO	DLE17	SN60 EBZ	DPS714	SN55 HKV	SP191	YR10 FFW	TA216	SN51 SYV
DE 13	YX58 DVP	DLE18	SN60 ECA	DPS715	SN55 HKW	SP192	YR10 FFX	TA217	SN51 SYW
DE 14	YX58 DVR	DPS582	SN51 TDV	DPS716	SN55 HKX	SP193	YR10 FFY	TA218	SN51 SYX
DE 15	YX58 DVT	DPS673	LG02 FHC	DPS717	SN55 HKY	SP194	YR10 FFZ	TLA 6	SN53 EUM
DE 16	YX58 DVU	DPS674	LG02 FHD	DPS718	SN55 HSD	SP195	YR10 FGA	TLA 8	SN53 EUP
DE 17	YX58 DVV	DPS675	LG02 FHE	SP 1	YN56 FCA	SP196	YR10 FGC		

A general view of **Kings Cross Bus Garage** on September 17th, 2013. The depot opened on July 10th, 2010 and the office and entrance can be seen at the far end of the road.

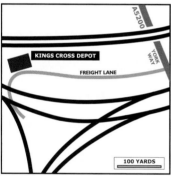

KINGS CROSS (KC)
1 Freight Lane, London N1 0FF
Operated by: Metroline
Location: TQ29928409 [51.540767, -0.127971]
Nearest Station: King's Cross (0.8 miles)
Nearest Bus Routes: 390 - York Way Railway Bridge (Stop A)
Bus Routes Serviced: 46/214 & 274

Metroline No.**DE999** on September 17th, 2013, moving west along Freight Lane before gaining access to **Kings Cross Bus Garage**.

A closer view of the wash plant at **Kings Cross Bus Garage** on September 17th, 2013 with Metroline No.**DE1334** alongside.

VEHICLE ALLOCATION

DE 999	LK09 EOA	DE1163	LK11 CWV	DE1322	LK12 AXA	DE1334	LK12 AYP	DLD701	LK55 KLU
DE1152	LK11 CWF	DE1164	LK11 CWW	DE1323	LK12 AXG	DE1335	LK12 AYZ	DLD702	LK55 KLV
DE1153	LK11 CWG	DE1165	LK11 CWX	DE1324	LK12 AXH	DE1336	LK12 AZA	DLD703	LK55 KLX
DE1154	LK11 CWJ	DE1166	LK11 CWY	DE1325	LK12 AXP	DLD207	LN51 KXO	DLD704	LK55 KLZ
DE1155	LK11 CWL	DE1167	LK11 CWZ	DE1326	LK12 AXR	DLD693	LK55 KLE	DLD705	LK55 KMA
DE1156	LK11 CWM	DE1168	LK11 CXA	DE1327	LK12 AXS	DLD694	LK55 KLF	DLD706	LK55 KME
DE1157	LK11 CWN	DE1169	LK11 CXB	DE1328	LK12 AXV	DLD695	LK55 KLJ	DLD707	LK55 KMF
DE1158	LK11 CWO	DE1170	LK11 CXC	DE1329	LK12 AXW	DLD696	LK55 KLL	DLD708	LK55 KMG
DE1159	LK11 CWP	DE1318	LK12 AWU	DE1330	LK12 AXZ	DLD697	LK55 KLM	DLD709	LK55 KMJ
DE1160	LK11 CWR	DE1319	LK12 AWX	DE1331	LK12 AYF	DLD698	LK55 KLO	DLD710	LK55 KMM
DE1161	LK11 CWT	DE1320	LK12 AWY	DE1332	LK12 AYG	DLD699	LK55 KLP	DLD711	LK55 KMO
DE1162	LK11 CWU	DE1321	LK12 AWZ	DE1333	LK12 AYN	DLD700	LK55 KLS		

LV | LEE VALLEY BUS GARAGE | ZONE 3

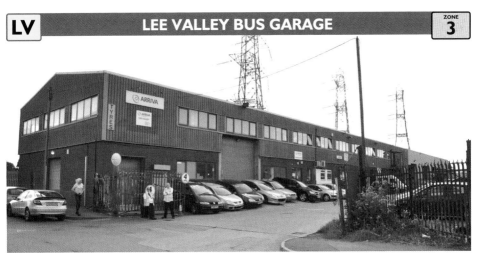

Lee Valley Bus Garage on August 20th, 2013. It was opened in 2005 to accommodate the articulated buses being deployed on Route No.149.

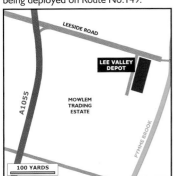

LEE VALLEY (LV)
Leeside Road, Tottenham, London N17 0SG
Operated by: Arriva London
Location: TQ35419148 [51.606237, -0.045974]
Nearest Station: Angel Road (0.5 miles)
Nearest Bus Routes: 192
Bus Routes Serviced: 34/318/341/397/444/657/
W3/W6 & W11

VEHICLE ALLOCATION

DLA293	Y493 UGC	DWL42	LF02 POA	ENS22	LJ12 BZF	T145	LJ60 AVR	T202	LJ61 CHF
DLA299	Y499 UGC	DWL43	LF02 POH	ENS23	LJ12 BYL	T146	LJ60 AVT	T203	LJ61 CHG
DLA348	LJ03 MKU	DWL45	LF52 UNW	ENS24	LJ12 BYM	T147	LJ60 AVU	T204	LJ61 CHH
DLA349	LJ03 MKV	DWL46	LF52 UNX	ENS25	LJ12 BYN	T148	LJ60 AVV	T205	LJ61 CHK
DLA350	LJ03 MKX	DWL47	LF52 UNY	ENS26	LJ12 BYO	T149	LJ60 AVW	T206	LJ61 CHL
DLA351	LJ03 MKZ	DWL48	LF52 UNZ	ENS27	LJ12 BYP	T150	LJ60 AVX	T207	LJ61 CHN
DLA352	LJ03 MLE	DWL49	LF52 UOA	ENS28	LJ12 BYR	T151	LJ60 AVY	T208	LJ61 CHO
DLA353	LJ03 MLF	DWL51	LF52 UOC	PDL 88	LF52 USH	T152	LJ60 AVZ	T209	LJ61 CHV
DLA354	LJ03 MLK	DWL52	LF52 UOD	PDL 89	LF52 USJ	T153	LJ60 AWA	T210	LJ61 CHX
DLA355	LJ03 MJX	EN16	GN57 BPF	PDL 90	LF52 USL	T154	LJ60 AWC	T211	LJ61 CGF
DLA356	LJ03 MJY	EN17	GN57 BPK	PDL101	LJ54 BBF	T155	LJ60 AVC	T212	LJ61 CGG
DLA357	LJ03 MKA	EN18	GN57 BPO	PDL102	LJ54 BBK	T156	LJ60 AVD	T213	LJ61 CGK
DLA358	LJ03 MKC	EN19	GN57 BPU	PDL103	LJ54 BBN	T157	LJ60 AVE	T214	LJ61 CGO
DLA359	LJ03 MKD	EN20	GN57 BPV	PDL104	LJ54 BBO	T158	LJ60 AVF	T215	LJ61 CGU
DLA360	LJ03 MKE	EN21	GN57 BPK	PDL105	LJ54 BBU	T159	LJ60 AVG	T216	LJ61 CGV
DLA361	LJ03 MKF	EN22	GN57 BPY	PDL106	LJ54 LHF	T160	LJ60 AVK	T217	LJ61 CGX
DLA362	LJ03 MKG	ENL19	LJ58 AWG	PDL107	LJ54 LHG	T161	LJ60 AVM	T218	LJ61 CGY
DLA363	LJ03 MKK	ENL20	LJ58 AVE	PDL108	LJ54 LHH	T162	LJ60 AVN	T219	LJ61 CGZ
DLA364	LJ03 MKL	ENS15	LJ12 BYY	PDL109	LJ54 LHK	T163	LJ60 AVO	T220	LJ61 CHC
DLA365	LJ03 MWE	ENS16	LJ12 BYZ	PDL110	LJ54 LHL	T164	LJ60 AVP	T221	LJ61 CFM
DLA366	LJ03 MWF	ENS17	LJ12 BZA	PDL121	LJ05 GPK	T165	LJ60 AUO	T222	LJ61 CFN
DLA367	LJ03 MWG	ENS18	LJ12 BZB	PDL122	LJ05 GPO	T166	LJ60 AUP	T223	LJ61 CFO
DLA368	LJ03 MWK	ENS19	LJ12 BZC	PDL137	SN06 BPE	T167	LJ60 AUR	T260	LJ61 LKL
DLA369	LJ03 MWL	ENS20	LJ12 BZD	PDL138	SN06 BPF	T168	LJ60 AUT		
DLA370	LJ03 MUY	ENS21	LJ12 BZE	PDL139	SN06 BPK	T201	LJ61 CHD		

53

Lee Interchange Bus Garage on September 17th, 2013 with Tower Transit Nos **DML44279** & **DN33625** in view. The garage was opened in 2007 to replace Stratford, Waterden Road which was removed to make way for the development of the Olympic Park.

LEE INTERCHANGE (LI)
151 Ruckholt Road, Leyton, London E10 5PB
Operated by: Tower Transit
Location: TQ37718596 [51.555692, -0.014951]
Nearest Tube Station: Leyton (0.6 miles)
Nearest Bus Routes: 308/N26 & W15
Bus Routes Serviced: 25/26/30/58/236/308/339/425/N26/N550/N551/RV1/W14 & W15

A general view of **Lee Interchange Bus Garage**, looking south from the railway bridge on Ruckholt Road on September 17th, 2013.

The entrance to **Lee Interchange Bus Garage** in Temple Mills Lane, looking northwest towards the main depot building on September 17th, 2013.

VEHICLE ALLOCATION

DM41444	LN51 DUA	DML44291	YX61 FYO	DN33625	SN11 BNU	TNL33036	LK51 UYE	VN36141	BJ11 EBP
DM41445	LN51 DUH	DML44292	YX61 FYP	DN33626	SN11 BNV	VN36101	BJ11 DSE	VN36142	BJ11 EAM
DM44167	YX60 DXL	DMV44221	YX12 AYZ	DN33627	SN11 BNX	VN36102	BJ11 DSZ	VN36143	BJ11 EAF
DM44168	YX60 DXM	DMV44222	YX12 AZA	DN33628	SN11 BNY	VN36103	BJ11 DSU	VN36144	BJ11 EAX
DM44169	YX60 DXO	DMV44223	YX12 AKK	DN33629	SN11 BNZ	VN36104	BJ11 DTF	VN36145	BJ11 EBG
DM44170	YX60 DXP	DMV44224	YX12 AKN	DN33630	SN11 BOF	VN36105	BJ11 DSV	VN36146	BJ11 EBL
DM44260	YX61 FZC	DMV44225	YX12 AEW	DN33631	SN11 BOH	VN36106	BJ11 DTV	VN36147	BJ11 EAK
DM44261	YX61 FZD	DMV44226	YX12 AEY	DN33632	SN11 BOJ	VN36107	BJ11 DTY	VN36148	BJ11 EAW
DM44262	YX61 FZE	DMV44227	YX12 AEO	DN33633	SN11 BOU	VN36108	BJ11 DTO	VN36149	BJ11 EAO
DM44263	YX61 FZF	DMV44228	YX12 AEP	DN33634	SN11 BOV	VN36109	BJ11 DUV	VN36150	BJ11 EBD
DM44264	YX61 FZG	DMV44229	YX12 AUA	DN33635	SN11 BPE	VN36110	BJ11 DUA	VN36151	BJ11 EBC
DM44265	YX61 FZH	DMV44230	YX12 AGY	DN33636	SN11 BPF	VN36111	BJ11 DVH	VN36152	BJ11 EAE
DM44266	YX61 FZJ	DMV44231	YX12 AXV	DN33637	SN11 BPK	VN36112	BJ11 DVF	VN36153	BJ11 DVX
DM44267	YX61 FZK	DMV44232	YX12 AFZ	DN33638	SN11 BPO	VN36113	BJ11 DVP	VN36154	BJ11 EAA
DM44268	YX61 FZL	DMV44233	YX12 AZN	DN33639	SN11 BPU	VN36114	BJ11 DVM	VN36155	BJ11 DZZ
DM44269	YX61 FZM	DMV44234	YX12 AJY	DN33640	SN11 BPV	VN36115	BJ11 DVL	VN36156	BJ11 DZY
DM44270	YX61 FZN	DMV44235	YX12 AGZ	DN33641	SN11 BPX	VN36116	BJ11 DUU	VN36157	BJ11 EAC
DMC42515	LK03 NKH	DMV44236	YX12 AON	DN33642	SN11 BPY	VN36117	BJ11 DVK	VN36158	BJ11 EAG
DMC42516	LK03 NKJ	DMV44250	YX12 AKP	DN33643	SN11 BPZ	VN36118	BJ11 DVC	VN36159	BJ11 EAP
DMC42517	LK03 NKL	DMV44251	YX12 AKU	DN33644	SN11 BRF	VN36119	BJ11 DSY	VN36160	BJ11 EAY
DMC42518	LK03 NKM	DMV44252	YX12 AKV	DN33645	SN11 BRV	VN36120	BJ11 DRZ	VN36161	BJ11 EBA
DML44171	YX11 AFK	DMV44253	YX12 AKY	DN33646	SN11 BRZ	VN36121	BJ11 DSO	VN36162	BJ11 EBK
DML44172	YX11 AFN	DMV44254	YX12 AEV	DN33647	SN11 BSO	VN36122	BJ11 DTK	VN36163	BJ11 EBM
DML44173	YX11 AFO	DMV44255	YX12 AHJ	DN33648	SN11 BSU	VN36123	BJ11 DTX	VN36164	BJ11 EBO
DML44174	YX11 AFU	DMV44256	YX12 AHK	DN33649	SN11 BSV	VN36124	BJ11 DTU	VN36165	BJ11 EBN
DML44175	YX11 AFV	DMV44257	YX12 ABF	DN33650	SN11 BSX	VN36125	BJ11 DVG	VN37842	BV10 WVM
DML44176	YX11 AFY	DMV44258	YX12 ABK	DN33651	SN11 BSY	VN36126	BJ11 DUY	VN37844	BV10 WWT
DML44177	YX11 AFZ	DMV44259	YX12 AWU	DN33652	SN11 BSZ	VN36127	BJ11 DVA	VN37847	BV10 WWE
DML44178	YX11 AGO	DN33612	SN11 BMU	DN33653	SN11 BTE	VN36128	BJ11 DVB	VN37849	BV10 WWG
DML44279	YX61 FYB	DN33613	SN11 BMV	DN33654	SN11 BTO	VN36129	BJ11 DVO	VN37850	BV10 WWH
DML44280	YX61 FYC	DN33614	SN11 BMY	DN33655	SN11 BTU	VN36130	BJ11 DVN	VN37851	BV10 WWJ
DML44281	YX61 FYD	DN33615	SN11 BMZ	DN33789	SN13 CGY	VN36131	BJ11 DVR	VN37852	BV10 WWK
DML44282	YX61 FYE	DN33616	SN11 BNA	DN33790	SN13 CGZ	VN36132	BJ11 DSX	VN37853	BV10 WWL
DML44283	YX61 FYF	DN33617	SN11 BNB	DN33791	SN13 CHC	VN36133	BJ11 DTN	VN37854	BV10 WWM
DML44284	YX61 FYG	DN33618	SN11 BND	DN33792	SN13 CHD	VN36134	BJ11 DTZ	VN37855	BV10 WWN
DML44285	YX61 FYH	DN33619	SN11 BNE	DN33793	SN13 CHF	VN36135	BJ11 DUH	VN37859	BV10 WWS
DML44286	YX61 FYJ	DN33620	SN11 BNF	DN33794	SN13 CHG	VN36136	BJ11 DVV	VN37860	BV10 WWB
DML44287	YX61 FYK	DN33621	SN11 BNJ	DN33795	SN13 CHH	VN36137	BJ11 DVW	VN37861	BV10 WWU
DML44288	YX61 FYL	DN33622	SN11 BNK	DN33796	SN13 CHJ	VN36138	BJ11 DVT	VN37862	BV10 WWX
DML44289	YX61 FYM	DN33623	SN11 BNL	DN33797	SN13 CHK	VN36139	BJ11 DVU	VN37863	BV10 WVY
DML44290	YX61 FYN	DN33624	SN11 BNO	DN33798	SN13 CHL	VN36140	BJ11 DZX	VN37864	BV10 WVZ

Stagecoach London No.15135 exiting from **Leyton Bus Garage** to take up duties on Route No.55 to Oxford Circus on September 17th, 2013.

LEYTON (T)
High Road Leyton, London E10 6AD
Operated by: Stagecoach London
Location: TQ38128797 [51.573806, -0.008546]
Nearest Station: Leyton Midland Road (0.3 miles)
Nearest Bus Routes: 20/48/55/56/69/97/230/257/357/W15/W16 & W19
Bus Routes Serviced: 48/55/56/69 (Night Service only)/97/179/215/275 & N55

The depot was opened by the London General Omnibus Company in 1912 to replace one that had been acquired from the London Metropolitan. It was badly damaged by bombing during WWII and not substantially rebuilt until 1955.

VEHICLE ALLOCATION

10113	LX12 DCZ	15126	LX59 CLV	15151	LX59 COJ	17523	LX51 FOD	17809	LX03 BXD
10114	LX12 DDA	15127	LX59 CLY	15152	LX59 COU	17524	LX51 FOF	17810	LX03 BXE
10115	LX12 DDE	15128	LX59 CLZ	15153	LX59 CPE	17525	LX51 FOH	17811	LX03 BXF
10116	LX12 DDF	15129	LX59 CME	15154	LX59 CPF	17541	LY02 OAN	17812	LX03 BXG
10117	LX12 DDJ	15130	LX59 CMF	15155	LX59 CPK	17543	LY02 OAP	17813	LX03 BXH
10118	LX12 DDK	15131	LX59 CMK	15156	LX59 CPN	17568	LV52 HEU	17814	LX03 BXJ
10119	LX12 DDL	15132	LX59 CMO	15157	LX59 CPO	17575	LV52 HFH	17826	LX03 BXZ
10120	LX12 DDN	15133	LX59 CMU	15158	LX59 CPU	17578	LV52 HFL	17827	LX03 BYA
10121	LX12 DDO	15134	LX59 CMV	15159	LX59 CPV	17745	LY52 ZFD	17828	LX03 BYB
10122	LX12 DDU	15135	LX59 CMY	15160	LX59 CPY	17746	LY52 ZFE	17851	LX03 BZE
10123	LX12 DDV	15136	LX59 CMZ	15161	LX59 CPZ	17747	LY52 ZFF	17852	LX03 BZF
10172	SN63 JVX	15137	LX59 CNA	15162	LX59 CRF	17749	LY52 ZFH	17853	LX03 BZG
10173	SN63 JVY	15138	LX59 CNC	15163	LX59 CRJ	17796	LX03 BWK	17871	LX03 NFT
10174	SN63 JVZ	15139	LX59 CNE	15164	LX59 CRK	17797	LX03 BWL	17873	LX03 NFV
10175	SN63 JWA	15140	LX59 CNF	15165	LX59 CRU	17798	LX03 BWM	17875	LX03 NFZ
10176	SN63 JWC	15141	LX59 CNJ	15166	LX59 CRV	17799	LX03 BWN	17876	LX03 NGE
10177	SN63 JWD	15142	LX59 CNK	15167	LX59 CRZ	17800	LX03 BWP	17877	LX03 NGF
10178	SN63 JWE	15143	LX59 CNN	15168	LX59 CSF	17801	LX03 BWU	17892	LX03 ORC
10179	SN63 JWF	15144	LX59 CNO	15169	LX59 CSO	17802	LX03 BWV	17905	LX03 ORY
10180	SN63 JWG	15145	LX59 CNU	15170	LX10 AUC	17803	LX03 BWW	17906	LX03 ORZ
10181	SN63 JWJ	15146	LX59 CNV	15171	LX10 AUE	17804	LX03 BWY	17907	LX03 OSA
10182	SN63 JWK	15147	LX59 CNY	15172	LX10 AUH	17805	LX03 BWZ	17908	LX03 OSB
10183	SN63 JWL	15148	LX59 CNZ	15173	LX10 AUH	17806	LX03 BXA		
15019	LX58 CFK	15149	LX59 COA	15174	LX10 AUJ	17807	LX03 BXB		
15125	LX59 CLU	15150	LX59 COH	17522	LX51 FOC	17808	LX03 BXC		

Mandela Way Bus Garage on August 31st, 2013.

MANDELA WAY (MW)
Unit 2, 5 Mandela Way, London SE1 5SS
Operated by: Go-Ahead London
Location: TQ33587871 [51.491317, -0.077672]
Nearest Station: Elephant & Castle (1.3 miles)
Nearest Bus Routes: 21/53/168/172/453 & N21 - Dunton Road (Stop EC)
Bus Routes Serviced: 1/42/453/507/521/624/658 & N1

East Thames Buses vacated Ash Grove (See Page 7) on October 13th, 2005 and moved to a brand new facility here. In 2009 the company was sold to London General (Go-Ahead London).

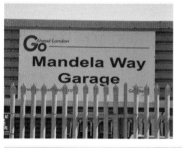

Go-Ahead London buses lined up in the yard at **Mandela Way Bus Garage** on August 31st, 2013.

VEHICLE ALLOCATION

DWL17	FJ54 ZDR	E176	SN61 BHJ	E191	SN61 BJO	ELS 5	YU02 GHD	VWL31	LF52 TJU
DWL37	FJ54 ZDC	E177	SN61 BHK	E192	SN61 BJU	ELS 6	YU02 GHA	VWL32	BX04 AZW
E163	SN61 BGF	E178	SN61 BHL	E193	SN61 BJV	ELS 7	YU02 GHN	VWL33	BX04 AZV
E164	SN61 BGK	E179	SN61 BHO	E194	SN61 BJX	ELS 8	YU02 GHO	VWL34	BX04 AZU
E165	SN61 BGO	E180	SN61 BHP	E195	SN61 BJY	ELS 9	YR52 VFJ	VWL35	BX04 AZZ
E166	SN61 BGU	E181	SN61 BHU	E196	SN61 BJZ	ELS10	YR52 VFH	VWL36	BX04 BAA
E167	SN61 BGV	E182	SN61 BHV	E197	SN61 BKA	ELS11	YR52 VFK	VWL37	BX04 BAU
E168	SN61 BGX	E183	SN61 BHW	E198	SN61 BKD	ELS12	YR52 VFL	VWL38	BX04 BAV
E169	SN61 BGY	E184	SN61 BHX	E199	SN61 BKE	ELS13	YR52 VFM	VWL39	BX04 BBE
E170	SN61 BGZ	E185	SN61 BHY	E200	SN61 BKF	ELS14	YR52 VFN	VWL40	BX04 BBF
E171	SN61 BHA	E186	SN61 BHZ	E201	SN61 BKG	PVL232	Y732 TGH	VWL41	BX04 BBJ
E172	SN61 BHD	E187	SN61 BJE	ELS 1	YU02 GHG	VWL27	LF52 THV	VWL42	BX04 BKL
E173	SN61 BGE	E188	SN61 BJF	ELS 2	YU02 GHH	VWL28	LF52 THX	VWL43	BX04 BKK
E174	SN61 BHE	E189	SN61 BJJ	ELS 3	YU02 GHJ	VWL29	LF52 THZ	VWL44	BX04 BKJ
E175	SN61 BHF	E190	SN61 BJK	ELS 4	YU02 GHK	VWL30	LF52 TJO	WVL271	LX06 ECE

Go-Ahead London No.**SOE21** passing **Merton Bus Garage** whilst working Route No.200 to Mitcham on September 19th, 2013.

MERTON (AL)
High Street, London SW19 1DN
Operated by: Go-Ahead London
Location: TQ26547030 [51.417402, -0.181738]
Nearest Tube Station: South Wimbledon (0.5 miles)
Nearest Bus Routes: 57/131/152/200/219 & N155 - Merton Abbey Savacentre (Stop E)
Bus Routes Serviced: 22/44/77/118/155/163/164/200/201/219/270/280/655 & N155

Merton Garage opened in 1913 and was the largest depot operated by the London General Omnibus Company. It was modernized in 1960 and further modernization in 1991 included the installation of a new roof and a repositioning of some of the ancillary buildings within the depot to improve the parking areas.

Go-Ahead London No.**DW2** parked inside **Merton Bus Garage** on September 19th, 2013.

The offices and amenities block in Wandle Bank, viewed on September 19th, 2013

VEHICLE ALLOCATION

DW 1	LF52 TKJ	E 92	LX57 CLV	PVL384	PJ53 NKZ	PVL419	LX54 GZZ	SOE19	LX09 AZB
DW 2	LF52 TKC	E 93	LX57 CLY	PVL385	PJ53 NLA	SE 1	LX07 BXH	SOE20	LX09 AZC
DW 3	LF52 TKD	E138	SN60 BZK	PVL386	PJ53 NLC	SE 2	LX07 BXJ	SOE21	LX09 AZD
DW 4	LF52 TJY	E139	SN60 BZL	PVL387	PJ53 NLD	SE 3	LX07 BXK	SOE22	LX09 AZF
DW 5	LF52 TJV	E140	SN60 BZM	PVL388	PJ53 NLE	SE 4	LX07 BXL	SOE23	LX09 AZG
DW 6	LF52 TJX	E141	SN60 BZO	PVL389	PJ53 NLF	SE 5	LX07 BXM	SOE24	LX09 AZJ
DW 7	LF52 TKO	E142	SN60 BZP	PVL390	LX54 HAA	SE 6	LX07 BXN	SOE25	LX09 AZL
DW 8	LF52 TKK	E143	SN60 BZR	PVL391	LX54 HAE	SE 7	LX07 BXO	SOE26	LX09 AZN
DW 9	LF52 TKT	E144	SN60 BZS	PVL392	LX54 HAO	SE 8	LX07 BXP	SOE27	LX09 AZO
DW11	LF52 TKN	E145	SN60 BZT	PVL393	LX54 HAU	SE 9	LX07 BXR	SOE28	LX09 AZP
DW12	LF52 TKA	E146	SN60 BZU	PVL394	LX54 HBA	SE10	LX07 BXS	WDL1	LX58 CWG
E 68	LX57 CJO	E147	SN60 BZV	PVL395	LX54 HBB	SE11	LX07 BXU	WS10	LJ13 GJU
E 69	LX57 CJU	E148	SN60 BZW	PVL396	LX54 GZG	SE12	LX07 BXV	WS11	LJ13 GJV
E 70	LX57 CJV	E149	SN60 BZX	PVL397	LX54 GZH	SE13	LX07 BXW	WS12	LJ13 GJY
E 71	LX57 CJY	E150	SN60 BZY	PVL398	LX54 GZK	SE14	LX07 BXY	WS13	LJ13 GJY
E 72	LX57 CJZ	E277	SN13 CJF	PVL399	LX54 GZL	SE15	LX07 BXZ	WS14	LJ13 GJZ
E 73	LX57 CKA	E278	SN13 CJJ	PVL400	LX54 GZM	SE16	LX07 BYA	WS15	LJ13 GKA
E 74	LX57 CKC	E279	SN13 CJO	PVL401	LX54 GZN	SOE 1	LX09 AYF	WS16	LJ13 GKC
E 75	LX57 CKD	E280	SN13 CJU	PVL402	LX54 GZO	SOE 2	LX09 AYG	WS17	LJ13 GKD
E 76	LX57 CKE	LDP198	SN51 UAL	PVL403	LX54 GZP	SOE 3	LX09 AYH	WS18	LJ13 GKE
E 77	LX57 CKF	PVL112	W512 WGH	PVL404	LX54 GZR	SOE 4	LX09 AYJ	WS19	LJ13 GKF
E 78	LX57 CKG	PVL215	Y815 TGH	PVL405	LX54 GZT	SOE 5	LX09 AYK	WS20	LJ13 GKG
E 79	LX57 CKJ	PVL371	PJ53 NKG	PVL406	LX54 GYV	SOE 6	I X09 AYI	WVI 101	LF52 ZNO
E 80	LX57 CKK	PVL372	PJ53 NKH	PVL407	LX54 GYW	SOE 7	LX09 AYM	WVL102	LF52 ZLZ
E 81	LX57 CKL	PVL373	PJ53 NKK	PVL408	LX54 GYY	SOE 8	LX09 AYN	WVL152	LX53 BEY
E 82	LX57 CKN	PVL374	PJ53 NKL	PVL409	LX54 GYZ	SOE 9	LX09 AYO	WVL206	LX05 EZC
E 83	LX57 CKO	PVL375	PJ53 NKM	PVL410	LX54 GZB	SOE10	LX09 AYP	WVL207	LX05 EZD
E 84	LX57 CKP	PVL376	PJ53 NKN	PVL411	LX54 GZC	SOE11	LX09 AYS	WVL208	LX05 EZE
E 85	LX57 CKU	PVL377	PJ53 NKO	PVL412	LX54 GZD	SOE12	LX09 AYT	WVL209	LX05 EZF
E 86	LX57 CKV	PVL378	PJ53 NKP	PVL413	LX54 GZE	SOE13	LX09 AYU	WVL210	LX05 EZG
E 87	LX57 CKY	PVL379	PJ53 NKR	PVL414	LX54 GZF	SOE14	LX09 AYV	WVL211	LX05 EZH
E 88	LX57 CLF	PVL380	PJ53 NKT	PVL415	LX54 GZU	SOE15	LX09 AYW		
E 89	LX57 CLJ	PVL381	PJ53 NKU	PVL416	LX54 GZV	SOE16	LX09 AYY		
E 90	LX57 CLN	PVL382	PJ53 NKW	PVL417	LX54 GZW	SOE17	LX09 AYZ		
E 91	LX57 CLO	PVL383	PJ53 NKX	PVL418	LX54 GZY	SOE18	LX09 AZA		

The entrance road off New Cross Road into **New Cross Bus Garage** on August 31st, 2013.

NEW CROSS (NX)
208 New Cross Road, London SE14 5UH
Operated by: Go-Ahead London
Location: TQ35977671 [51.473044, -0.044027]
Nearest Station: New Cross Gate (300 yards)
Nearest Bus Routes: 36/136/171/177/343/436/
N89/N136,N171/N343 & P13 - New Cross Bus
Garage (Stop K)
Bus Routes Serviced: 21/36/108/129/171/225/
321/436/N21 & N171

New Cross was opened as a tram depot by London County Council on
May 15th, 1905; closed to trams by London Transport on July 6th, 1952
and subsequently utilized as an omnibus depot.

Go-Ahead London No.**E253** turning into the approach road to **New Cross Bus Garage** off New Cross Road on
August 31st, 2013.

New Cross Bus Garage viewed from the entrance in Pepys Road on August 31st, 2013.

VEHICLE ALLOCATION

DP192	EJ52 WXF	E227	SN61 DFG	ED 6	AE06 HCH	PVL324	PJ52 LWC	WVL296	LX59 CZO
DWL16	BX04 BXM	E228	SN61 DFJ	ED 7	AE06 HCJ	PVL325	PJ52 LWD	WVL297	LX59 CZP
DWL18	FJ54 ZDP	E246	YX12 FPA	ED 8	AE06 HCK	PVL343	PF52 WPT	WVL298	LX59 CZR
DWL19	FJ54 ZDT	E247	YX12 FPF	EH 6	SN61 BLJ	PVL344	PF52 WPU	WVL299	LX59 CZS
DWL21	FJ54 ZDV	E248	YX12 FPC	EH 7	SN61 BLK	PVL345	PF52 WPV	WVL300	LX59 CZT
DWL22	FJ54 ZDW	E249	YX12 FPD	EH 8	SN61 BLV	PVL346	PF52 WPW	WVL301	LX59 CZU
DWL26	FJ54 ZFA	E250	YX12 FPF	EH 9	SN61 DAA	PVL347	PF52 WPX	WVL302	LX59 CZV
DWL27	FJ54 ZTV	E251	YX12 FPG	EH10	SN61 DAO	PVL348	PF52 WPY	WVL386	LX11 CVL
DWL31	FJ54 ZTZ	E252	YX12 FPJ	EH11	SN61 DAU	PVL349	PF52 WPZ	WVL387	LX11 CVM
DWL32	FJ54 ZUA	E253	YX12 FPK	EH12	SN61 DBO	PVL350	PF52 WRA	WVL388	LX11 CVN
DWL34	FJ54 ZUD	E254	YX12 FPL	EH13	SN61 DBU	PVL351	PF52 WRC	WVL389	LX11 CVO
DWL36	FJ54 ZVB	E255	YX12 FPN	EH14	SN61 DBV	PVL352	PF52 WRD	WVL390	LX11 CVP
E 94	LX08 EBP	E256	YX12 FPO	EH15	SN61 DBX	PVL353	PF52 WRE	WVL391	LX11 CVR
E 95	LX08 EBU	E257	YX12 FPP	EH16	SN61 DBY	PVL354	PF52 WRG	WVL392	LX11 CVS
E 96	LX08 EBV	E258	YX12 FPT	EH17	SN61 DBZ	PVL355	PL03 AGZ	WVL393	LX11 CVT
E 97	LX08 EBZ	E259	YX12 FPU	EH18	SN61 DCE	WVL274	LX59 CYL	WVL394	LX11 CVU
E 98	LX08 ECA	E260	YX12 FPV	EH19	SN61 DCO	WVL275	LX59 CYO	WVL395	LX11 CVV
E 99	LX08 ECC	E261	SN62 DDE	EH20	SN61 DCU	WVL276	LX59 CYP	WVL396	LX11 CVW
E208	SN61 DCZ	E262	SN62 DDO	LDP209	SN51 UAY	WVL277	LX59 CYS	WVL397	LX11 CVY
E209	SN61 DDA	E263	SN62 DDX	LDP210	SN51 UAZ	WVL278	LX59 CYT	WVL398	LX11 CVZ
E210	SN61 DDE	E264	SN62 DFL	LDP273	LX06 EYT	WVL279	LX59 CYU	WVL399	LX11 CWA
E211	SN61 DDF	E265	SN62 DFX	LDP274	LX06 EYU	WVL280	LX59 CYV	WVL400	LX11 CWC
E212	SN61 DDJ	E266	SN62 DGF	LDP275	LX06 EYV	WVL281	LX59 CYW	WVL401	LX11 CWD
E213	SN61 DDK	E267	SN62 DGU	LDP276	LX06 EYW	WVL282	LX59 CYY	WVL402	LX11 CWE
E214	SN61 DDL	E268	SN62 DHA	LDP277	LX06 FBD	WVL283	LX59 CYZ	WVL403	LX11 CWG
E215	SN61 DDO	E269	SN62 DHX	LDP278	LX06 FBE	WVL284	LX59 CZA	WVL404	LX11 CWJ
E216	SN61 DDU	E270	SN62 DHZ	LDP279	LX06 FAA	WVL285	LX59 CZB	WVL405	LX11 CWK
E217	SN61 DDV	E271	SN62 DJO	LDP280	LX06 FAF	WVL286	LX59 CZC	WVL406	LX11 CWL
E218	SN61 DDX	E272	SN62 DKJ	PVL151	X551 EGK	WVL287	LX59 CZD	WVL407	LX11 CWM
E219	SN61 DDY	E273	SN62 DLY	PVL159	X559 EGK	WVL288	LX59 CZF	WVL408	LX11 CWN
E220	SN61DDZ	E274	SN62 DLZ	PVL169	X569 EGK	WVL289	LX59 CZG	WVL409	LX11 CWO
E221	SN61 DEU	E275	SN62 DMV	PVL170	X707 EGK	WVL290	LX59 CZH	WVL410	LX11 CWP
E222	SN61 DFA	ED 1	AE06 HCA	PVL319	PJ52 LVW	WVL291	LX59 CZJ	WVL411	LX11 CWR
E223	SN61 DFC	ED 2	AE06 HCC	PVL320	PJ52 LVX	WVL292	LX59 CZK	WVL412	LX11 CWT
E224	SN61 DFD	ED 3	AE06 HCD	PVL321	PJ52 LVY	WVL293	LX59 CZL		
E225	SN61 DFE	ED 4	AE06 HCF	PVL322	PJ52 LVZ	WVL294	LX59 CZM		
E226	SN61 DFF	ED 5	AE06 HCG	PVL323	PJ52 LWA	WVL295	LX59 CZN		

The entrance to **Northumberland Park Bus Garage** on August 20th, 2013.

NORTHUMBERLAND PARK (NP)
Marsh Lane, Tottenham, London N17 0XB
Operated by: Go-Ahead London
Location: TQ35089080 [51.600213, -0.050748]
Nearest Station: Northumberland Park (400 yards)
Nearest Bus Routes: 192
Bus Routes Serviced: 20/191/231/257/259/299/327/357/389/399/476/491/616/692/699/W4/W10 & W16

The garage was opened in 1991 to accommodate vehicles used on the Walthamstow Citybus operation. Through a subsequent management buyout and then purchase by First Group it operated buses under the First Capital branding until the depot was sold to the Go-Ahead group on March 28th, 2012.

The exit road out of **Northumberland Park Bus Garage** on August 20th, 2013, with the office block visible on the left of the picture.

Go-Ahead Nos **WVN22**, **EN18** & **EN7** parked in the yard at **Northumberland Park Bus Garage** on August 20th, 2013.

VEHICLE ALLOCATION

DMN 1	LT02 NUK	PVN 5	LK03 NHV	WS21	LJ13 GKK	WVL459	LJ61 NUP	WVN23	LK59 FDU
E276	SN13 CJE	PVN 6	LK03 NHX	WS22	LJ13 GKL	WVL460	LJ61 NUU	WVN24	BG59 FXA
EN 1	SN58 CDY	SEN 1	YX60 FUA	WS23	LJ13 GKN	WVL461	LJ61 NUV	WVN25	BG59 FXB
EN 2	SN58 CDZ	SEN 2	YX60 FUB	WS24	LJ13 GKO	WVL462	LJ61 NUW	WVN26	BG59 FXC
EN 3	SN58 CEA	SEN 3	YX60 FUD	WS25	LJ13 GKP	WVL463	LJ61 NUX	WVN27	BG59 FXD
EN 4	SN58 CEF	SEN 4	YX60 FUE	WS26	LJ13 GKU	WVL464	LJ61 NUY	WVN28	BG59 FXE
EN 5	SN58 CEJ	SEN 5	YX60 FUF	WS27	LJ13 GKV	WVL465	LJ61 NVA	WVN29	BG59 FXF
EN 6	SN58 CEK	SEN 6	YX60 FUG	WS28	LJ13 GKX	WVL466	LJ61 NVB	WVN30	BG59 FXH
EN 7	SN58 CEO	SEN 7	YX60 FUH	WS29	LJ13 GKY	WVL467	LJ61 NWW	WVN31	BV10 WVD
EN 8	SN58 CEU	SEN 8	YX60 FUJ	WS30	LJ13 GKZ	WVN 1	LK59 FEP	WVN32	BV10 WVE
EN 9	SN58 CEV	SEN 9	YX60 FUM	WS31	LJ13 GLF	WVN 2	LK59 FET	WVN33	BV10 WVF
EN10	SN58 CEX	SEN10	YX60 FUO	WS32	LJ13 GLK	WVN 3	LK59 FEU	WVN34	BV10 WVG
EN11	SN58 CEY	SEN11	YX60 FUP	WVL189	LX05 FBC	WVN 4	LK59 FDV	WVN35	BV10 WVH
EN12	SN58 CFA	SEN12	YX60 FUT	WVL190	LX05 EZV	WVN 5	LK59 FDX	WVN36	BV10 WVJ
EN13	SN58 CFD	SEN13	YX11 FYS	WVL191	LX05 EZW	WVN 6	LK59 FDY	WVN37	BV10 WVK
EN14	SN58 CFE	SEN14	YX11 FYT	WVL192	LX05 EZZ	WVN 7	LK59 FDZ	WVN38	BV10 WVL
EN15	SN58 CFF	SEN15	YX11 FYU	WVL193	LX05 EZK	WVN 8	LK59 FEF	WVN39	BV10 WWA
EN16	SN58 CFG	SEN16	YX11 FYV	WVL194	LX05 EZL	WVN 9	LK59 FEG	WVN40	BV10 WWC
EN17	SN58 CFJ	SEN17	YX11 FYW	WVL195	LX05 EZM	WVN10	LK59 FEH	WVN41	BV10 WWD
EN18	LK08 FLH	SEN18	YX11 FYY	WVL196	LX05 EZN	WVN11	LK59 FEO	WVN42	BV10 WWF
EN19	LK08 FLJ	SEN19	YX11 FYZ	WVL197	LX05 EZO	WVN12	LK59 FDG	WVN43	BV10 WWO
EN20	LK08 FLL	SEN20	YX11 AGU	WVL198	LX05 EZP	WVN13	LK59 FEJ	WVN44	BV10 WWP
EN21	LK08 FLM	SEN21	YX61 FYT	WVL199	LX05 EZR	WVN14	LK59 FEM	WVN45	BV10 WWR
EN22	LK08 FLN	SEN22	YX61 FYU	WVL200	LX05 EZS	WVN15	LK59 FDE	WVN46	BL61 ACY
EN23	LK08 FLP	SEN23	YX61 FYV	WVL201	LX05 EZT	WVN16	LK59 FDF	WVN47	BL61 ACX
EN24	LK08 FLR	SEN24	YX61 FYW	WVL202	LX05 EZU	WVN17	LK59 FDJ	WVN48	BL61 ADU
PVL113	W513 WGH	SEN25	YX61 FYY	WVL203	LX05 EYZ	WVN18	LK59 FDL	WVN49	BL61 ACZ
PVN 1	LK03 NHF	SEN26	YX61 FYZ	WVL204	LX05 EZA	WVN19	LK59 FDM	WVN50	BL61 ADV
PVN 2	LK03 NHG	SEN27	YX61 FZA	WVL205	LX05 EZB	WVN20	LK59 FDN	WVN51	BL61 ADO
PVN 3	LK03 NHP	SEN28	YX61 FZB	WVL457	LJ61 NUM	WVN21	LK59 FDO	WVN52	BL61 ADX
PVN 4	LK03 NHT	SEN29	YX61 FZZ	WVL458	LJ61 NUO	WVN22	LK59 FDP	WVN53	BL61 ADZ

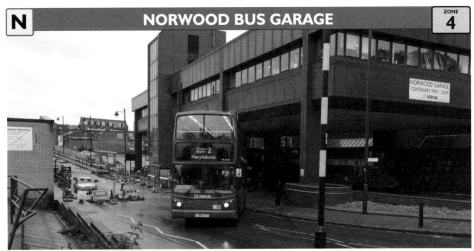

Arriva London No. **VLA62** departing from **Norwood Bus Garage** on October 16th, 2013.

NORWOOD (N)
Ernest Avenue, West Norwood, London SE27 0HN
Operated by: Arriva London
Location: TQ31957174 [51.429335, -0.103346]
Nearest Station: West Norwood (0.2 miles)
Nearest Bus Routes: 2/196/315/432/468/690/N2/ N68 & X68 - West Norwood, West Norwood Bus Garage (Stop U)
Bus Routes Serviced: 2/59/133/415/417/432/ 690/N2 & N137

The garage was originally opened in 1909 by the London General Omnibus Company and totally rebuilt between 1981 and 1984.

VEHICLE ALLOCATION

DLA173	W373 VGJ	T 99	LJ59 LYY	VLA 8	LJ03 MXY	VLA 34	LJ53 BDZ	VLA 60	LJ04 LFR
DLA174	W374 VGJ	T100	LJ59 LYZ	VLA 9	LJ03 MXZ	VLA 35	LJ53 BEO	VLA 61	LJ04 LFS
DLA179	W379 VGJ	T101	LJ59 LZA	VLA 10	LJ03 MYA	VLA 36	LJ53 BBV	VLA 62	LJ04 LFT
DLA180	W433 WGJ	T102	LJ59 LZB	VLA 11	LJ03 MYB	VLA 37	LJ53 BBX	VLA 63	LJ04 YWS
DLA233	X433 FGP	T103	LJ59 LZC	VLA 12	LJ03 MYC	VLA 38	LJ53 BBZ	VLA 64	LJ04 YWT
DLA235	X435 FGP	T104	LJ59 LYA	VLA 13	LJ03 MYD	VLA 39	LJ53 BCF	VLA 65	LJ04 YWU
DLA253	X453 FGP	T105	LJ59 LYC	VLA 14	LJ03 MYF	VLA 40	LJ53 BCK	VLA 66	LJ04 YWV
DLA254	X454 FGP	T106	LJ59 LYD	VLA 15	LJ03 MXH	VLA 41	LJ53 BCO	VLA 67	LJ04 YWW
DLA255	X507 GGO	T107	LJ59 LYF	VLA 16	LJ03 MXK	VLA 42	LJ53 BCU	VLA 68	LJ04 YWX
DLA273	Y473 UGC	T108	LJ59 LYG	VLA 17	LJ03 MXL	VLA 43	LJ53 BCV	VLA 69	LJ04 YWY
DLA275	Y475 UGC	T109	LJ59 LYH	VLA 18	LJ03 MXM	VLA 44	LJ53 BCX	VLA 70	LJ04 YWZ
T 84	LJ59 LZD	T110	LJ59 LYK	VLA 19	LJ03 MXN	VLA 45	LJ53 BCY	VLA 71	LJ04 YXA
T 85	185 CLT	T111	LJ59 LYO	VLA 20	LJ03 MXP	VLA 46	LJ53 BAA	VLA 72	LJ04 YXB
T 86	LJ59 LZF	T112	LJ59 LYP	VLA 21	LJ53 BFK	VLA 47	LJ53 BAO	VLA 73	LJ04 YWE
T 87	LJ59 LZG	T113	LJ59 LYS	VLA 22	LJ53 BFL	VLA 48	LJ53 BAU	VLA 74	LJ54 BGO
T 88	LJ59 LZH	T114	LJ59 LXP	VLA 23	LJ53 BFM	VLA 49	LJ53 BAV	VLA 75	LJ54 BEO
T 89	LJ59 LZK	T115	LJ59 LXR	VLA 24	LJ53 BFN	VLA 50	LJ53 BBE	VLA 76	LJ54 BEU
T 90	LJ59 LZL	T116	LJ59 LXS	VLA 25	LJ53 BFO	VLA 51	LJ53 BBF	VLA 77	LJ54 BFA
T 91	LJ59 LZM	T117	LJ59 LXT	VLA 26	LJ53 BCZ	VLA 52	LJ53 BBK	VLA 78	LJ54 BFE
T 92	LJ59 LZN	VLA 1	LJ03 MYP	VLA 27	LJ53 BDE	VLA 53	LJ53 BBN	VLA101	LJ54 BCO
T 93	593 CLT	VLA 2	LJ03 MYR	VLA 28	LJ53 BDF	VLA 54	LJ53 BBO	VLA104	LJ05 BKY
T 94	LJ59 LYT	VLA 3	LJ03 MYS	VLA 29	LJ53 BDO	VLA 55	LJ53 BBU	VLA105	LJ05 BKZ
T 95	LJ59 LYU	VLA 4	LJ03 MYT	VLA 30	LJ53 BDU	VLA 56	LJ04 LFL	VLA106	LJ05 BLF
T 96	LJ59 LYV	VLA 5	LJ03 MXV	VLA 31	LJ53 BDV	VLA 57	LJ04 LFM	VLA107	LJ05 BLK
T 97	LJ59 LYW	VLA 6	LJ03 MXW	VLA 32	LJ53 BDX	VLA 58	LJ04 LFN	VLA108	LJ05 BLN
T 98	398 CLT	VLA 7	LJ03 MXX	VLA 33	LJ53 BDY	VLA 59	LJ04 LFP		

Arriva London Nos **T85** & **T111** in the yard at the east end of **Norwood Bus Garage** on October 16th, 2013.

Arriva London No.**VLA44** parked alongside of the offices at **Norwood Bus Garage** on October 16th, 2013.

The entrance to **Orpington Bus Garage** on September 21st, 2013 on the occasion of an open day to celebrate thirty years of Metrobus. The depot was enlarged and modernized in 2005.

ORPINGTON (MB)

Farnborough Hill, Green Street Green, Orpington, Kent BR6 6DA

Operated by: Metrobus
Location: TQ45486394 [51.356492, 0.087531]
Nearest Station: Chelsfield (1.1 miles)
Nearest Bus Routes: 358/402/R8 & R11 - Farnborough Hill Bus Garage (K)
Bus Routes Serviced: 119 (Night Services only)/126/138/146/161/162/181/233/261/284/320/336/352/353/358/367/464/654/B14/R1/R2/R3/R4/R6/R8/R9& R11

Orpington Garage was originally the sole depot operated by Metrobus until Croydon (See Page 30) opened in December 2005.

The maintenance building at **Orpington Bus Garage** on September 21st, 2013.

Buses of varying vintage, including Nos **T1030**, **VDN34215**, **DM541356**, **529**, **609** & **RML2699**, line up at the open day at **Orpington Bus Garage** on September 21st, 2013.

VEHICLE ALLOCATION

101	YJ56 WVF	184	YX62 DZU	279	SN03 YBT	605	YM55 SWY	762	YX13 AHL
102	YJ56 WVG	185	YX13 AJO	280	SN03 YBX	606	YN06 JXS	901	YN55 PZC
142	LT02 ZDR	186	YX13 AJU	281	SN03 YBY	607	YM55 SXA	902	YN55 PZD
143	LT02 ZDS	187	YX13 AJV	282	SN03 YBZ	608	YM55 SXB	903	YN55 PZE
148	YX60 FTO	188	YX13 AJY	283	SN03 YCD	609	YM55 SXC	904	YN55 PZF
149	YX60 FTP	228	PO56 JEU	284	SN03 YCE	610	YM55 SXD	905	YN55 PZG
150	YX60 FTT	229	PO56 JFA	285	SN03 YCF	611	YM55 SXE	906	YN55 PZH
151	YX60 FTU	230	PO56 JFE	456	YN03 DFC	612	YM55 SXF	907	YN55 PZJ
152	YX60 FTV	231	PO56 JFF	457	YU52 XVR	613	YN06 JXT	908	YN55 PZL
153	YX60 FTY	232	PO56 JFG	458	YN03 DFD	614	YM55 SXH	909	YN55 PZM
154	YX60 FTZ	233	PO56 JFJ	459	YN03 DFE	701	PN07 KRK	910	YN55 PZO
155	YX60 FUV	234	PO56 JFK	460	YN03 DFG	702	PN07 KRO	911	YN55 PZP
156	YX60 FUW	235	PO56 JFN	461	YN03 DFJ	703	PN07 KRU	912	YN55 PZR
157	YX60 FUY	236	PO56 JFU	462	YN03 DFK	704	PN07 KRV	913	YN55 PZU
158	YX60 FVA	251	SN54 GPV	465	YN03 DFU	705	PN07 KRX	914	YN55 PZV
159	YX60 FVB	252	SN54 GPX	466	YN03 DFV	731	YX11 CTE	915	YN55 PZW
160	YX60 FVC	253	SN54 GPY	467	YN03 DFX	732	YX11 CTF	916	YN55 PZX
161	YX60 FVD	254	SN54 GPZ	468	YN03 DFY	733	YX11 CTK	930	YN56 FDD
162	YX60 FVE	255	SN54 GRF	479	YN53 RYM	740	YX13 AFF	931	YN56 FDE
163	YX61 ENC	256	SN54 GRK	514	YN53 RXF	741	YX13 AFJ	932	YN56 FDF
164	YX61 ENE	257	PN06 UYL	515	YN53 RXG	742	YX13 AFK	933	YN56 FDG
165	YX61 ENF	258	PN06 UYM	516	YN53 RXH	743	YX13 AFN	934	YN56 FDJ
166	YX61 ENH	259	PN06 UYO	517	YN53 RXJ	744	YX13 AFO	937	YN56 FDM
167	YX61 ENJ	260	PN06 UYP	518	YN53 RXK	745	YX13 AFU	938	YN56 FDO
168	YX61 ENK	261	PN06 UYR	519	YN53 RXL	746	YX13 AFV	939	YN56 FDP
169	YX61 ENL	262	PN06 UYS	520	YN53 RXM	747	YX13 AFY	940	YN56 FDU
170	YX61 ENM	263	PN06 UYT	521	YN53 RXO	748	YX13 AFZ	941	YN56 FDV
171	YX61 ENN	264	PN06 UYU	522	YN53 RXP	749	YX13 AGO	942	YN56 FDX
172	YX61 ENO	265	PN06 UYV	523	YN53 RXR	750	YX13 AGU	943	YN56 FDY
173	YX61 ENP	266	PN06 UYW	524	YN53 RXT	751	YX13 AGV	944	YN56 FDZ
174	YX61 ENR	267	PN06 UYX	525	YN53 RXU	752	YX13 AGY	945	YN56 FEF
175	YX61 ENT	268	PN06 UYY	526	YN53 RXV	753	YX13 AGZ	946	YN56 FEG
176	YX61 ENU	271	SN03 YBA	527	YN53 RXW	754	YX13 AHA	974	YR10 BCE
177	YX61 ENV	272	SN03 YBB	528	YN53 RXX	755	YX13 AHC	975	YR10 BCF
178	YX61 ENW	273	SN03 YBC	529	YN53 RXY	756	YX13 AHD	976	YR10 BCK
179	YX62 DYH	274	SN03 YBG	530	YN53 RXZ	757	YX13 AHE	977	YR10 BCO
180	YX62 DYN	275	SN03 YBH	601	YM55 SWU	758	YX13 AHF	978	YR10 BCU
181	YX62 DYS	276	SN03 YBK	602	YM55 SWV	759	YX13 AHG		
182	YX62 DZE	277	SN03 YBR	603	YN06 JXR	760	YX13 AHJ		
183	YX62 DZN	278	SN03 YBS	604	YM55 SWX	761	YX13 AHK		

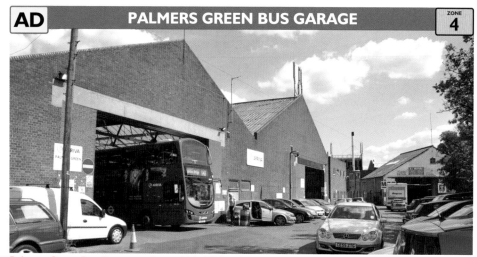

Palmers Green Bus Garage on August 20th, 2013 with Arriva London No.**DW510** leaving to take up duties on the Route No.141 service to London Bridge.

PALMERS GREEN (AD)
Regents Avenue, Palmers Green, London N13 5UR
Operated by: Arriva London
Location: TQ31029218 [51.613207, -0.019065]
Nearest Station: Palmers Green (0.5 miles)
Nearest Bus Routes: 34/102/121/329/629 (North Circular Road/Palmers Green)
Bus Routes Serviced: 34/102/125/329 & 629

A general view of the inside of the building at **Palmers Green Bus Garage** on August 20th, 2013 with No.**DLP98** parked in the entrance. The depot was opened in July 1912 by the London General Omnibus Company and modernized in 1952 and 1974.

VEHICLE ALLOCATION

DLP 68	LJ51 DLF	DLP 98	LF52 URC	T 6	LJ08 CVX	T 35	LJ08 CUA	T268	LJ61 LJU
DLP 72	LJ51 DLV	DLP100	LF52 URE	T 7	LJ08 CVY	T 36	LJ08 CUC	T269	LJ61 LJV
DLP 74	LJ51 DLY	DLP102	LF52 URH	T 8	LJ08 CVZ	T 37	LJ08 CUG	T270	LJ61 LJX
DLP 84	LJ51 ORK	DLP103	LF52 URJ	T 9	LJ08 CWA	T 38	LJ08 CUH	T271	LJ61 LHP
DLP 85	LJ51 ORL	DLP104	LF52 URK	T 10	LJ08 CWC	T 39	LJ08 CUK	T272	LJ61 LHR
DLP 87	LF02 PKC	DLP105	LF52 URL	T 11	LJ08 CVF	T 40	LJ08 CUO	T273	LJ61 LHT
DLP 89	LF02 PKE	DLP106	LF52 URM	T 27	LJ08 CVB	T 41	LJ08 CSO	T274	LJ61 LHU
DLP 90	LF02 PKJ	DLP107	LF52 UPP	T 28	LJ08 CVC	T261	LJ61 LJC	T275	LJ61 LHV
DLP 91	LF52 URS	DLP110	LF52 UPT	T 29	LJ08 CVD	T262	LJ61 LJE	T276	LJ61 LHW
DLP 92	LF52 URT	T 1	LJ08 CVS	T 30	330 CLT	T263	LJ61 LJF	T277	LJ61 LHX
DLP 93	LF52 URU	T 2	LJ08 CVT	T 31	LJ08 CTV	T264	LJ61 LJK	T278	LJ61 LHY
DLP 94	LF52 URV	T 3	3 CLT	T 32	LJ08 CTX	T265	LJ61 LJL		
DLP 95	LF52 URW	T 4	LJ08 CVV	T 33	LJ08 CTY	T266	LJ61 LJN		
DLP 97	LF52 URB	T 5	205 CLT	T 34	LJ08 CTZ	T267	LJ61 LJO		

Park Royal Bus Garage on June 22nd, 2013 with the wash plant in view. The depot was opened on May 26th, 2007 by NCP-Challenger and occupies the site of a former Metroline garage that had been closed in 2005.

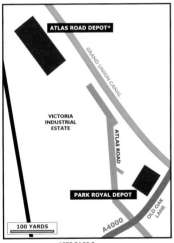

*SEE PAGE 8

PARK ROYAL (PK)
Atlas Road, Harlesden, London NW10 6DN
Operated by: London United
Location: TQ21438259 [51.529245, -0.251003]
Nearest Station: Willesden Junction (0.5 miles)
Nearest Bus Routes: 228 & 266 - Old Oak Common, Old Oak Common Lane (Stop J)
Bus Routes Serviced: 220/283/440 & E11

London United No.DE75 parked outside of **Park Royal Bus Garage** on June 22nd, 2013.

VEHICLE ALLOCATION

ADE46	YX62 BBO	ADE60	YX62 BKO	DE 74	SK07 DXZ	OV52	YJ58 PJO	OV66	YJ09 EZD
ADE47	YX62 BBZ	ADE61	YX62 BLZ	DE 75	SK07 DYC	OV53	YJ58 PJU	SDE11	SK07 HLM
ADE48	YX62 BCK	ADE62	YX62 BMV	DE 76	SK07 DYD	OV54	YJ09 EZE	SDE12	SK07 HLO
ADE49	YX62 BCV	ADE63	YX62 BMY	DE 77	SK07 DYF	OV55	YJ09 EZF	SDE13	SK07 HLO
ADE50	YX62 BFL	ADE64	YX62 BNO	DE 78	SK07 DYG	OV56	YJ09 EYT	SDE14	SK07 HLP
ADE51	YX62 BFU	ADE65	YX62 BNV	DE 79	SK07 DYH	OV57	YJ09 EYU	SDE15	SK07 HLR
ADE52	YX62 BGE	ADE66	YX62 BPF	DE 80	SK07 DYJ	OV58	YJ09 EYV	SDE16	SK07 HLU
ADE53	YX62 BGF	ADE67	YX62 BPO	DE 81	SK07 DYM	OV59	YJ09 EYW	SDE17	SK07 HLV
ADE54	YX62 BHD	ADE68	YX62 BPU	DE 82	SK07 DYN	OV60	YJ09 EYX	TA282	LG02 FDZ
ADE55	YX62 BHW	ADE69	YX62 BPZ	DE 83	SK07 DYO	OV61	YJ09 EYY	TA283	LG02 FEF
ADE56	YX62 BJF	ADE70	YX62 BUA	DE 84	SK07 DYP	OV62	YJ09 EYZ		
ADE57	YX62 BJU	ADE71	YX62 BUE	OV12	YJ58 VBO	OV63	YJ09 EZA		
ADE58	YX62 BJZ	ADE72	YX62 BVN	OV50	YJ58 PHY	OV64	YJ09 EZB		
ADE59	YX62 BKF	ADE73	YX62 BWO	OV51	YJ58 PHZ	OV65	YJ09 EZC		

Peckham Bus Garage on August 31st, 2013. It was opened in 1994 to replace one that had been sited in the town and its origins, as a former council yard, were still apparent.

PECKHAM (PM)
Blackpool Road, London SE15 3SU
Operated by: Go-Ahead London
Location: TQ34587629 [51.469371, -0.064478]
Nearest Station: Peckham Rye (0.3 miles)
Nearest Bus Routes: 12/37/63/78/197/343/363/
N63/N343 & P12 - Heaton Road (Stop X)
Bus Routes Serviced: 36/37/63/363/N63/P12 & X68

London Central-branded Go-Ahead London No.**E20** parked up in the yard at **Peckham Bus Garage** on August 31st, 2013.

VEHICLE ALLOCATION

E 16	LX06 EZL	E 34	LX06 ECT	PVL342	PJ52 LWX	WVL 85	LF52 ZNT	WVL318 LX59 DBU
E 17	LX06 EZM	E 35	LX06 ECV	SE153	YX61 DVA	WVL 86	LF52 ZNU	WVL319 LX59 DBV
E 18	LX06 EZN	E 36	LX06 FKL	SE154	YX61 DVB	WVL100	LF52 ZNN	WVL320 LX59 DBY
E 19	LX06 EZO	E 37	LX06 FKM	SE155	YX61 DVC	WVL303	LX59 CYA	WVL321 LX59 DBZ
E 20	LX06 EZP	E 61	LX07 BYG	SE156	YX61 DVF	WVL304	LX59 CYC	WVL322 LX59 DCE
E 21	LX06 EZR	PVL329	PJ52 LWH	SE157	YX61 DVG	WVL305	LX59 CYE	WVL323 LX59 DCF
E 22	LX06 EZS	PVL330	PJ52 LWK	SE158	YX61 DVH	WVL306	LX59 CYF	WVL324 LX59 DCO
E 23	LX06 EZT	PVL331	PJ52 LWL	SE159	YX61 DVJ	WVL307	LX59 CYG	WVL325 LX59 DCU
E 24	LX06 EYY	PVL332	PJ52 LWM	SE160	YX61 DVK	WVL308	LX59 CYH	WVL326 LX59 DCV
E 25	LX06 EYZ	PVL333	PJ52 LWN	SE161	YX61 DVL	WVL309	LX59 CYJ	WVL327 LX59 DCY
E 26	LX06 EZA	PVL334	PJ52 LWO	SE162	YX61 DVM	WVL310	LX59 CYK	WVL328 LX59 DCZ
E 27	LX06 EZB	PVL335	PJ52 LWP	SE163	YX61 DVN	WVL311	LX59 CZW	WVL329 LX59 DDA
E 28	LX06 EZC	PVL336	PJ52 LWR	SE164	YX61 DVO	WVL312	LX59 CZY	WVL330 LX59 DDE
E 29	LX06 EZD	PVL337	PJ52 LWS	SE165	YX61 DVP	WVL313	LX59 CZZ	WVL331 LX59 DDF
E 30	LX06 EZE	PVL338	PJ52 LWT	SE166	YX61 DVR	WVL314	LX59 DAA	WVL332 LX59 DDJ
E 31	LX06 EZF	PVL339	PJ52 LWU	WVL 79	LF52 ZPK	WVL315	LX59 DAO	WVL333 LX59 DDK
E 32	LX06 EZG	PVL340	PJ52 LWV	WVL 81	LF52 ZPM	WVL316	LX59 DAU	
E 33	LX06 EZH	PVL341	PJ52 LWW	WVL 82	LF52 ZNP	WVL317	LX59 DBO	

Perivale (West) Bus Garage on July 20th, 2013 with Metroline Nos **MM817, TE907, VP619, TP434** & **MM780** parked on the forecourt.

PERIVALE (WEST) (PA)
Unit 12, Perivale Industrial Park, Horsenden Lane, South Greenford UB6 7RL
Operated by: Metroline
Location: TQ16608343 [51.537651, -0.320144]
Nearest Tube Station: Perivale (300 yards)
Nearest Bus Routes: 297 - Perivale (Stop PF)
Bus Routes Serviced: 7/79/90/105/297/395/611/ E6 & N7

VEHICLE ALLOCATION

DE1150	LK10 BZT	MM780	LK07 AYM	MM826	LK57 AYX	SEL764	LK57 KAU	VW1194	LK11 CYJ
DE1151	LK10 BZU	MM781	LK07 AYN	MM827	LK57 AYY	SEL803	LK57 KAX	VW1195	LK11 CYL
DE1171	LK11 CXD	MM782	LK57 EHS	SEL739	LK07 AZV	SEL804	LK57 KBE	VW1196	LK11 CYO
DE1172	LK11 CXE	MM783	LK57 EHT	SEL740	LK07 AZW	SEL805	LK57 KBF	VW1197	LK11 CYP
DE1173	LK11 CXF	MM784	LK57 EHU	SEL741	LK07 AZY	SEL806	LK57 KBJ	VW1198	LK11 CYS
DE1174	LK11 CXG	MM785	LK57 EHV	SEL742	LK07 AZZ	SEL807	LK57 KBN	VW1199	LK11 CYT
DE1598	YX58 DUA	MM786	LK57 EHW	SEL743	LK07 BAA	SEL808	LK57 KBO	VW1200	LK11 CYU
DE1599	YX58 DUH	MM787	LK57 EHX	SEL744	LK07 BAO	SEL809	LK08 DVY	VW1201	LK11 CYV
DE1600	YX58 DUJ	MM788	LK57 EHY	SEL745	LK07 BAU	VW1175	LK11 CXJ	VW1202	LK61 BJE
DE1601	YX58 DUU	MM789	LK57 EHZ	SEL746	LK07 BBE	VW1176	LK11 CXL	VW1203	LK61 BJF
DE1602	YX58 DVY	MM790	LK57 EJA	SEL747	LK07 BBF	VW1177	LK11 CXM	VW1204	LK61 BJJ
DE1603	YX58 DVZ	MM810	LK57 AYD	SEL748	LK07 BBJ	VW1178	LK11 CXN	VW1205	LK61 BMU
DE1604	YX58 DWA	MM811	LK57 AYE	SEL749	LK07 BBN	VW1179	LK11 CXO	VW1206	LK61 BMV
DE1605	YX58 DWC	MM812	LK57 AYF	SEL750	LK07 BBO	VW1180	LK11 CXP	VW1207	LK61 BMY
DE1606	YX58 DWD	MM813	LK57 AYG	SEL751	LK07 BBU	VW1181	LK11 CXR	VW1208	LK61 BMZ
DE1607	YX58 DWE	MM814	LK57 AYH	SEL752	LK07 BBV	VW1182	LK11 CXS	VW1209	LK61 BNA
DE1608	YX58 DWF	MM815	LK57 AYJ	SEL753	LK07 BBX	VW1183	LK11 CXT	VW1210	LK61 BNB
DE1609	YX58 DWG	MM816	LK57 AYL	SEL754	LK07 BBZ	VW1184	LK11 CXU	VW1211	LK61 BNE
DE1610	YX58 DWJ	MM817	LK57 AYM	SEL755	LK07 BCE	VW1185	LK11 CXV	VW1212	LK61 BNF
DE1611	YX58 DWL	MM818	LK57 AYN	SEL756	LK07 BCF	VW1186	LK11 CXW	VW1213	LK61 BNJ
DP1010	RL51 DNX	MM819	LK57 AYO	SEL757	LK07 BCO	VW1187	LK11 CXX	VW1214	LK61 BNL
DP1011	RL51 DOJ	MM820	LK57 AYP	SEL758	LK07 BCU	VW1188	LK11 CXY	VW1215	LK61 BNN
DP1012	RL51 DOH	MM821	LK57 AYS	SEL759	LK07 BCZ	VW1189	LK11 CXZ	VW1216	LK61 BNO
DP1015	RL51 DOU	MM822	LK57 AYT	SEL760	LK07 BCX	VW1190	LK11 CYA		
DP1016	RL51 DNU	MM823	LK57 AYU	SEL761	LK07 BCY	VW1191	LK11 CYE		
MM778	LK07 AYJ	MM824	LK57 AYV	SEL762	LK07 BCZ	VW1192	LK11 CYF		
MM779	LK07 AYL	MM825	LK57 AYW	SEL763	LK07 BDE	VW1193	LK11 CYH		

Plumstead Bus Garage viewed from the higher level of the A206 Plumstead Road on September 7th, 2013. The entrance to the depot is the one on the left, with Stagecoach London No.17963 in the centre of the picture and nearest the camera.

PLUMSTEAD (PD)
Pettman Crescent, Plumstead, London SE28 0BJ
Operated by: Stagecoach London
Location: TQ44737901 [51.491297, 0.083571]
Nearest Station: Plumstead (0.2 miles)
Nearest Bus Routes: 122/177/180/422/472 & N1 -
Plumstead, Plumstead Road, Plumstead Station
(Stop WM)
Bus Routes Serviced: 51/53/96/99/122/177/291/
386/469/472/601/602 & 672

Plumstead Depot was opened in 1981 and replaced Plumstead (AM) and Abbey Wood (AW) garages.

The south side of **Plumstead Bus Garage**, viewed on September 7th, 2013.

Stagecoach London No. 17839 passing **Plumstead Bus Garage** along the A206 Plumstead Road on September 7th, 2013.

VEHICLE ALLOCATION

10196	SN63 NCA	15074	LX09 AEY	17540	LY02 OAG	17964	LX53 JZG	19830	LX11 BLZ
15036	LX58 CGY	15075	LX09 AEZ	17560	LY02 OBM	19742	LX11 BBK	19831	LX11 BMO
15037	LX58 CGZ	15076	LX09 AFA	17561	LV52 USF	19743	LX11 BBN	19832	LX11 BMU
15038	LX58 CHC	15077	LX09 AFE	17563	LV52 HDU	19744	LX11 BBO	19833	LX11 BMV
15039	LX58 CHD	15078	LX09 AFF	17566	LV52 HDZ	19745	LX11 BBV	19834	LX11 BMY
15040	LX09 AAO	15079	LX09 AFJ	17567	LV52 HEJ	19746	LX11 BBZ	34366	LV52 HGC
15041	LX09 AAU	15080	LX09 AFK	17570	LV52 HFB	19747	LX11 BCE	34374	LV52 HGM
15042	LX09 AAV	15081	LX09 AFN	17571	LV52 HFC	19748	LX11 BCF	34377	LX03 BZJ
15043	LX09 AAY	15082	LX09 AFO	17572	LV52 HFD	19749	LX11 BCK	34378	LX03 BZK
15044	LX09 AAZ	15083	LX09 AFU	17573	LV52 HFE	19750	LX11 BCO	34379	LX03 BZL
15045	LX09 ABF	15084	LX09 AFV	17590	LV52 HFZ	19751	LX11 BCU	34380	LX03 BZM
15046	LX09 ABK	15085	LX09 AFY	17591	LV52 HGA	19752	LX11 BCV	34381	LX03 BZN
15047	LX09 ABN	15086	LX09 AFZ	17789	LX03 BWC	19753	LX11 BCY	34382	LX03 BZP
15048	LX09 ABO	15087	LX09 AGO	17790	LX03 BWD	19754	LX11 BCZ	34383	LX03 BZR
15049	LX09 ABU	15088	LX09 AGU	17836	LX03 BYM	19755	LX11 BDE	34384	LX03 BZS
15050	LX09 ABV	15089	LX09 AGV	17837	LX03 BYN	19806	LX11 BJO	34385	LX03 BZT
15051	LX09 ABZ	15090	LX09 AGY	17838	LX03 BYP	19807	LX11 BJU	34386	LX03 BZU
15052	LX09 ACF	15091	LX09 AGZ	17839	LX03 BYR	19808	LX11 BJV	36268	LX11 AVZ
15053	LX09 ACJ	15092	LX09 AHA	17840	LX03 BYS	19809	LX11 BJY	36269	LX11 AWC
15054	LX09 ACO	15093	LX09 AHC	17866	LX03 NFL	19810	LX11 BJZ	36270	LX11 AWF
15055	LX09 ADZ	15094	LX09 AHD	17945	LX53 JYH	19811	LX11 BKA	36271	LX11 AWG
15056	LX09 AEA	15095	LX09 AHE	17946	LX53 JYJ	19812	LX11 BKD	36272	LX11 AWH
15057	LX09 AEB	15096	LX09 AHF	17947	LX53 JYK	19813	LX11 BKE	36273	LX11 AWJ
15058	LX09 AEC	17404	Y404 NHK	17948	LX53 JYL	19814	LX11 BKF	36274	LX11 AWM
15059	LX09 AED	17427	Y441 NHK	17949	LX53 JYN	19815	LX11 BKG	36275	LX11 AWN
15060	LX09 AEE	17441	Y441 NHK	17950	LX53 JYO	19816	LX11 BKJ	36327	LX58 CCN
15061	LX09 AEF	17466	LX51 FLC	17951	LX53 JYP	19817	LX11 BKK	36328	LX58 CCO
15062	LX09 AEG	17484	LX51 FMC	17952	LX53 JYR	19818	LX11 BKL	36329	LX58 CCU
15063	LX09 AEJ	17486	LX51 FME	17953	LX53 JYT	19819	LX11 BKN	36330	LX58 CCV
15064	LX09 AEK	17487	LX51 FMF	17954	LX53 JYU	19820	LX11 BKO	36331	LX58 CCY
15065	LX09 AEL	17503	LX51 FNF	17955	LX53 JYV	19821	LX11 BKU	36332	LX58 CDE
15066	LX09 AEM	17504	LX51 FNG	17956	LX53 JYW	19822	LX11 BKV	36333	LX58 CDF
15067	LX09 AEN	17505	LX51 FNH	17957	LX53 JYY	19823	LX11 BKY	36334	LX58 CDK
15068	LX09 AEO	17506	LX51 FNJ	17958	LX53 JYZ	19824	LX11 BKZ	36335	LX58 CDN
15069	LX09 AEP	17508	LX51 FNL	17959	LX53 JZA	19825	LX11 BLF	36336	LX58 CDO
15070	LX09 AET	17511	LX51 FNO	17960	LX53 JZC	19826	LX11 BLJ	36337	LX58 CDU
15071	LX09 AEU	17512	LX51 FNP	17961	LX53 JZD	19827	LX11 BLK	36555	LX13 CYW
15072	LX09 AEV	17537	LY02 OAC	17962	LX53 JZE	19828	LX11 BLN		
15073	LX09 AEW	17538	LY02 OAD	17963	LX53 JZF	19829	LX11 BLV		

73

Potters Bar Bus Garage on August 20th, 2013 with Metroline No.**DEL854** parked on the exit road.

100 YARDS

POTTERS BAR DEPOT

HOLLIES WAY

HIGH STREET

B156

A1000

OAKMERE LANE

PARKFIELD OPEN SPACE

POTTERS BAR (PB)
High Street, Potters Bar, Hertfordshire EN6 5BE
Operated by: Metroline
Location: TL26130146 [51.697737, -0.176436]
Nearest Station: Potters Bar (0.5 miles)
Nearest Bus Routes: 84/242/312/398 & PB1 - Potters Bar, Bus Garage
Bus Routes Serviced: 82/217/234/263/383/384/634/N20/N91/W8 & W9

The depot was opened in 1930 by "Overground", a subsidiary of the London General Omnibus Company, and during WWII and the early 1950s was also utilized as a bus storage facility. Its location, on the northern fringe of London bus operations, made it vulnerable to closure but it survived and was eventually taken over by Metroline.

VEHICLE ALLOCATION

DEM1337	LK62 DAA	TE 936	LK09 EKR	TE1430	LK62 DYG	TP 439	LK03 GGV	TPL241	LN51 KXU
DEM1338	LK62 DAO	TE 937	LK09 EKT	TE1431	LK62 DYH	TP 440	LK03 GGX	TPL248	LN51 KYC
DEM1339	LK62 DBZ	TE 938	LK58 KHC	TE1432	LK62 DYN	TP 441	LK03 GGY	TPL249	LN51 KYE
DEM1340	LK62 DCE	TE 939	LK58 KHD	TE1433	LK62 DYO	TP 442	LK03 GGZ	TPL250	LN51 KYF
DEM1341	LK62 DCF	TE 940	LK58 KHE	TE1434	LK13 BEU	TP 443	LK03 GHA	TPL251	LN51 KYG
DEM1342	LK62 DCY	TE 941	LK58 KHF	TE1435	LK13 BEY	TP 444	LK03 GHB	TPL253	LN51 KYJ
DEM1343	LK62 DDU	TE 942	LK58 KHG	TE1436	LK13 BFA	TP 445	LK03 GHD	TPL254	LN51 KYK
DEM1344	LK62 DDY	TE 943	LK58 KHH	TE1437	LK13 BFF	TP 446	LK03 GHF	TPL255	LN51 KYO
DEM1345	LK62 DDZ	TE 944	LK09 EKU	TE1438	LK13 BFJ	TP 447	LK03 GHG	TPL276	LR02 BBJ
DEM1346	LK62 DEU	TE 945	LK58 KHL	TE1439	LK13 BFL	TP 448	LK03 GHH	TPL277	LR02 BBK
DEM1347	LK62 DFF	TE 946	LK58 KHM	TE1440	LK13 BFM	TP 449	LK03 GHJ	TPL278	LR02 BBN
DEM1348	LK62 DFJ	TE 947	LK58 KHO	TE1441	LK13 BFN	TP 450	LK03 GHN	TPL279	LR02 BBO
DEM1349	LK62 DFP	TE 948	LK58 KHP	TE1442	LK13 BFO	TP 452	LK03 GHV	TPL280	LR02 BBU
DEM1350	LK62 DFY	TE 949	LK58 KHR	TE1443	LK13 BFP	TP 453	LK03 GHX	TPL281	LR02 BBV
DEM1351	LK62 DGF	TE 950	LK58 KHT	TE1444	LK13 BFU	TP 454	LK03 GHY	TPL282	LR02 BBX
DEM1352	LK62 DGO	TE 951	LK58 KHU	TE1445	LK13 BFV	TP 455	LK03 GHZ	TPL284	LR02 BCE
DEM1353	LK62 DHC	TE1420	LK62 DXM	TE1446	LK13 BFX	TP 456	LK03 GJF	TPL285	LR02 BCF
DEM1354	LK62 DHD	TE1421	LK62 DXP	TE1447	LK13 BFY	TP 457	LK03 GJG	TPL287	LR02 BCO
DEM1355	LK62 DHE	TF1422	LK62 DXS	TP 405	LK03 CEU	TP 458	LK03 GJU	TPL288	LR02 BCU
DEM1356	LK62 DHG	TE1423	LK62 DXT	TP 407	LK03 CEX	TP 459	LK03 GJV	TPL290	LR02 BCX
DEM1357	LK62 DHP	TE1424	LK62 DXX	TP 431	LK03 GFX	TP 460	LK03 GJX	TPL291	LR02 BCY
DEM1358	LK62 DHU	TE1425	LK62 DXY	TP 434	LK03 GGA	TP 461	LK03 GJY	TPL292	LR02 BCZ
DEM1359	LK62 DHV	TE1426	LK62 DYA	TP 435	LK03 GGF	TP 462	LK03 GJZ	TPL293	LR02 BDE
DLD178	Y238 NLK	TE1427	LK62 DYC	TP 436	LK03 GGJ	TP 463	LK03 GKA	TPL294	LR02 BDF
DP1009	RL51 DOA	TE1428	LK62 DYD	TP 437	LK03 GGP	TP 464	LK03 GKC	TPL295	LR02 BDO
DP1013	RL51 DNY	TE1429	LK62 DYF	TP 438	LK03 GGU	TP 465	LK03 GKD		

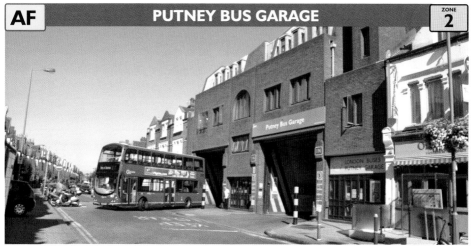

Go-Ahead London No. **WVL25** departing from **Putney Bus Garage** on August 31st, 2013.

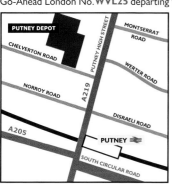

PUTNEY (AF)
Chelverton Road, London SW15 1RN
Operated by: Go-Ahead London
Location: TQ23937528 [51.462632, -0.217141]
Nearest Station: Putney (0.2 miles)
Nearest Bus Routes: 14/39/74/85/93/424 & 430 - (Putney Exchange) Putney
Bus Routes Serviced: 14/22/74/85/424/430/670/ N22 & N74

Originally known as Chelverton Road, it can trace its origins back to the 1880s when it was a horse bus depot, becoming a motorized omnibus garage in 1912. It was modernized in 1935 and re-named as Putney in 1963 following the closure of Putney Bridge. The depot was again modernized and refurbished in 1986.

VEHICLE ALLOCATION

LDP151	Y851 TGH	WVL 20	LG02 KHV	WVL 46	LF52 ZRE	WVL153	LX53 BGE	WVL179	LX05 FBV
LDP281	LX06 FAJ	WVL 21	LG02 KHW	WVL 47	LF52 ZRG	WVL154	LX53 BFK	WVL180	LX05 FAA
LDP282	LX06 FAK	WVL 22	LG02 KHX	WVL 48	LF52 ZRJ	WVL155	LX53 BDY	WVL181	LX05 FAF
LDP283	LX06 FAM	WVL 23	LG02 KHY	WVL 49	LF52 ZRK	WVL156	LX53 BBZ	WVL182	LX05 FAJ
LDP284	LX06 FAO	WVL 24	LG02 KHZ	WVL 50	LF52 ZRL	WVL157	LX53 BAA	WVL183	LX05 FAK
LDP285	LX06 FAU	WVL 25	LG02 KJA	WVL 51	LF52 ZRN	WVL158	LX53 BDO	WVL184	LX05 FAM
LDP286	LX06 FBA	WVL 26	LG02 KJE	WVL 52	LF52 ZPN	WVL159	LX53 BAO	WVL185	LX05 FAO
VE1	LX58 CWK	WVL 27	LG02 KJF	WVL 53	LF52 ZPO	WVL160	LX05 FBY	WVL186	LX05 FAU
VE2	LX58 CWL	WVL 28	LF52 ZSO	WVL 54	LF52 ZPP	WVL161	LX05 FBZ	WVL187	LX05 FBA
VE3	LX58 CWM	WVL 29	LF52 ZSP	WVL 55	LF52 ZPR	WVL162	LX05 FCA	WVL188	LX05 FBB
WHV32	LJ62 KFD	WVL 30	LF52 ZSR	WVL 56	LF52 ZPS	WVL163	LX05 FCC	WVL497	LJ62 KXZ
WHV33	LJ62 KFF	WVL 31	LF52 ZST	WVL 57	LF52 ZPU	WVL164	LX05 FCD	WVL498	LJ62 KYA
WHV34	LJ62 KFU	WVL 32	LF52 ZRO	WVL 58	LF52 ZPV	WVL165	LX05 FCE	WVL499	LJ62 KYG
WHV35	LJ62 KGF	WVL 33	LF52 ZRP	WVL 59	LF52 ZPW	WVL166	LX05 FCF	WVL500	LJ62 KOX
WHV36	LJ62 KGG	WVL 34	LF52 ZRR	WVL 60	LF52 ZPX	WVL167	LX05 FBD	WVL501	LJ62 KZD
WHV37	LJ62 KGN	WVL 35	LF52 ZRT	WVL 61	LF52 ZPY	WVL168	LX05 FBE	WVL502	LJ62 KZP
WHV38	LJ62 KGY	WVL 36	LF52 ZRU	WVL 62	LF52 ZTG	WVL169	LX05 FBF	WVL503	LJ62 KBY
WHV39	LJ62 KHF	WVL 37	LF52 ZRV	WVL 63	LF52 ZTH	WVL170	LX05 FBJ	WVL504	LJ62 KCU
WHV40	LJ62 KHV	WVL 38	LF52 ZRX	WVL 64	LF52 ZTJ	WVL171	LX05 FBK	WVL505	LJ62 KDV
WHV41	LJ62 KKP	WVL 39	LF52 ZRY	WVL 65	LF52 ZTK	WVL172	LX05 FBL	WVL506	LJ62 KDZ
WVL 14	LG02 KHM	WVL 40	LF52 ZRZ	WVL 66	LF52 ZTL	WVL173	LX05 FBN	WVL507	LJ62 KLC
WVL 15	LG02 KHO	WVL 41	LF52 ZSD	WVL 67	LF52 ZTM	WVL174	LX05 FBO	WVL508	LJ62 KLS
WVL 16	LG02 KHP	WVL 42	LF52 ZPZ	WVL 68	LF52 ZTN	WVL175	LX05 FBU		
WVL 17	LG02 KHR	WVL 43	LF52 ZRA	WVL 69	LF52 ZTO	WVL176	LX05 EZJ		
WVL 18	LG02 KHT	WVL 44	LF52 ZRC	WVL 70	LF52 ZTP	WVL177	LX05 EYM		
WVL 19	LG02 KHU	WVL 45	LF52 ZRD	WVL 71	LF52 ZTR	WVL178	LX05 EYO		

Go-Ahead London's **Rainham Bus Garage** on September 18th, 2013 with No.**PVL96** parked in the yard.

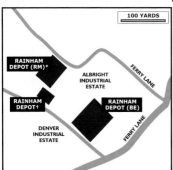

100 YARDS

RAINHAM (BE)

Unit 4, Denver Industrial Estate, Ferry Lane, Rainham, Essex RM13 9DD
Operated by: Go-Ahead London
Location: TQ51778172 [51.514064, 0.185806]
Nearest Station: Rainham (0.4 miles)
Nearest Bus Routes: 372 - Rainham, Rainham (London) (Stop B)
Bus Routes Serviced: 167/193/300/347/362/364/368/376/462/498/608/646/648/649/650/651/652/656/667/674/679/686/EL1/EL2 & W19

*SEE PAGE 77 †SEE PAGE 109

VEHICLE ALLOCATION

DMN 2	LN51 DWL	ED20	LX07 BYL	PVN16	LK03 NJZ	SE 46	LX10 AVD	WVL103	LF52 ZMO
DMN 3	LN51 DWM	ED21	LX07 BYM	PVN17	LK03 NKA	SE 94	SN11 FFZ	WVL104	LF52 ZMU
DMN 4	LN51 DWO	ED22	LX07 BYN	SE 18	SK07 DZM	SE 95	SN11 FGA	WVL334	LX59 DDL
DMN 5	LN51 DWP	ED23	LX07 BYO	SE 19	SK07 DZN	SE 96	SN11 FGC	WVL335	LX59 DDN
DMN 6	LN51 DWU	ED24	LX07 BYP	SE 20	SK07 DZO	SE 97	SN11 FGD	WVL336	LX59 DDO
DMN 7	LT02 NUM	ED25	LX07 BYR	SE 21	SN57 DWG	SE 98	SN61 BKO	WVL337	LX59 DDU
DMN 8	LT02 NUO	ED26	LX07 BYS	SE 22	SN57 DWJ	SE 99	SN61 BKU	WVL338	LX59 DDV
DMN 9	LT02 NUP	ED27	LX07 BYT	SE 23	SN57 DWK	SE100	SN61 BKV	WVL339	LX59 DDY
DMN10	LT02 NUU	EN25	LK57 EJN	SE 24	SN57 DWL	SE101	SN61 BKX	WVL340	LX59 DDZ
DMN11	LT02 NUV	EN26	LK57 EJO	SE 25	SN57 DWM	SE102	SN61 BKY	WVL341	LX59 DEU
DMN12	LT02 NVE	EN27	LK08 FKX	SE 26	SN57 DWO	SE103	SN61 BKZ	WVL342	LX59 DFA
DMN13	LT52 WUP	LDP208	SN51 UAX	SE 27	SN57 DWP	SE104	YX61 BWA	WVL343	LX59 DFC
DMN14	LT52 WUO	PVL 66	W466 WGH	SE 28	SN57 DWU	SEN30	YX61 FZO	WVL344	LX59 DFD
DMN15	LT02 NVH	PVL 67	W467 WGH	SE 29	SN57 DWV	SEN31	YX61 FZP	WVL345	LX59 DFE
DMN16	LT02 NVJ	PVL 68	W468 WGH	SE 30	SN57 DWW	SEN32	YX61 FZR	WVL346	LX59 DFF
DMN17	LT52 WUM	PVL 69	W469 WGH	SE 31	SN57 DWX	SEN33	YX61 FZS	WVL347	LX59 DFG
DMN18	LT52 WUR	PVL 70	W578 DGU	SE 32	SN57 DWY	SEN34	YX61 FZT	WVL348	LX59 DFJ
DP208	SN56 AYC	PVL 95	W495 WGH	SE 33	SN57 DWZ	SEN35	YX61 FZU	WVL349	LX59 DFK
ED 9	AE56 OUH	PVL 96	W496 WGH	SE 34	SN57 DXA	SEN36	YX61 FZV	WVL454	LJ61 GWP
ED10	AE56 OUJ	PVL110	W401 WGH	SE 35	SN57 DXB	SEN37	YX61 FZW	WVL 75	LF52 ZPE
ED11	AE56 OUK	PVN 7	LK03 NHY	SE 36	YN08 DMY	WS 1	LJ12 CGF	WVL 77	LF52 ZPH
ED12	AE56 OUL	PVN 8	LK03 NHZ	SE 38	LX10 AUR	WS 2	LJ12 CGG	WVL 90	LF52 ZNY
ED13	AE56 OUM	PVN 9	LK03 NJE	SE 39	LX10 AUT	WS 3	LJ12 CGK	WVL 91	LF52 ZNZ
ED14	AE56 OUN	PVN10	LK03 NJF	SE 40	LX10 AUU	WS 4	LJ12 CGO	WVL 97	LF52 ZNK
ED15	AE56 OUO	PVN11	LK03 NJJ	SE 41	LX10 AUV	WS 5	LJ12 CGU	WVL 98	LF52 ZNL
ED16	AE56 OUP	PVN12	LK03 NJN	SE 42	LX10 AUW	WS 6	LJ12 CGV		
ED17	AE56 OUS	PVN13	LK03 NJV	SE 43	LX10 AUY	WS 7	LJ12 CGX		
ED18	LX07 BYJ	PVN14	LK03 NJX	SE 44	LX10 AVB	WS 8	LJ12 CGY		
ED19	LX07 BYK	PVN15	LK03 NJY	SE 45	LX10 AVC	WS 9	LJ12 CGZ		

The entrance to Stagecoach London's **Rainham Bus Garage** on September 18th, 2013.

*SEE PAGE 76 †SEE PAGE 109

RAINHAM (RM)
Unit 2, Albright Industrial Estate, Ferry Lane, Rainham, Essex RM13 9BU
Operated by: Stagecoach London
Location: TQ51648186 [51.515326, 0.183993]
Nearest Station: Rainham (0.5 mile)
Nearest Bus Routes: 372 - Rainham, Rainham (London) (Stop B)
Bus Routes Serviced: 165/174/248/252/256/287/365 & 372

VEHICLE ALLOCATION

10165	SN63 JVO	15016	LX58 CFF	19712	LX11 AYT	19733	LX11 AZW	36564	LX13 CZG
10166	SN63 JVP	15017	LX58 CFG	19713	LX11 AYU	19786	LX11 BGZ	36565	LX13 CZH
10167	SN63 JVR	15020	LX58 CFL	19714	LX11 AYV	19787	LX11 BHA	36566	LX13 CZJ
10168	SN63 JVT	15021	LX58 CFM	19715	LX11 AYW	19788	LX11 BHD	36567	LX13 CZK
10169	SN63 JVU	15022	LX58 CFN	19716	LX11 AYY	19789	LX11 BHE	36568	LX13 CZL
10170	SN63 JVV	15023	LX58 CFO	19717	LX11 AYZ	19790	LX11 BHF	36569	LX13 CZM
10171	SN63 JVW	15024	LX58 CFP	19718	LX11 AZA	19791	LX11 BHJ	36570	LX13 CZN
15001	LX58 CDV	15025	LX58 CFU	19719	LX11 AZB	19792	LX11 BHK	36571	LX13 CZO
15002	LX58 CDY	15026	LX58 CFV	19720	LX11 AZC	19793	LX11 BHL	36572	LX13 CZP
15003	LX58 CDZ	15027	LX58 CFY	19721	LX11 AZD	36338	LX09 ACU	36573	LX13 CZR
15004	LX58 CEA	15028	LX58 CFZ	19722	LX11 AZF	36339	LX09 ACV	36574	LX13 CZS
15005	LX58 CEF	15029	LX58 CGE	19723	LX11 AZG	36341	LX09 ACZ	36575	LX13 CZT
15006	LX58 CEJ	15030	LX58 CGF	19724	LX11 AZJ	36342	LX09 ADO	36576	LX13 CZU
15007	LX58 CEK	15031	LX58 CGG	19725	LX11 AZL	36556	LX13 CYY	36577	LX13 CZV
15008	LX58 CEN	15032	LX58 CGK	19726	LX11 AZN	36557	LX13 CYZ	36578	LX13 CZW
15009	LX58 CEO	15033	LX58 CGO	19727	LX11 AZO	36558	LX13 CZA	36579	LX13 CZY
15010	LX58 CEU	15034	LX58 CGU	19728	LX11 AZP	36559	LX13 CZB	36580	LX13 CZZ
15011	LX58 CEV	15035	LX58 CGV	19729	LX11 AZR	36560	LX13 CZC		
15012	LX58 CEY	17425	LX51 FJZ	19730	LX11 AZT	36561	LX13 CZD		
15014	LX58 CFD	17519	LX51 FNY	19731	LX11 AZU	36562	LX13 CZE		
15015	LX58 CFE	19711	LX11 AYS	19732	LX11 AZV	36563	LX13 CZF		

A general view of **Romford Bus Garage** on September 18th, 2013. In this picture the entrance is at the left end of the building, off Seymer Road and the exit is on Park Drive.

ROMFORD (NS)
North Street, Romford, Essex RM1 1DS
Operated by: Stagecoach London
Location: TQ50788948 [51.583947, 0.175049]
Nearest Station: Romford (1.3 miles)
Nearest Bus Routes: 66/103/175/247/294/296/365/375/575/649 & 650 - Romford Bus Garage (Stop NS)
Bus Routes Serviced: 86/103/175/247/256/294/296/496 & N86

Romford Garage was opened in 1953 to supplement a garage at Hornchurch. It was originally known as North Street to differentiate it from another Romford garage located in London Road.

Stagecoach London No.10156 on the Park Drive exit road at **Romford Bus Garage** on September 18th, 2013.

VEHICLE ALLOCATION

10155	EU62 AXT	17764	LX03 BUW	17867	LX03 NFM	17993	LX53 KCA	18477	LX55 ESF
10156	EU62 AXV	17765	LX03 BVA	17868	LX03 NFN	17994	LX53 KCC	18478	LX55 ESG
10157	EU62 AYB	17766	LX03 BVB	17869	LX03 NFP	17995	LX53 KCE	18479	LX55 ESN
10158	EU62 AYE	17767	LX03 BVC	17870	LX03 NFR	17996	LX53 KCF	18480	LX55 ESO
10159	EU62 AZA	17768	LX03 BVD	17874	LX03 NFY	17997	LX53 KCG	19734	LX11 AZZ
10160	EU62 AZO	17769	LX03 BVE	17976	LX53 JZV	17998	LX53 KCJ	19735	LX11 BAA
10161	EU62 AAE	17770	LX03 BVF	17977	LX53 JZW	17999	LX04 GCU	19736	LX11 BAO
10162	EU62 AAO	17771	LX03 BVG	17978	LX53 KAE	18451	LX05 LLM	19737	LX11 BAU
10163	EU62 ADZ	17772	LX03 BVH	17979	LX53 KAJ	18452	LX05 LLN	19738	LX11 BAV
17559	LY02 OBL	17773	LX03 BVJ	17980	LX53 KAK	18453	LX05 LLO	19739	LX11 BBE
17562	LV52 HDO	17774	LX03 BVK	17981	LX53 KAO	18465	LX55 EPP	19740	LX11 BBF
17564	LV52 HDX	17775	LX03 BVL	17982	LX53 KAU	18466	LX55 EPU	19741	LX11 BBJ
17565	LV52 HDY	17776	LX03 BVM	17983	LX53 KBE	18467	LX55 EPV	36261	LX11 AVP
17569	LV52 HFA	17777	LX03 BVN	17984	LX53 KBF	18468	LX55 EPY	36262	LX11 AVR
17574	LV52 HFF	17778	LX03 BVP	17985	LX53 KBJ	18469	LX55 EPZ	36263	LX11 AVT
17577	LV52 HFK	17791	LX03 BWE	17986	LX53 KBK	18470	LX55 ERJ	36264	LX11 AVU
17748	LY52 ZFG	17792	LX03 BWF	17987	LX53 KBN	18471	LX55 ERK	36265	LX11 AVV
17759	LX03 BUF	17793	LX03 BWG	17988	LX53 KBO	18472	LX55 ERO	36266	LX11 AVW
17760	LX03 BUH	17829	LX03 BYC	17989	LX53 KBP	18473	LX55 ERU	36267	LX11 AVY
17761	LX03 BUP	17830	LX03 BYD	17990	LX53 KBV	18474	LX55 ERV		
17762	LX03 BUU	17835	LX03 BYL	17991	LX53 KBY	18475	LX55 ERY		
17763	LX03 BUV	17854	LX03 BZH	17992	LX53 KBZ	18476	LX55 ERZ		

The Seymer Road entrance to **Romford Bus Garage** on September 18th, 2013.

The interior of **Romford Bus Garage**, viewed from the Seymer Road entrance on September 18th, 2013.

Shepherds Bush Bus Garage on August 17th, 2013 with London United No.**DE36** in view.

SHEPHERDS BUSH (S)
Wells Road, London W12 8DA
Operated by: London United
Location: TQ23237957 [51.501662, -0.226015]
Nearest Tube Station: Goldhawk Road (Adjacent)
Nearest Bus Routes: 94 & 237 - Goldhawk Road (Stop K)
Bus Routes Serviced: 49/72/94/148/220 (Night Service only)/272/C1 & N97

London United No.**ADH12** parked in the rear entrance to **Shepherds Bush Bus Garage** on August 17th, 2013.

A general view of the interior of **Shepherds Bush Bus Garage** on August 17th, 2013 with London United No.**VA91** parked in the entrance.

VEHICLE ALLOCATION

ADH 3	SN60 BXX	DE 39	YX09 HKH	DE101	SN10 CCA	SP112	YR59 FYT	TLA17	SN53 KHR
ADH 4	SN60 BXY	DE 40	YX09 HKJ	DE102	SN10 CCD	SP113	YR59 FYU	TLA18	SN53 KHT
ADH 5	SN60 BXZ	DE 41	YX09 HKK	DE103	SN10 CCE	SP114	YR59 FYV	TLA19	SN53 KHU
ADH 6	SN60 BYA	DE 42	YX09 HKL	DE104	SN10 CCF	SP115	YR59 FYW	TLA20	SN53 KHV
ADH 7	SN60 BYB	DE 43	YX09 HKM	DE105	SN10 CCJ	SP116	YR59 FYX	TLA21	SN53 KHW
ADH 8	SN60 BYC	DE 44	YX09 HKN	DE106	SN10 CCK	SP117	YR59 FYY	TLA22	SN53 KHX
ADH 9	SN60 BYD	DE 45	YX09 HKO	DE107	SN10 CCO	SP118	YR59 FYZ	TLA23	SN53 KHY
ADH10	SN60 BYF	DE 46	YX09 HKP	DE108	SN10 CCU	SP119	YR59 FZA	TLA24	SN53 KHZ
ADH11	SN60 BYG	DE 47	YX09 HKT	DPS624	SK02 XGT	SP120	YR59 FZB	TLA25	SN53 KJA
ADH12	SN60 BYH	DE 48	YX09 HKU	DPS669	LG02 FGX	SP121	YR59 FZC	TLA26	SN53 KJE
ADH13	SN60 BYJ	DE 49	YX09 HKV	DPS688	SN03 LFD	SP122	YR59 FZD	TLA27	SN53 KJF
ADH14	SN60 BYK	DE 85	SK07 DYS	SLE43	YN55 NKM	SP123	YR59 FZE	TLA29	SN53 KJK
ADH15	SN60 BYL	DE 86	SK07 DYT	SLE44	YN55 NKO	SP124	YR59 FZF	TLA30	SN53 KJO
ADH16	SN60 BYM	DE 87	SK07 DYU	SP 29	YN08 DHU	SP125	YR59 FZG	VA62	V178 OOE
ADH17	SN60 BYO	DE 88	SK07 DYV	SP 30	YN08 DHV	SP126	YT59 PBF	VA64	V180 OOE
ADH18	SN60 BYP	DE 89	SK07 DYW	SP 31	YN08 DHX	SP127	YT59 PBO	VA91	W124 EON
ADH19	SN60 BYR	DE 90	SK07 DYX	SP 32	YN08 DHY	SP128	YT59 PBV	VE 1	PG04 WGN
ADH20	SN60 BYS	DE 91	SK07 DYY	SP 33	YN08 DHZ	SP129	YT59 PBX	VE 2	PG04 WGP
ADH21	SN60 BYT	DE 92	YX58 DXA	SP 34	YN08 MTU	SP130	YT59 PBY	VE 3	PG04 WGU
ADH22	SN60 BYU	DE 93	SN10 CAV	SP 35	YN08 MRV	SP131	YT59PBZ	VE 4	PG04 WGV
DE 32	YX09 HKA	DE 94	SN10 CAX	SP 36	YN08 MRX	SP132	YT59 PCF	VE 5	PG04 WGW
DE 33	YX09 HKB	DE 95	SN10 CBF	SP 37	YN08 MRY	SP133	YT59 PCO	VE 6	PG04 WGX
DE 34	YX09 HKC	DE 96	SN10 CBO	SP 39	YP58 ACJ	SP134	YT59 PCU	VE 7	PG04 WGY
DE 35	YX09 HKD	DE 97	SN10 CBU	SP 40	YP58 ACO	SP135	YT59 PBU	VE 8	PG04 WGZ
DE 36	YX09 HKE	DE 98	SN10 CBX	SP109	YR59 FYO	TLA 1	SN53 EUF	VE10	PG04 WHB
DE 37	YX09 HKF	DE 99	SN10 CBY	SP110	YR59 FYP	TLA 2	SN53 EUH		
DE 38	YX09 HKG	DE100	SN10 CBY	SP111	YR59 FYS	TLA 7	SN53 EUO		

The entrance to **Silvertown Bus Garage** on September 7th, 2013 with Go-Ahead London No.**SE143** parked in front of the wash plant.

SILVERTOWN (SI)
Factory Road, Silvertown, London E16 2EL
Operated by: Go-Ahead London
Location: TQ42727987 [51.499516, 0.054142]
Nearest DLR Station: King George V (0.4 miles)
Nearest Bus Routes: 474 & 573 - Fernhill Street (Stop C)
Bus Routes Serviced: 150/276/474/541/549/673/D6/D7 & D8

Go-Ahead London Nos **DP195**, **WVL451** & **SE117** standing in the yard at **Silvertown Bus Garage** on September 7th, 2013.

VEHICLE ALLOCATION

ED28	LX07 BYU	SE119	YX61 BYA	SE137	YX61 BWN	SO3	BV55 UCW	WVL422	LX11 FHV
PVL 97	W497 WGH	SE120	YX61 BWU	SE138	YX61 BWO	SO4	BV55 UCX	WVL423	LX11 FHW
PVL115	W415 WGH	SE121	YX61 BWV	SE139	YX61 BWP	SO5	BV55 UCY	WVL424	LX11 FHY
SE 17	LX07 BYB	SE122	YX61 BWW	SE140	YX61 BVY	WVL 72	LF52 ZPB	WVL425	LX11 FHZ
SE105	YX61 BWB	SE123	YX61 BWY	SE141	YX61 BVZ	WVL 73	LF52 ZPC	WVL426	LX11 FJA
SE106	YX61 BWC	SE124	YX61 BWZ	SE142	YX61 BXK	WVL 84	LF52 ZNS	WVL427	LX11 FJC
SE107	YX61 BWD	SE125	YX61 BXA	SE143	YX61 BXL	WVL 92	LF52 ZND	WVL428	LX11 FJD
SE108	YX61 BWE	SE126	YX61 BXB	SE144	YX61 BXM	WVL 94	LF52 ZNG	WVL429	LX11 FJE
SE109	YX61 BYD	SE127	YX61 BXC	SE145	YX61 BXN	WVL 95	LF52 ZNH	WVL430	LX11 FJF
SE110	YX61 BYF	SE128	YX61 BXD	SE146	YX61BXO	WVL413	LX11 CWU	WVL431	LX11 FJJ
SE111	YX61 BYG	SE129	YX61 BXE	SE147	YX61 BXP	WVL414	IX11 CWV	WVL432	LX11 FJK
SE112	YX61 BXR	SE130	YX61 BWF	SE148	YX61 DTO	WVL415	LX11 CWW	WVL433	LX11 FJN
SE113	YX61 BXS	SE131	YX61 BWG	SE149	YX61 DTU	WVL416	LX11 CWY	WVL434	LX11 FJO
SE114	YX61 BXU	SE132	YX61 BWH	SE150	YX61 DTV	WVL417	LX11 CWZ	WVL451	LJ61 GWM
SE115	YX61 BXV	SE133	YX61 BWJ	SE151	YX61 DTY	WVL418	LX11 CXA	WVL452	LJ61 GWN
SE116	YX61 BXW	SE134	YX61 BWK	SE152	YX61 DTZ	WVL419	LX11 CXB	WVL453	LJ61 GWO
SE117	YX61 BXY	SE135	YX61 BWL	SO1	BV55 UCT	WVL420	LX11 CXC		
SE118	YX61 BXZ	SE136	YX61 BWM	SO2	BV55 UCU	WVL421	LX11 CXD		

South Mimms Bus Garage viewed on August 20th, 2013.

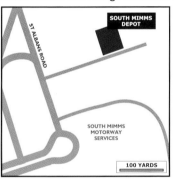

SOUTH MIMMS (SM)
South Mimms Service Area, Potters Bar,
Hertfordshire EN6 3NE
Operated by: Sullivan Buses
Location: TL22960048 [51.689652, -0.222587]
Nearest Station: Potters Bar (2.6 miles)
Nearest Bus Routes: 398 & 615 - South Mimms,
Motorway Service Station (Southbound)
Bus Routes Serviced: 298/626/628/653/683 & 688
(Plus Rail Replacement Bus Services for TfL)

Sullivan Buses Nos **TAL123, DEL1, TPL927, ALX2, VPL1704 & WVL1** parked inside
South Mimms Bus Garage on August 20th, 2013.

VEHICLE ALLOCATION

AE 1	MS10 SUL	ALX1	V116 MEV	DP82	V782 FKH	ELV 4	PN02 XBY	TN2	PO51 UML
AE 2	SN57 DXH	ALX2	V117 MEV	DP92	V792 FKH	ELV 5	PA04 CYH	TN3	PO51 UMR
AE 3	SN57 DXK	ALX3	V119 MEV	DP96	V796 FKH	ELV 6	PL51 LGG	TPL926	EY03 FNK
AE 4	NH11 SUL	ALX4	V139 MEV	DPS574	SN51 SZK	ELV 7	PO04 ADU	TPL927	EY03 FNL
AE 5	AH11 SUL	ALX5	V142 MEV	DPS575	SN51 SZL	ELV 8	PO04 OOE	VP113	W459 BCW
AE11	CJ61 SUL	ALX6	LY02 OAX	DPS576	SN51 SZO	ELV 9	PO04 OOF	VP119	W466 BCW
AE12	DS61 SUL	DEL1	PJ52 BYP	DPS577	SN51 SZP	ELV10	PO04 OOG	VPL174	X157 JOP
AE13	KR61 SUL	DN1	X2 SUL	DT4	G504 VYE	PDL26	PJ02 PZZ	WVL1	GD52 SYC
AE14	KS61 SUL	DN2	DN02 SUL	ELV 1	EL04 SUL	TAL123	X343 HLL	WVL2	FJ57 CYZ
AE15	TW6 1SUL	DN3	SC02 SUL	ELV 2	PN02 XCR	TAL132	X332 HLL	WVL3	FJ57 CZD
AE16	SB61 SUL	DN4	CN02 SUL	ELV 3	PL51 LGD	TN1	PO51 UMH	WVL4	FJ57 CZE

The entrance to **Stamford Brook Bus Garage** on August 17th, 2013. Following closure to trams it became a trolleybus depot in 1935 and, later, an omnibus works and store. It was leased out in 1963 but, in 1966, was used as a garage for British Airways bus services. It became a bus garage in 1980, was closed in 1996 and used as a bus store and re-opened in 1999.

STAMFORD BROOK (V)
72-74 Chiswick High Road, London W4 1SF
Operated by: London United
Location: TQ21587867 [51.493877, -0.250044]
Nearest Tube Station: Stamford Brook (0.4 miles)
Nearest Bus Routes: 27/190/237/267/
391/H91/N9& N11 - Turnham Green,
Stamford Brook Bus Garage (Stop PP)
Bus Routes Serviced: 9/10/27/391 & 419

It was opened as a horse tram depot by the West Metropolitan Tramways in 1883/4 and electrified in 1901. At this point it was converted to a works with a further tram shed added on the western side. The depot closed to trams on May 5th, 1932.

VEHICLE ALLOCATION

ADH 1	SN58 EOR	ADH45	YX62 FSS	LT76	LTZ 1076	OV 6	YJ58 VBF	SP148	YP59 OEG
ADH 2	SN58 EOS	ADH46	YX62 FTD	LT77	LTZ 1077	OV 7	YJ58 VBG	SP149	YP59 OEH
ADH23	YX62 FAU	ADH47	YX62 FTF	LT78	LTZ 1078	OV 8	YJ58 VBK	SP150	YP59 OEJ
ADH24	YX62 FCM	ADH48	YX62 FTP	LT79	LTZ 1079	OV 9	YJ58 VBL	SP151	YP59 OEK
ADH25	YX62 FDD	ADH49	YX62 FTZ	LT80	LTZ 1080	OV10	YJ58 VBM	SP152	YP59 OEL
ADH26	YX62 FDY	ADH50	YX62 FUT	LT81	LTZ 1081	OV11	YJ58 VBN	SP153	YP59 OEM
ADH27	YX62 FFB	ADH51	YX62 FTU	LT82	LTZ 1082	OV13	YJ58 VBP	SP154	YP59 OEN
ADH28	YX62 FFG	DPS583	SN51 TAV	LT83	LTZ 1083	OV14	YJ58 VBT	SP155	YP59 OEO
ADH29	YX62 FHA	DPS664	LG02 FGN	LT84	LTZ 1084	OV15	YJ58 VBU	SP156	YP59 OER
ADH30	YX62 FHO	DPS701	SN55 HKD	LT85	LTZ 1085	OV16	YJ58 VBV	SP157	YP59 OES
ADH31	YX62 FJD	DPS702	SN55 HKE	LT86	LTZ 1086	OV17	YJ58 VBX	SP158	YP59 OET
ADH32	YX62 FJV	DPS703	SN55 HKF	LT87	LTZ 1087	OV18	YJ58 VBX	SP159	YP59 OEU
ADH33	YX62 FKE	DPS704	SN55 HKG	LT88	LTZ 1088	OV19	YJ58 VBZ	SP160	YP59 OEV
ADH34	YX62 FKK	DPS705	SN55 HKH	LT89	LTZ 1089	SP137	YP59 ODT	SP161	YP59 OEW
ADH35	YX62 FLH	DPS706	SN55 HKJ	LT90	LTZ 1090	SP138	YP59 ODU	SP162	YP59 OEX
ADH36	YX62 FME	DPS719	SN55 HSE	LT91	LTZ 1091	SP139	YP59 ODV	VE 9	PG04 WHA
ADH37	YX62 FMG	DPS720	SN55 HKZ	LT92	LTZ 1092	SP140	YP59 ODW	VLE 3	PG04 WHE
ADH38	YX62 FMV	LT69	LTZ 1069	LT93	LTZ 1093	SP141	YP59 ODX	VLE 5	PG04 WHH
ADH39	YX62 FNZ	LT70	LTZ 1070	LT94	LTZ 1094	SP142	YP59 OEA	VLE 7	PG04 WHK
ADH40	YX62 FOA	LT71	LTZ 1071	OV 1	YJ58 VBA	SP143	YP59 OEB	VLE 8	PG04 WHL
ADH41	YX62 FPC	LT72	LTZ 1072	OV 2	YJ58 VBB	SP144	YP59 OEC	VLE22	PA04 CYE
ADH42	YX62 FPF	LT73	LTZ 1073	OV 3	YJ58 VBC	SP145	YP59 OED	VLE23	PA04 CYF
ADH43	YX62 FPK	LT74	LTZ 1074	OV 4	YJ58 VBD	SP146	YP59 OEE		
ADH44	YX62 FSE	LT75	LTZ 1075	OV 5	YJ58 VBE	SP147	YP59 OEF		

Stamford Hill Bus Garage on September 17th, 2013 with London Arriva No.**HV75** leaving the depot whilst London Arriva No.**HV83** can be seen further along Rookwood Road, parked outside of the entrance.

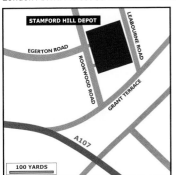

STAMFORD HILL (SF)
Rookwood Road, London N16 6SS
Operated by: Arriva London
Location: TQ34078790 [51.574106, -0.066831]
Nearest Station: Stamford Hill (0.4 miles)
Nearest Bus Routes: 67/76/149/243/253/254/318/ 349 & 476
Bus Routes Serviced: 67/73/253/N73 & N253

It was opened as an electric tram depot by London County Council on February 9th, 1907 and closed by London Transport on February 5th, 1939. It was then utilized as a trolleybus depot and subsequently as an omnibus garage. Stamford Hill Garage closed in 1995, reopened in 1996, closed once more in 2000 and finally reopened again in July 2002.

VEHICLE ALLOCATION

DW428	LJ11 ADO	DW453	LJ61 CEX	HV 40	LJ11 EFL	HV 65	LJ62 BAU	VLW176	LJ03 MPV
DW429	LJ11 ADU	DW454	LJ61 CEY	HV 41	LJ11 EFM	HV 66	LJ62 BCU	VLW177	LJ03 MLL
DW430	LJ11 ADV	DW455	LJ61 CFD	HV 42	LJ11 EFN	HV 67	LJ62 BND	VLW178	LJ03 MLN
DW431	LJ11 ADX	DW456	LJ61 CFE	HV 43	LJ11 EFO	HV 68	LJ62 BPV	VLW179	LJ03 MLV
DW432	LJ11 ADZ	DW457	LJ61 CFF	HV 44	LJ11 EFP	HV 69	LJ62 BSO	VLW180	LJ03 MLX
DW433	LJ11 AEA	DW458	LJ61 CFG	HV 45	LJ11 EFR	HV 70	LJ62 BTO	VLW181	LJ03 MLY
DW434	LJ11 ABK	DW459	LJ61 CDX	HV 46	LJ11 EEU	HV 71	LJ62 BTY	VLW182	LJ03 MLZ
DW435	LJ11 ABN	DW460	LJ61 CDY	HV 47	LJ62 BEO	HV 72	LJ62 BVE	VLW183	LJ03 MMA
DW436	LJ11 ABO	DW461	LJ61 CDZ	HV 48	LJ62 BGK	HV 73	LJ62 BVP	VLW184	LJ03 MME
DW437	LJ11 ABU	DW462	LJ61 CEA	HV 49	LJ62 BGX	HV 74	LJ62 BVY	VLW185	LJ03 MMF
DW438	LJ11 ABV	DW463	LJ61 CEF	HV 50	LJ62 BHY	HV 75	LJ62 BWF	VLW186	LJ03 MMK
DW439	LJ11 ABX	DW464	LJ61 CEK	HV 51	LJ62 BKU	HV 76	LJ62 BWP	VLW187	LJ03 MKM
DW440	LJ11 ABZ	HV 27	LJ11 EFT	HV 52	LJ62 BKX	HV 77	LJ62 BFZ	VLW188	LJ03 MKN
DW441	LJ11 ACF	HV 28	LJ11 EFU	HV 53	LJ62 BMZ	HV 78	LJ62 BGZ	VLW189	LJ03 MYN
DW442	LJ11 ACO	HV 29	LJ11 EFV	HV 54	LJ62 BNE	HV 79	LJ62 BHF	VLW190	LJ03 MXR
DW443	LJ11 ACU	HV 30	LJ11 EFW	HV 55	LJ62 BNL	HV 80	LJ62 BJK	VLW191	LJ03 MXS
DW444	LJ11 AAE	HV 31	LJ11 EFX	HV 56	LJ62 BNU	HV 81	LJ62 BJX	VLW192	LJ03 MXT
DW445	LJ11 AAF	HV 32	LJ11 EFY	HV 57	LJ62 BXD	HV 82	LJ13 FDD	VLW193	LJ03 MXU
DW446	LJ61 CFA	HV 33	LJ11 EFZ	HV 58	LJ62 BXF	HV 83	LJ13 FDE	VLW194	LJ03 MWX
DW447	LJ61 CFK	HV 34	LJ11 EGC	HV 59	LJ62 BYT	VLW170	LJ03 MOA	VLW195	LJ53 BEU
DW448	LJ61 CFL	HV 35	LJ11 EGD	HV 60	LJ62 BYU	VLW171	LJ03 MOF	VLW196	LJ53 BEY
DW449	LJ61 CDV	HV 36	LJ11 EFE	HV 61	LJ62 BZH	VLW172	LJ03 MOV	VLW197	LJ53 BFA
DW450	LJ11 AAX	HV 37	LJ11 EFF	HV 62	LJ62 BZR	VLW173	VLT 173	VLW198	LJ53 BFE
DW451	LJ11 AAY	HV 38	LJ11 EFG	HV 63	LJ62 BZY	VLW174	LJ03 MPF	VLW199	LJ53 BFF
DW452	LJ61 CEV	HV 39	LJ11 EFK	HV 64	LJ62 BAO	VLW175	LJ03 MPU		

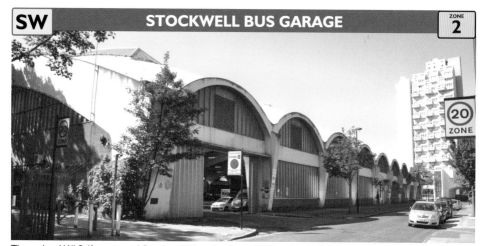

The author Will Self nominated **Stockwell Bus Garage** in 2011 as London's most important building. This is the exit, fronting onto Lansdowne Way on August 31st, 2013.

STOCKWELL (SW)
Binfield Road, London SW4 6ST
Operated by: Go-Ahead London
Location: TQ30417669 [51.473431, -0.124235]
Nearest Tube Station: Stockwell (0.2 miles)
Nearest Bus Routes: 22/024/025/026/88/A3 & N2 - South Lambeth Road, Stockwell Station (Stop A)
Bus Routes Serviced: 11/19/87/88/170/196/315/333/337/639/670/N11/N19/N44 & N87

This Grade 2* Listed building was opened in 1952 and featured the largest area of uninterrupted floor space enclosed by a single roof in Europe – some 73,750 ft². Due to post WWII material shortages, principally steel, the roof was designed as a whale-back structure and constructed in reinforced concrete.

The somewhat less-imposing office block and entrance off Binfield Road into **Stockwell Bus Garage** on August 31st, 2013. Part of the concrete roof can be seen between the office and the bus on the right.

Go-Ahead London No.**E38**, operating on Route No.196, passing **Stockwell Bus Garage** on Lansdowne Way on August 31st, 2013.

VEHICLE ALLOCATION

DP193	EU53 PXY	E151	SN11 BTY	LDP291	LX06 EZW	WHV19	LJ61 NVE	WVL119	LX03 ECV
DP194	EU53 PXZ	E152	SN11 BTZ	LT41	LTZ 1041	WHV20	LJ61 NVF	WVL120	LX03E CW
DP195	EU53 PYA	E153	SN11 BUA	LT42	LTZ 1042	WHV21	LJ61 NVG	WVL121	LX03 ECY
DP196	EU53 PYB	E154	SN11 BUE	LT43	LTZ 1043	WHV22	LJ61 NVH	WVL122	LX53 AZP
DP197	EU53 PYD	E155	SN11 BUF	LT44	LTZ 1044	WHV23	LJ61 NVK	WVL123	LX53 AZR
DP198	EU53 PYF	E156	SN11 BUH	LT45	LTZ 1045	WHV24	LJ61 NVL	WVL124	LX53 AZT
DP199	EU53 PYG	E157	SN11 BUJ	LT46	LTZ 1046	WHV25	LJ61 NVM	WVL125	LX53 AZU
DP200	EU53 PYH	E158	SN11 BUO	LT47	LTZ 1047	WHV26	LJ61 NVN	WVL150	LX53 BJO
DP201	EU53 PYJ	E159	SN11 BUP	LT48	LTZ 1048	WHV27	LJ12 CHH	WVL450	LJ61 GWL
DP202	EU53 PYL	E160	SN11 BUU	LT49	LTZ 1049	WHV28	LJ61 NVP	WVL468	LJ61 NWX
DP203	EU53 PYO	E161	SN11 BUV	LT50	LTZ 1050	WHV29	LJ61 NVR	WVL469	LJ12 CHC
DP204	EU53 PYP	E162	SN11 BUW	LT51	LTZ 1051	WHV30	LJ61 NVS	WVL470	LJ61 NWZ
DP205	BT04 BUS	EH 1	LX58 DDJ	LT52	LTZ 1052	WHV31	LJ12 CHK	WVL471	LJ61 NXA
DP209	SN56 AYD	EH 2	LX58 DDK	LT53	LTZ 1053	WVL 1	LG02 KGP	WVL472	LJ61 NXB
E 1	SN06 BNA	EH 3	LX58 DDL	LT54	LTZ 1054	WVL 2	LG02 KGU	WVL473	LJ61 NXC
E 2	SN06 BNB	EH 4	LX58 DDN	LT55	LTZ 1055	WVL 3	LG02 KGV	WVL474	LJ61 NXD
E 3	SN06 BND	EH 5	LX58 DDO	LT56	LTZ 1056	WVL 4	LG02 KGX	WVL475	LJ61 NXE
E 4	SN06 BNE	EH21	YX13 BJE	LT57	LTZ 1057	WVL 5	LG02 KGY	WVL476	LJ61 NXF
E 5	SN06 BNF	EH22	YX13 BJF	LT58	LTZ 1058	WVL 6	LG02 KGZ	WVL477	LJ61 NWL
E 6	SN06 BNJ	EH23	YX13 BJJ	LT59	LTZ 1059	WVL 7	LG02 KHA	WVL478	LJ61 NWM
E 7	SN06 BNK	EH24	YX13 BJK	LT60	LTZ 1060	WVL 8	LG02 KHE	WVL479	LJ61 NWN
E 8	SN06 BNL	EH25	YX13 BJO	LT61	LTZ 1061	WVL 9	LG02 KHF	WVL480	LJ61 NWO
E 9	SN06 BNO	EH26	YX13 BJU	LT62	LTZ 1062	WVL 10	LG02 KHH	WVL481	LJ12 CHD
E 10	SN06 BNU	EH27	YX13 BJV	LT63	LTZ 1063	WVL 11	LG02 KHJ	WVL482	LJ61 NWR
E 11	SN06 BNV	EH28	YX13 BJY	LT64	LTZ 1064	WVL 12	LG02 KHK	WVL483	LJ12 CHF
E 12	SN06 BNX	EH29	YX13 BJZ	LT65	LTZ 1065	WVL 13	LG02 KHL	WVL484	LJ12 CHG
E 13	SN06 BNY	EH30	YX13 BKA	LT66	LTZ 1066	WVL105	LX03 EXV	WVL485	LJ61 NWU
E 14	SN06 BNZ	EH31	YX13 BKD	LT67	LTZ 1067	WVL106	LX03 EXW	WVL486	LJ61 NWV
E 15	SN06 BOF	EH32	YX13 BKE	LT68	LTZ 1068	WVL107	LX03 EXZ	WVL487	LJ61 NXZ
E 38	LX06 FKN	EH33	YX13 BKF	PVL203	X503 EGK	WVL108	LX03 EXU	WVL488	LJ61 NWA
E 57	LX07 BYH	EH34	YX13 BKG	SE47	YX60 EOE	WVL109	LX03 EDR	WVL489	LJ61 NWB
E129	SN60 BZA	EH35	YX13 BKJ	SE48	YX60 EOF	WVL110	LX03 EDU	WVL490	LJ61 NWC
E130	SN60 BZB	EH36	YX13 BKK	SE49	YX60 EOG	WVL111	LX03 EDV	WVL491	LJ61 NWD
E131	SN60 BZC	EH37	YX13 BKL	SE50	YX60 EOH	WVL112	LX03 EEA	WVL492	LJ61 NWE
E132	SN60 BZD	EH38	YX13 BKN	SE51	YX60 EOJ	WVL113	LX03 EEB	WVL493	LJ61 NWF
E133	SN60 BZE	LDP204	SN51 UAT	SE52	YX60 EOK	WVL114	LX03 EEF	WVL494	LJ61 NWG
E134	SN60 BZF	LDP287	LX06 FBB	SE53	YX60 EOL	WVL115	LX03 EEG	WVL495	LJ61 NWH
E135	SN60 BZG	LDP288	LX06 FBC	SE54	YX60 EOO	WVL116	LX03 EEH	WVL496	LJ62 KXX
E136	SN60 BZH	LDP289	LX06 EZU	WHV17	LJ61 NVC	WVL117	LX03 EEJ		
E137	SN60 BZJ	LDP290	LX06 EZV	WHV18	LJ61 NVD	WVL118	LX03 EEM		

The main, Bushey Road, entrance to **Sutton Bus Garage** on October 16th, 2013.

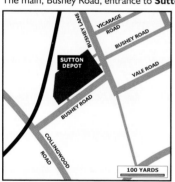

SUTTON (A)
Bushey Road, Sutton SM1 1QJ
Operated by: Go-Ahead London
Location: TQ25456488 [51.369433, -0.199093]
Nearest Station: West Sutton (0.7 miles)
Nearest Bus Routes: 80 & 613 - Sutton Bus Garage/ Bushey Road
Bus Routes Serviced: 80/93/151/154/164/213/413 & N155

The garage was opened in January 1924 by the London General Omnibus Company with a capacity of about 100 buses. It won the Bus Garage of the Year Award for 2004 and in 2013 ran buses branded as "London General".

VEHICLE ALLOCATION

DOE 1	LX58 CWN	DOE21	LX58 CXL	DOE41	LX09 BXK	PVL282	PJ02 RCF	SE171	YX61 EKK
DOE 2	LX58 CWO	DOE22	LX58 CXN	DOE42	LX09 BXL	PVL283	PJ02 RCO	SE172	YX61 EKL
DOE 3	LX58 CWP	DOE23	LX58 CXO	DOE43	LX09 BXM	PVL284	PJ02 RCU	SE173	YX61 EKM
DOE 4	LX58 CWR	DOE24	LX58 CXP	DOE44	LX09 BXO	PVL285	PJ02 RCV	SE174	YX61 EKN
DOE 5	LX58 CWT	DOE25	LX58 CXR	DOE45	LX09 AXU	PVL286	PJ02 RCX	SOE29	LX09 AZR
DOE 6	LX58 CWU	DOE26	LX58 CXS	DOE46	LX09 AXV	PVL287	PJ02 RCY	SOE30	LX09 AZT
DOE 7	LX58 CWV	DOE27	LX58 CXT	DOE47	LX09 AXW	PVL288	PJ02 RCZ	SOE31	LX09 BXP
DOE 8	LX58 CWW	DOE28	LX58 CXU	DOE48	LX09 AXY	PVL289	PJ02 RDO	SOE32	LX09 BXR
DOE 9	LX58 CWY	DOE29	LX58 CXV	DOE49	LX09 AXZ	PVL290	PJ02 RDU	SOE33	LX09 BXS
DOE10	LX58 CWZ	DOE30	LX58 CXW	DOE50	LX09 AYA	PVL291	PJ02 RDV	SOE34	LX09EVB
DOE11	LX58 CXA	DOE31	LX58 CXY	DOE51	LX09 AYB	PVL292	PJ02 RDX	SOE35	LX09 EVC
DOE12	LX58 CXB	DOE32	LX58 CXZ	DOE52	LX09 AYC	PVL293	PJ02 RDY	SOE36	LX09 EVD
DOE13	LX58 CXC	DOE33	LX58 CYA	DOE53	LX09 AYD	PVL294	PJ02 RDZ	SOE37	LX09 EVF
DOE14	LX58 CXD	DOE34	LX58 CYC	DOE54	LX09 AYE	PVL295	PJ02 REU	SOE38	LX09 EVG
DOE15	LX58 CXE	DOE35	LX58 CYE	E 58	LX07 BYC	PVL296	PJ02 RFE	SOE39	LX09 EVH
DOE16	LX58 CXF	DOE36	LX58 CYF	E 59	LX07 BYD	PVL297	PJ02 RFF	SOE40	LX09 EVJ
DOE17	LX58 CXG	DOE37	LX58 CYG	E 60	LX07 BYF	SE167	YX61 EKF	WVL74	LF52 ZPD
DOE18	LX58 CXH	DOE38	LX09 BXG	LDP197	SN51 UAK	SE168	YX61 EKG	WVL76	LF52 ZPG
DOE19	LX58 CXJ	DOE39	LX09 BXH	LDP201	SN51 UAP	SE169	YX61 EKH		
DOE20	LX58 CXK	DOE40	LX09 BXJ	PVL281	PJ02 RBZ	SE170	YX61 EKJ		

Thornton Heath Bus Garage on September 21st, 2013 with Arriva London No.**ENX17** inside the depot.

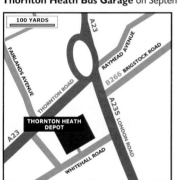

THORNTON HEATH (TH)
Whitehall Road, Thornton Heath CR7 6AB
Operated by: Arriva London
Location: TQ32166765 [51.392508, -0.114847]
Nearest Station: Thornton Heath (0.9 miles)
Nearest Bus Routes: 64/109/289/N64 & N109 - Thornton Heath Pond (Stop J)
Bus Routes Serviced: 198/250/255/289/410 & 450

This garage was built on the site of Thornton Heath Tram Depot which was opened on October 9th, 1879 by the Croydon Tramways Company and closed by London Transport on December 31st, 1949. Thornton Heath was rebuilt and partially operational prior to the official reopening as an omnibus garage in 1951.

VEHICLE ALLOCATION

DLA373	LJ03 MVE	DWL 5	Y805 DGT	DWS14	LJ53 NGG	PDL112	LJ54 LHN	T127	LJ10 HVG
DLA374	LJ03 MSY	DWL 6	Y806 DGT	DWS15	LJ53 NGN	PDL113	LJ54 LHO	T128	LJ10 HVH
DLA375	LJ03 MTE	DWL 7	LJ51 DDK	DWS16	LJ53 NFE	PDL114	LJ54 LHP	T129	LJ10 HVK
DLA376	LJ03 MTF	DWL 8	LJ51 DDL	DWS17	LJ53 NFF	PDL124	LJ56 APZ	T130	LJ10 HVL
DLA377	LJ03 MTK	DWL 9	LJ51 DDN	DWS18	LJ53 NFG	PDL125	LJ56 ARF	T131	LJ10 HTZ
DLA378	LJ03 MTU	DWL10	LJ51 DDO	ENX 9	LJ12 BYS	PDL126	LJ56 ARO	T132	LJ10 HUA
DLA379	LJ03 MTV	DWL11	LJ51 DDU	ENX10	LJ12 BYT	PDL127	LJ56 ARU	T133	LJ10 HUH
DLA380	LJ03 MTY	DWL16	LJ51 DEU	ENX11	LJ12 BYU	PDL128	LJ56 ARX	T134	LJ10 HUK
DLA381	LJ03 MTZ	DWS 1	LJ53 NGZ	ENX12	LJ12 BYV	PDL129	LJ56 ARZ	T135	LJ10 HUO
DLA382	LJ03 MUA	DWS 2	LJ53 NHA	ENX13	LJ12 BXY	PDL130	LJ56 ASO	T136	LJ10 HUP
DLA383	LJ03 MUB	DWS 3	LJ53 NHB	ENX14	LJ12 BXZ	PDL131	LJ56 ASU	T137	LJ10 HUU
DLA384	LJ03 MYU	DWS 4	LJ53 NHC	ENX15	LJ12 BYA	PDL132	LJ56 ASV	T138	LJ10 HUV
DLA385	LJ03 MYV	DWS 5	LJ53 NHD	ENX16	LJ12 BYB	PDL133	LJ56 ASX	T139	LJ10 HUY
DLA386	LJ03 MYX	DWS 6	LJ53 NFT	ENX17	LJ12 BYC	PDL134	LJ56 AOW	T140	LJ10 HUZ
DLA387	LJ03 MYY	DWS 7	LJ53 NFU	ENX18	LJ12 BYD	PDL135	LJ56 AOX	T141	LJ10 HTT
DLA388	LJ03 MYZ	DWS 8	LJ53 NFV	ENX19	LJ12 BYF	PDL136	LJ56 AOY	T142	LJ10 HTU
DLA389	LJ03 MZD	DWS 9	LJ53 NFX	PDL 97	LJ54 BAO	T122	LJ10 HVB	T143	LJ10 HTV
DWL 1	Y801 DGT	DWS10	LJ53 NFY	PDL 98	LJ54 BAU	T123	LJ10 HVC	T144	LJ10 HTX
DWL 2	Y802 DGT	DWS11	LJ53 NFZ	PDL 99	LJ54 BAV	T124	LJ10 HVD		
DWL 3	Y803 DGT	DWS12	LJ53 NGE	PDL100	LJ54 BBE	T125	LJ10 HVE		
DWL 4	Y804 DGT	DWS13	LJ53 NGF	PDL111	LJ54 LHM	T126	LJ10 HVF		

The entrance to **Tolworth Garage** on October 16th, 2013 with London United Nos **TA320** & **SDE5** amongst those in view. The wash unit can be seen on the left and the main depot buildings on the right. It opened in 2002 with a nominal capacity of 100 buses.

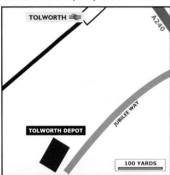

TOLWORTH (TV)
Kingston Road, Tolworth KT5 9NU
Operated by: London United
Location: TQ196965409 [51.375715, -0.280689]
Nearest Station: Tolworth (300 yards)
Nearest Bus Routes: 406/418/965 & K2 - Tolworth, Tolworth (Stop A)
Bus Routes Serviced: 57/265/613/665/965/K2 & K4

London United No.**DPS685** on the approach road to **Tolworth Bus Garage** on October 16th, 2013.

VEHICLE ALLOCATION

DE 57	SK07 DXE	DPS626	SK02 XGV	DPS691	SN03 LFG	TA239	LG02 FBD	VLE 4	PG04 WHF
DE 58	SK07 DXF	DPS641	LG02 FFK	DPS692	SN03 LFH	TA240	LG02 FBE	VLE 6	PG04 WHJ
DE 59	SK07 DXG	DPS642	LG02 FFL	DPS693	SN03 LFJ	TA241	LG02 FBF	VLE 9	PG04 WHM
DE 60	SK07 DXH	DPS643	LG02 FFM	DPS721	SN55 HLA	TA242	LG02 FBJ	VLE10	PG04 WHN
DE 61	SK07 DXJ	DPS644	LG02 FFN	DPS722	SN55 HLC	TA243	LG02 FBK	VLE11	PG04 WHP
DE 62	SK07 DXL	DPS645	LG02 FFO	SDE 1	YX08 MFO	TA244	LG02 FBL	VLE12	PG04 WHR
DE 63	SK07 DXM	DPS646	LG02 FFP	SDE 2	YX08 MFV	TA245	LG02 FBN	VLE13	PG04 WHS
DE 64	SK07 DXO	DPS647	LG02 FFR	SDE 3	YX08 MFY	TA246	LG02 FBO	VLE14	PG04 WHT
DE 65	SK07 DXP	DPS648	LG02 FFS	SDE 4	YX08 MDZ	TA247	LG02 FBU	VLE15	PG04 WHU
DE 66	SK07 DXR	DPS649	LG02 FFT	SDE 5	YX08 MFN	TA248	LG02 FBV	VLE16	PG04 WHV
DE 67	SK07 DXS	DPS650	LG02 FFU	SDE 6	YX08 MEU	TA249	LG02 FBX	VLE17	PG04 WHW
DE 70	SK07 DXV	DPS651	LG02 FFV	SDE 7	YX08 MEV	TA250	LG02 FBY	VLE18	PG04 WHX
DE 72	SK07 DXX	DPS652	LG02 FFW	SDE 8	YX08 MFA	TA281	LG02 FDY	VLE19	PG04 WHZ
DPS579	SN51 TAU	DPS653	LG02 FFX	SDE 9	YX08 MHM	TA284	LG02 FEH	VLE20	PG04 WJA
DPS580	SN51 TBY	DPS654	LG02 FFY	SDE10	YX08 MFK	TA285	LG02 FEJ	VLE21	PA04 CYC
DPS588	SN51 TCJ	DPS656	LG02 FGA	TA230	LG02 FAF	TA286	LG02 FEK	VLE24	PA04 CYG
DPS589	SN51 TCY	DPS657	LG02 FGC	TA231	LG02 FAJ	TA312	SN03 DZJ	VLE26	PA04 CYJ
DPS590	SN51 TDZ	DPS658	LG02 FGD	TA234	LG02 FAO	TA320	SN03 DZW		
DPS591	SN51 TBU	DPS660	LG02 FGF	TA235	LG02 FAU	TLA 5	SN53 EUL		
DPS592	SN51 TCK	DPS662	LG02 FGK	TA236	LG02 FBA	VLE 1	PG04 WHC		
DPS625	SK02 XGU	DPS666	LG02 FGP	TA238	LG02 FBC	VLE 2	PG04 WHD		

Tottenham Bus Garage on September 17th, 2013.

TOTTENHAM (AR)
Philip Lane, Tottenham, London N15 4JB
Operated by: Arriva London
Location: TQ33688957 [51.588761, -0.072042]
Nearest Tube Station: Tottenham Hale (0.5 miles)
Nearest Bus Routes: 41/76/123/149/230/243/259/
279/318/341/349/476 & W4 (Philip Lane/High Road)
Bus Routes Serviced: 41/67/76/123/149/230/243/
N41 & N76

The garage was built in 1913 by the Metropolitan Electric Tramway Company to house the omnibuses utilized to support their tram services.

VEHICLE ALLOCATION

DW298	LJ10 CVE	DW322	LJ60 AYB	DW541	LJ13 CFA	HV 2	LJ09 KOE	HV 26	LJ60 JGZ
DW299	LJ10 CVF	DW323	LJ60 AYC	DW542	LJ13 CFD	HV 3	LJ09 KOU	VLA 79	LJ54 BFF
DW300	LJ10 CVG	DW324	LJ60 AYD	DW543	LJ13 CFE	HV 4	LJ09 KOH	VLA 80	LJ54 BFK
DW301	LJ10 CVH	DW325	LJ60 AYE	DW544	LJ13 CFF	HV 5	LJ09 KOV	VLA 81	LJ54 BFL
DW302	LJ10 CVK	DW326	LJ60 AXH	DW545	LJ13 CFG	HV 6	LJ09 KOW	VLA 82	LJ54 BFM
DW303	LJ10 CVL	DW327	LJ60 AXK	DW546	LJ13 CFK	HV 7	LJ60 AWY	VLA 83	LJ54 BFN
DW304	LJ10 CVM	DW328	LJ60 AXM	DW547	LJ13 CFL	HV 8	LJ60 AWZ	VLA 84	LJ54 BFO
DW305	LJ10 CVN	DW329	LJ60 AXN	DW548	LJ13 CFM	HV 9	LJ60 AXA	VLA 85	LJ54 BCY
DW306	LJ10 CVO	DW330	LJ60 AXO	DW549	LJ13 CDV	HV 10	LJ60 AXB	VLA 86	LJ54 BCZ
DW307	LJ10 CVP	DW331	LJ60 AXP	DW550	LJ13 CDX	HV 11	LJ60 AXC	VLA 87	LJ54 BDE
DW308	LJ10 CUO	DW332	LJ60 AXR	DW551	LJ13 CDY	HV 12	LJ60 AXD	VLA 88	LJ54 BDF
DW309	LJ10 CUU	DW333	LJ60 AXS	DW552	LJ13 CDZ	HV 13	LJ60 AXF	VLA 89	LJ54 BDO
DW310	LJ10 CUV	DW334	LJ60 AXT	DW553	LJ13 CEA	HV 14	LJ60 AXG	VLA 90	LJ54 BDU
DW311	LJ10 CUW	DW335	LJ60 AXU	DW554	LJ13 CEF	HV 15	LJ60 AWF	VLA 91	LJ54 BDV
DW312	LJ10 CUX	DW336	LJ60 AWW	DW555	LJ13 CEK	HV 16	LJ60 AWG	VLA 92	LJ54 BDX
DW313	LJ10 CUY	DW401	LJ11 AEO	DW579	LT63 UKA	HV 17	LJ60 AWH	VLA 93	LJ54 BDY
DW314	LJ10 CVA	DW402	LJ11 AEP	DW580	LT63 UKB	HV 18	LJ60 AWM	VLA 94	LJ54 BDZ
DW315	LJ10 CVB	DW534	LJ13 CLN	DW581	LT63 UKC	HV 19	LJ60 AWN	VLA 95	LJ54 BBV
DW316	LJ10 CVC	DW535	LJ13 CLO	DW582	LT63 UKD	HV 20	LJ60 AWO	VLA 96	LJ54 BBX
DW317	LJ10 CVD	DW536	LJ13 CLV	DW583	LT63 UKE	HV 21	LJ60 AWP	VLA 97	LJ54 BBZ
DW318	LJ60 AXX	DW537	LJ13 CLX	DW584	LT63 UKF	HV 22	LJ60 AWR	VLA 98	LJ54 BCE
DW319	LJ60 AXY	DW538	LJ13 CLY	DW585	LT63 UKG	HV 23	LJ60 AWU	VLA 99	LJ54 BCF
DW320	LJ60 AXZ	DW539	LJ13 CEV	DW586	LT63 UKH	HV 24	LJ60 AWV	VLA100	LJ54 BCK
DW321	LJ60 AYA	DW540	LJ13 CEX	HV 1	LJ09 KRU	HV 25	LJ60 JGY		

Abellio No.8749 leaving its home depot, **Twickenham Bus Garage**, on August 17th, 2013.

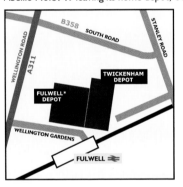

TWICKENHAM (TF)
The Old Tram Depot, Stanley Road, Twickenham, Middlesex TW2 5NT
Operated by: Abellio
Location: TQ14817191 [51.434862, -0.347518]
Nearest Station: Fulwell (Adjacent)
Nearest Bus Routes: 33/281/481 & 681 - Fulwell, Fulwell (Stop C)
Bus Routes Serviced: 117/235/290/481/490/969/ H20/H25/H26/K1/K3/R68 & R70

For a potted history of Fulwell Depot, please see Page 38.

NB Both London United* and Abellio utilize this depot with the former occupying the west end and Abellio the east. (*See Page 38)

VEHICLE ALLOCATION

8447	RD02 BJK	8112	DK04 SUU	8515	LJ08 CZZ	8567	YX11 HPA	8752	RN52 FYO
8448	RD02 BJO	8116	MX56 HYR	8529	YX10 FEF	8568	YX11 HPC	8753	RN52 FZA
8449	RD02 BJU	8117	MX56 HYS	8530	YX10 FEG	8569	YX11 HPE	8788	YX12 GHA
8450	RD02 BJV	8118	YX13 EHE	8531	YX10 FEH	8570	YX11 HPF	8789	YX12 GHB
8451	RD02 BJX	8119	YX13 EHF	8532	YX10 FEJ	8571	YX11 HPJ	8790	YX12 GHD
8478	KP02 PWV	8120	YX13 EHG	8533	YX10 FEK	8572	YX61 BXG	8791	YX12 GHF
8479	KP02 PVE	8121	YX13 EHH	8534	YX10 FEM	8573	YX11 HPL	8792	YX12 GHG
8480	KP02 PUK	8122	YX13 EHJ	8535	YX10 FEO	8574	YX11 HPN	8793	YX12 GHH
8481	KP02 PVU	8123	YX13 EHK	8536	YX10 FEP	8575	YX11 HOA	8806	YX13 EFM
8482	KM02 HGF	8124	YX13 EHL	8537	YX10 FET	8577	YX61 GAA	8807	YX13 EFN
8483	KP02 PUJ	8125	YX13 EHM	8538	YX10 FEU	8578	YX61 GAO	8808	YX13 EFO
8484	KM02 HGE	8126	YX13 EHN	8539	YX10 FEV	8579	YX61 GAU	8809	YX13 EFP
8485	KU52 YKO	8127	YX13 EHO	8540	YX10 FFA	8580	YX61 GBE	8810	YX13 EFR
8486	KU52 YKR	8460	RL02 FOT	8541	YX10 FFB	8581	YX61 GBF	8811	YX13 EFS
8487	KU52 YKS	8461	RL02 FOU	8542	YX10 FFC	8582	YX61 GBO	8812	YX13 EFT
8033	BU05 HFN	8462	RL02 FVM	8543	YX10 FFD	8743	RN52 EYK	8813	YX13 EFU
8101	LJ56 VSP	8507	LJ08 CZP	8544	YX10 FFE	8744	RN52 EYL	8814	YX13 EFV
8102	LJ56 VST	8508	LJ08 CZR	8545	YX10 FFG	8745	RN52 FPA	8815	YX13 EFW
8103	LJ56 VSU	8509	LJ08 CZS	8546	YX10 FFH	8746	RN52 FPC	8816	YX13 EFY
8104	LJ56 VSV	8510	LJ08 CZT	8547	YX10 FFJ	8747	RN52 FRD	8817	YX13 EFZ
8105	LJ56 VSX	8511	LJ08 CZU	8548	YX10 FFK	8748	RN52 FRF		
8106	LJ56 VSY	8512	LJ08 CZV	8549	YX10 FFL	8749	RN52 FVR		
8110	SN04 EGD	8513	LJ08 CZX	8550	YX10 FFM	8750	RN52 FVS		
8111	SN04 EFJ	8514	LJ08 CZY	8551	YX10 FFN	8751	RN52 FXD		

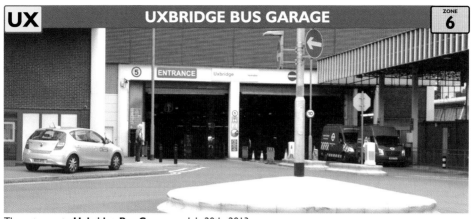

The entrance to **Uxbridge Bus Garage** on July 20th, 2013.

UXBRIDGE (UX)
Bakers Road, Uxbridge, Middlesex UB8 1RJ
Operated by: Metroline
Location: TQ05688423 [51.546962, -0.477681]
Nearest Tube Station: Uxbridge (Adjacent)
Nearest Bus Routes: Uxbridge Bus Station adjacent
Bus Routes Serviced: 331/607/A10/U1/U2/U3/U4/
U5 & U10

Metroline No.**VW1562** leaving **Uxbridge Bus Garage** on July 20th, 2013 to run on Route No.607 to White City.

VEHICLE ALLOCATION

DC1540	LK03 NLE	DC1557	LK53 FDP	DE1597	LK08 FLZ	DE1814	YX10 BGK	TP1536	LK03 UFU
DC1541	LK03 NLF	DC1558	LK53 FDU	DE1798	YX10 BFA	DE1815	YX10 BGO	TP1537	LK03 UFV
DC1542	LK03 NLG	DC1559	LK53 FDV	DE1799	YX10 BFE	DE1816	YX10 BGU	TP1538	LK03 UFW
DC1543	LK03 NLJ	DE1583	LK08 FNF	DE1800	YX10 BFF	DE1895	YX60 BZN	TP1539	LK03 UFX
DC1544	LK03 NLL	DE1584	LK08 FNG	DE1801	YX10 BFJ	DE1896	YX60 BZO	VW1560	LK55 ACU
DC1545	LK03 NLM	DE1585	LK08 FNH	DE1802	YX10 BFK	TP 433	LK03 GFZ	VW1561	LK55 AAE
DC1546	LK03 NLT	DE1586	LK08 FKT	DE1803	YX10 BFL	TP1525	LK03 UFD	VW1562	LK55 AAF
DC1547	LK03 NFY	DE1587	LK08 FKU	DE1804	YX10 BFM	TP1526	LK03 UFE	VW1563	LK55 AAJ
DC1548	LK03 NFZ	DE1588	LK08 FKV	DE1805	YX10 BFN	TP1527	LK03 UFG	VW1564	LK55 AAN
DC1549	LK53 FDC	DE1589	LK08 FKW	DE1806	YX10 BFO	TP1528	LK03 UFJ	VW1565	LK55 AAU
DC1550	LK53 FDE	DE1590	LK08 FLC	DE1807	YX10 BFP	TP1529	LK03 UFL	VW1566	LK55 AAV
DC1551	LK53 FDF	DE1591	LK08 FLD	DE1808	YX10 BFU	TP1530	LK03 UFM	VW1567	LK55 AAX
DC1552	LK53 FDG	DE1592	LK08 FLE	DE1809	YX10 BFV	TP1531	LK03 UFN	VW1568	LK55 AAY
DC1553	LK53 FDJ	DE1593	LK08 FLF	DE1810	YX10 BFY	TP1532	LK03 UFP	VW1569	LK55 AAZ
DC1554	LK53 FDM	DE1594	LK08 FLG	DE1811	YX10 BFZ	TP1533	LK03 UFR	VW1570	LK55 ABF
DC1555	LK53 FDN	DE1595	LK08 FLV	DE1812	YX10 BGE	TP1534	LK03 UFS		
DC1556	LK53 FDO	DE1596	LK08 FLW	DE1813	YX10 BGF	TP1535	LK03 UFT		

The Camberwell New Road exit of **Walworth Bus Garage** on August 31st, 2013. When solely a tram depot it was known as Camberwell but, with the introduction of buses in 1950, the name was changed to avoid confusion with the bus garage on the opposite side of the road.

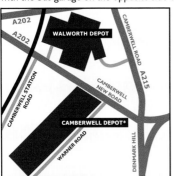

*SEE PAGE 24

WALWORTH (WL)
301 Camberwell New Road, London SE5 0TF
Operated by: Abellio
Location: TQ32387691 [51.475568, -0.095708]
Nearest Station: Denmark Hill (0.7 miles)
Nearest Bus Routes: 36/185/436 & N136 - Warner Road (Stop H)
Bus Routes Serviced: 35/40/100/172/188/343/381/484/N35/N343 & N381

Two tram depots were opened on this site by the Pimlico, Peckham & Greenwich Street Tramways Company in 1871 and 1873. They were enlarged prior to sustaining bomb damage during WWII and then substantially rebuilt before closure to trams by London Transport on October 7th, 1951. The depot was then used exclusively as an omnibus garage.

The less-than auspicious entrance off Camberwell Road to **Walworth Bus Garage** on August 31st, 2013. The entrance to the garage building can be identified by the sign board visible above the wall.

Go-Ahead London No.**PVL311** passing the Camberwell Road entrance to **Walworth Bus Garage** on August 31st, 2013.

VEHICLE ALLOCATION

2401	SN61 DFL	8329	YX10 EBM	9020	BX54 DJZ	9069	BX55 XNZ	9459	LJ09 CDY
2402	SN61 DFO	8330	YX11 AHA	9034	BX55 XMH	9070	LF06 YRC	9460	LJ09 CDZ
2403	SN61 DFP	8331	YX11 AHC	9035	BX55 XMJ	9428	LJ09 CAA	9461	LJ09 CEA
2404	SN61 DFU	8332	YX11 AHD	9036	BX55 XMK	9429	LJ09 CAE	9462	LJ09 CEF
2405	SN61 DFV	8333	YX11 AHE	9037	BX55 XML	9430	LJ09 CAO	9463	LJ09 CEK
2406	SN61 DFX	8334	YX11 AHF	9038	BX55 XMM	9431	LJ09 CAU	9464	LJ09 CEN
2407	SN61 DFY	8335	YX11 AHG	9039	BX55 XMO	9432	LJ09 CAV	9465	LJ09 CEO
2408	SN61 DFZ	8336	YX11 AHJ	9040	BX55 XMP	9433	LJ09 CAX	9466	LJ09 CEU
2409	SN61 DGE	8337	YX11 AHK	9041	BX55 XMR	9434	LJ09 CBF	9741	YN51 KUW
2410	SN61 DGF	8338	YX11 AHL	9042	BX55 XMS	9435	LJ09 CBO	9744	YN51 KVA
2411	SN61 DGO	8339	YX11 AHN	9043	BX55 XMT	9436	LJ09 CBU	9747	YN51 KVD
2412	SN61 DGU	8340	YX11 AHO	9044	BX55 XMU	9437	LJ09 CBV	9753	YN51 KVK
2413	SN61 DGV	8341	YX11 AHP	9045	LF55 CZA	9438	LJ09 CBX	9756	YN51 KVO
8053	X313 KRV	8342	YX11 AHU	9046	BX55 XMW	9439	LJ09 CBY	9761	YN51 KVU
8301	BX54 DKA	9001	BX54 DHJ	9047	BX55 XMZ	9440	LJ09 CCA	9828	LG52 XYJ
8302	BX54 DKD	9002	BX54 DHK	9048	LF55 CYZ	9441	LJ09 CCD	9829	LG52 XWD
8303	BX54 DKE	9003	BX54 DHL	9049	LF55 CYY	9442	LJ09 CCE	9830	KN52 NCE
8304	BX54 DKF	9004	BX54 DHM	9050	LF55 CYX	9443	LJ09 CCF	9832	KN52 NDD
8305	BX54 DKJ	9005	BX54 DHN	9051	LF55 CYW	9444	LJ09 CCK	9833	KN52 NDE
8306	BX54 DKK	9006	BX54 DHO	9052	LF55 CYV	9445	LJ09 CCN	9834	KN52 NDO
8307	BX54 DKL	9007	BX54 DHP	9053	LF55 CZB	9446	LJ09 CCO	9835	KN52 NDG
8308	BX54 DKO	9008	BX54 DHV	9054	BX55 XNG	9447	LJ09 CCU	9836	KN52 NDJ
8309	BX54 DKU	9009	BX54 DHY	9055	BX55 XNJ	9448	LJ09 CCX	9837	KN52 NDY
8310	BX54 DKV	9010	BX54 DHZ	9056	BX55 XNK	9449	LJ09 CCY	9838	KN52 NDZ
8318	BX54 DLU	9011	BX54 DJD	9057	BX55 XNL	9450	LJ09 CCZ	9839	KN52 NEJ
8321	YX10 EBA	9012	BX54 DJE	9058	BX55 XNM	9451	LJ09 CDE	9840	KN52 NEO
8322	YX10 EBC	9013	BX54 DJF	9059	BX55 XNN	9452	LJ09 CDF	9841	KN52 NEU
8323	YX10 EBD	9014	BX54 DJJ	9060	BX55 XNO	9453	LJ09 CDK	9842	KN52 NEY
8324	YX10 EBF	9015	BX54 DJK	9061	BX55 XNP	9454	LJ09 CDN	9843	KN52 NFA
8325	YX10 EBG	9016	BX54 DJO	9062	BX55 XNR	9455	LJ09 CDO		
8326	YX10 EBJ	9017	BX54 DJU	9063	BX55 XNS	9456	LJ09 CDU		
8327	YX10 EBK	9018	BX54 DJV	9064	BX55 XNT	9457	LJ09 CDV		
8328	YX10 EBL	9019	BX54 DJY	9065	BX55 XNU	9458	LJ09 CDX		

Waterloo Bus Garage on September 17th, 2013. It was opened during the 1980s as a Red Arrow garage and currently only operates on Mondays to Fridays.

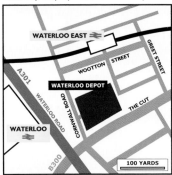

WATERLOO (RA)
Cornwall Road, London SE1 8TE
Operated by: Go-Ahead London
Location: TQ31327993 [51.503001, -0.109617]
Nearest Station: Waterloo East (300 yards)
Nearest Bus Routes: 59/68/168/171/172/176/N68/ N171 & X68 - Waterloo Station, Waterloo Rd (Stop D)
Bus Routes Serviced: 507 & 521

Go-Ahead London No.**MEC39** parked inside **Waterloo Bus Garage** on September 17th, 2013.

The wash plant at **Waterloo Bus Garage** on September 17th, 2013.

VEHICLE ALLOCATION

MEC 1	BG09 JJK	MEC11	BD09 ZPR	MEC21	BD09 ZRC	MEC31	BD09 ZVW	MEC41	BD09 ZWH
MEC 2	BG09 JJL	MEC12	BD09 ZPS	MEC22	BD09 ZRE	MEC32	BD09 ZVX	MEC42	BT09 GOH
MEC 3	BG09 JJU	MEC13	BD09 ZPT	MEC23	BD09 ZRF	MEC33	BD09 ZVY	MEC43	BT09 GOJ
MEC 4	BG09 JJV	MEC14	BD09 ZPU	MEC24	BD09 ZRG	MEC34	BD09 ZVZ	MEC44	BT09 GOK
MEC 5	BG09 JJX	MEC15	BD09 ZPV	MEC25	BD09 ZRJ	MEC35	BD09 ZWA	MEC45	BT09 GOP
MEC 6	BG09 JJY	MEC16	BD09 ZPW	MEC26	BD09 ZRK	MEC36	BD09 ZWB	MEC46	BT09 GOU
MEC 7	BG09 JJZ	MEC17	BD09 ZPX	MEC27	BF59 NHJ	MEC37	BD09 ZWC	MEC47	BT09 GOX
MEC 8	BG09 JKE	MEC18	BD09 ZPY	MEC28	BD09 ZVT	MEC38	BD09 ZWE	MEC48	BT09 GPE
MEC 9	BG09 JKF	MEC19	BD09 ZPZ	MEC29	BD09 ZVU	MEC39	BD09 ZWF	MEC49	BT09 GPF
MEC10	BG09 JKJ	MEC20	BD09 ZRA	MEC30	BD09 ZVV	MEC40	BD09 ZWG	MEC50	BT09 GPJ

Waterside Way Bus Garage on September 19th, 2013 with the wash plant in view on the left.

WATERSIDE WAY (PL)
Waterside Way, London SW17 0HB
Operated by: Go-Ahead London
Location: TQ26337125 [51.426166, -0.184204]
Nearest Station: Haydons Road (0.7 miles)
Nearest Bus Routes: 493 - Waterside Way (Stop SR)
Bus Routes Serviced: 39/485/493 & G1

Go-Ahead London No.**LDP222** parked in the yard at **Waterside Way Bus Garage** on September 19th, 2013.

The small office and amenities block at **Waterside Way Bus Garage** on September 19th, 2013.

VEHICLE ALLOCATION

LDP211	SK52 MMU	LDP221	SK52 MLU	LDP266	LX05 EYT	SE175	SN12 AUM	SE185	SN12 AVB
LDP212	SK52 MMV	LDP222	SK52 MLV	LDP267	LX05 EYU	SE176	SN12 AVO	SE186	SN12 AVC
LDP213	SK52 MMX	LDP223	SK52 MLX	LDP268	LX05 EYV	SE177	SN12 AUP	SE187	SN12 AVD
LDP214	SK52 MOA	LDP224	SK52 MLY	LDP269	LX05 EYW	SE178	SN12 AUR	SE188	SN12 AVE
LDP215	SK52 MOF	LDP225	SK52 MLZ	LDP270	LX05 EYY	SE179	SN12 AUT	SE189	SN12 AVF
LDP216	SK52 MOU	LDP226	SK52 MMA	LDP271	LX05 EXZ	SE180	SN12 AUU	SE190	SN12 AVG
LDP217	SK52 MOV	LDP227	SK52 MME	LDP272	LX05 EYA	SE181	SN12 AUV	SE191	SN12 AVJ
LDP218	SK52 MPE	LDP263	LX05 EYP	LDP292	LX06 EZZ	SE182	SN12 AUW	SE192	SN12 AVK
LDP219	SK52 MPF	LDP264	LX05 EYR	LDP293	LX06 EZJ	SE183	SN12 AUX	SE193	SN12 AVL
LDP220	SK52 MPO	LDP265	LX05 EYS	LDP294	LX06 EZK	SE184	SN12 AUY		

A general view of **West Ham Bus Garage** on September 7th, 2013 with Stagecoach London Routemaster No.**RM1941** parked on the right and the wash plant on the left. Also visible is a Northwind 100 Wind Turbine which, combined with rainwater harvesting, timber structural beams, biomass heating and a living roof aims to reduce the CO_2 output from the depot by around 25%.

WEST HAM (WH)
Stephenson Street, Canning Town, London E16 4SA
Operated by: Stagecoach London
Location: TQ39048248 [51.522566, 0.003046]
Nearest DLR Station: Star Lane (0.4 miles)
Nearest Bus Routes: 276 & 323 - Manor Road, Star Lane (Stop L)
Bus Routes Serviced: 15/69/86/97/104/115/147 /158/238/241/262/323/330/473/488 & D3

West Ham Garage was opened in February 2008 and replaced two depots in Stratford. It was fully operational by November 2009 and officially opened on July 14th, 2010. With a nominal capacity for 300 vehicles it is the largest bus garage in the UK and the training centre and head office for the East London Bus Group.

The south end of **West Ham Bus Garage** on September 7th, 2013. The site was originally occupied by a Parcelforce building and this was demolished in 2007 to facilitate the construction of the depot. It replaced Stratford and Waterden Road garages which were both removed to make way for the Olympic Park.

The wash plant at **West Ham Bus Garage** on September 7th, 2013 with Stagecoach London Routemaster No.**RM1968** occupying the left hand bay.

VEHICLE ALLOCATION

10101	LX12 DAU	17550	LY02 OBB	17920	LX03 OSU	18251	LX04 FYU	19865	LX12 CZU		
10102	LX12 DBO	17551	LY02 OBC	17921	LX03 OSV	18252	LX04 FYV	19866	LX12 CZV		
10103	LX12 DBU	17552	LY02 OBD	17922	LX03 OSW	18253	LX04 FYW	19867	LX12 CZW		
10104	LX12 DBV	17553	LY02 OBE	17923	LX03 OSY	18254	LX04 FYY	19868	LX12 CZY		
10105	LX12 DBY	17554	LY02 OBF	17924	LX03 OSZ	18255	LX04 FYZ	19869	LX12 CZZ		
10106	LX12 DBZ	17555	LY02 OBG	17925	LX03 OTA	18256	LX04 FZA	19870	LX12 DAA		
10107	LX12 DCE	17556	LY02 OBH	17926	LX03 OTB	18257	LX04 FZB	19871	LX12 DAO		
10108	LX12 DCF	17557	LY02 OBJ	17927	LX03 OTC	18258	LX04 FZC	36339	LX09 ACV		
10109	LX12 DCO	17576	LV52 HFJ	17928	LX03 OTD	18259	LX04 FZD	36340	LX09 ACY		
10110	LX12 DCU	17580	LV52 HFN	17929	LX03 OTE	18260	LX04 FZE	36344	LX09 ADV		
10111	LX12 DCV	17586	LV52 HFU	17931	LX03 OTF	18261	LX04 FZF	36345	LX59 ANF		
10112	LX12 DCY	17588	LV52 HFX	17931	LX03 OTG	18262	LX04 FZG	36346	LX59 ANP		
15018	LX58 CFJ	17589	LV52 HFY	17932	LX03 OTH	18263	LX04 FZH	36347	LX59 ANR		
17452	Y452 NHK	17815	LX03 BXK	17933	LX03 OTJ	18264	LX04 FZJ	36348	LX59 ANU		
17454	Y454 NHK	17816	LX03 BXL	17934	LX53 JXU	18265	LX04 FZK	36349	LX59 ANV		
17460	Y529 NHK	17817	LX03 BXM	17935	LX53 JXV	18266	LX05 BVY	36350	LX59 AOA		
17489	LX51 FMJ	17820	LX03 BXR	17936	LX53 JXW	18267	LX05 BVZ	36351	LX59 AOB		
17490	LX51 FMK	17821	LX03 BXS	17937	LX53 JXY	18268	LX05 BWA	36352	LX59 AOC		
17493	LX51 FMO	17822	LX03 BXU	17938	LX53 JYA	18269	LX05 BWB	36353	LX59 AOD		
17494	LX51 FMP	17823	LX03 BXV	17939	LX53 JYB	18270	LX05 BWC	36354	LX59 AOE		
17495	LX51 FMU	17824	LX03 BXW	17940	LX53 JYC	18271	LX05 BWD	36355	LX59 AOF		
17497	LX51 FMY	17825	LX03 BXY	17941	LX53 JYD	18272	LX05 BWE	36356	LX59 AOG		
17498	LX51 FMZ	17834	LX03 BYJ	17942	LX53 JYE	18273	LX05 BWF	36357	LX59 AOH		
17499	LX51 FNA	17847	LX03 BZA	17943	LX53 JYF	18274	LX05 BWG	36358	LX59 AOJ		
17500	LX51 FNC	17848	LX03 BZB	17944	LX53 JYG	18275	LX05 BWH	36359	LX59 AOK		
17501	LX51 FND	17849	LX03 BZC	18232	LX04 FXY	18276	LX05 BWJ	36360	LX59 AOL		
17509	LX51 FNM	17850	LX03 BZD	18233	LX04 FXZ	18277	LX05 BWK	36361	LX59 AOM		
17515	LX51 FNT	17865	LX03 NFK	18236	LX04 FYC	18454	LX05 LLP	36362	LX59 ECF		
17516	LX51 FNU	17889	LX03 OPY	18237	LX04 FYD	18456	LX55 EPC	36363	LX59 ECJ		
17518	LX51 FNW	17890	LX03 OPZ	18238	LX04 FYE	18457	LX55 EPD	36364	LX59 ECN		
17520	LX51 FNZ	17891	LX03 ORA	18239	LX04 FYF	18458	LX55 EPE	36365	LX59 ECT		
17521	LX51 FOA	17909	LX03 OSC	18240	LX04 FYG	18459	LX55 EPF	36366	LX59 ECV		
17527	LX51 FOK	17910	LX03 OSD	18241	LX04 FYH	18460	LX55 EPJ	36367	LX59 ECW		
17528	LX51 FOM	17911	LX03 OSE	18242	LX04 FYJ	18461	LX55 EPK	36368	LX59 ECY		
17529	LX51 FON	17912	LX03 OSG	18243	LX04 FYK	18462	LX55 EPL	36369	LX59 ECZ		
17530	LX51 FOP	17913	LX03 OSJ	18244	LX04 FYL	19000	LX55 HGC	36370	LX59 EDC		
17535	LY02 OAA	17914	LX03 OSK	18245	LX04 FYM	19859	LX12 CZN	36371	LX59 EDF		
17536	LY02 OAB	17915	LX03 OSL	18246	LX04 FYN	19860	LX12 CZO	36372	LX59 EDJ		
17545	LY02 OAU	17916	LX03 OSM	18247	LX04 FYP	19861	LX12 CZP	36373	LX59 EDK		
17546	LY02 OAV	17917	LX03 OSN	18248	LX04 FYR	19862	LX12 CZR	36374	LX59 EDL		
17547	LY02 OAW	17918	LX03 OSP	18249	LX04 FYS	19863	LX12 CZS	36375	LX59 EDO		
17549	LY02 OAZ	17919	LX03 OSR	18250	LX04 FYT	19864	LX12 CZT				

Westbourne Park Bus Garage on August 17th, 2013 with Tower Transit Nos **DNH3900** & **DN33785** in the exit road. It opened in 1981 and its adjacency to the A40 Westway flyover can clearly be seen.

NB PART OF THE DEPOT IS UNDER THE A40 WESTWAY

Westbourne Park replaced two older garages; the small and inadequate Middle Row (X), and the larger former trolleybus depot at Stonebridge (SE).

WESTBOURNE PARK (X)
Great Western Road, London W9 3NW
Operated by: Tower Transit
Location: TQ24948188 [51.521445, -0.200732]
Nearest Tube Station: Westbourne Park (200 yards)
Nearest Bus Routes: 28/31/328/N28 & N31 - Westbourne Park (Stop A)
Bus Routes Serviced: 9H/23/70 & 295

Routemaster buses parked on the north side of **Westbourne Park Bus Garage** on August 17th, 2013.

VEHICLE ALLOCATION

DML44313	YX12 AAJ	DML44323	YX12 AVJ	DN33780	SN12 AVW	VN37953	BN61 MXB	VN37990	BF62 UYC
DML44314	YX12 AEA	DML44324	YX12 AYF	DN33781	SN12 AVX	VN37954	BN61 MXA	VN37991	BF62 UYE
DML44315	YX12 AED	DML44325	YX12 AZW	DN33782	SN12 AVY	VN37955	BN61 MXE	VN37992	BF62 UYG
DML44316	YX12 AEF	DML44326	YX12 DHZ	DN33783	SN12 AVZ	VN37956	BN61 MXD	VN37993	BF62 UYD
DML44317	YX12 AEU	DML44327	YX12 DJD	DN33784	SN12 AWA	VN37957	BN61 MXH	VN37994	BF62 UYH
DML44318	YX12 AOF	DML44328	YX12 DJE	DN33785	SN12 AWB	VN37958	BN61 MXC	VN37995	BF62 UYJ
DML44319	YX12 AFV	DN33776	SN12 AVR	DN33786	SN12 EHB	VN37959	BN61 MXF	VN37996	BF62 UYK
DML44320	YX12 AMK	DN33777	SN12 AVT	DN33787	SN12 EHC	VN37961	BN61 MXL		
DML44321	YX12 ARZ	DN33778	SN12 AVU	VN37943	BK10 MFZ	VN37988	BF62 UYB		
DML44322	YX12 AXU	DN33779	SN12 AVV	VN37952	BN61 MWZ	VN37989	BF62 UYA		

The entrance to **Willesden Junction Bus Garage** on November 2nd, 2013.

WILLESDEN JUNCTION (WJ)
46 Station Road, London NW10 4XB
Operated by: Metroline
Location: TQ21588306 [51.533149, -0.247045]
Nearest Station: Willesden Junction (300 yards)
Nearest Bus Routes: 228 & 266 - Willesden Junction (Stop M)
Bus Routes Serviced: 18/187/206/226/228 & N18

Willesden Junction Depot — Metroline

VEHICLE ALLOCATION

DE1620	YX58 FPA	DE1644	YX58 FOV	DE1668	YX09 AEY	VW1848	BF60 UUJ	VW1872	BF60 VJA
DE1621	YX58 FPC	DE1645	YX58 FRC	DE1669	YX09 AEZ	VW1849	BF60 UUG	VW1873	BF60 VHY
DE1622	YX58 FPD	DE1646	YX58 FRD	DE1670	YX09 AFA	VW1850	BF60 UUK	VW1874	BF60 VJC
DE1623	YX58 FPE	DE1647	YX58 HVA	DE1671	YX09 AFE	VW1851	BF60 UUH	VW1875	BF60 VJK
DE1624	YX58 FPF	DE1648	YX58 HVB	DE1672	YX09 AFF	VW1852	BF60 UUL	VW1876	BF60 VJJ
DE1625	YX58 FPG	DE1649	YX58 HVM	DE1673	YX09 AFJ	VW1853	BF60 UUN	VW1877	BF60 VJE
DE1626	YX58 FPJ	DE1650	YX09 AEA	DE1674	YX09 AFK	VW1854	BF60 UUM	VW1878	BF60 VHZ
DE1627	YX58 FPK	DE1651	YX09 AEB	DEL1970	YX12 AOS	VW1855	BF60 UUO	VW1879	BF60 VJG
DE1628	YX58 FPL	DE1652	YX09 AEC	DEL1971	YX12 AOT	VW1856	BF60 UUR	VW1880	BF60 VJD
DE1629	YX58 FPN	DE1653	YX09 AED	DEL1972	YX12 AFU	VW1857	BF60 UUP	VW1881	BF60 VJL
DE1630	YX58 FPO	DE1654	YX09 AEE	DEL1973	YX12 AFK	VW1858	BF60 UUT	VW1882	BF60 VJU
DE1631	YX58 FPT	DE1655	YX09 AEF	DEL1974	YX12 AZG	VW1859	BF60 UUS	VW1883	BF60 VJV
DE1632	YX58 FPU	DE1656	YX09 AEG	DEL1975	YX12 AFO	VW1860	BF60 UUX	VW1884	BF60 UVB
DE1633	YX58 FPV	DE1657	YX09 AEJ	DEL1976	YX12 AVT	VW1861	BF60 UUY	VW1885	BF60 UVA
DE1634	YX58 FPY	DE1658	YX09 AEK	DEL1977	YX12 AYK	VW1862	BF60 UUV	VW1886	BF60 UVD
DE1635	YX58 FOF	DE1659	YX09 AEL	DEL1978	YX12 ATN	VW1863	BF60 UUZ	VW1887	BF60 UVG
DE1636	YX58 FOH	DE1660	YX09 AEM	DEL1979	YX12 ATK	VW1864	BF60 VHP	VW1888	BF60 UVH
DE1637	YX58 FOJ	DE1661	YX09 AEN	DEL1980	YX12 APK	VW1865	BF60 VHR	VW1889	BF60 UVC
DE1638	YX58 FOK	DE1662	YX09 AEO	VW1842	BF60 UUA	VW1866	BF60 VHV	VW1890	BF60 UVE
DE1639	YX58 FOM	DE1663	YX09 AEP	VW1843	BF60 UUB	VW1867	BF60 VHU	VW1891	BF60 VJM
DE1640	YX58 FON	DE1664	YX09 AET	VW1844	BF60 UTZ	VW1868	BF60 VHW	VW1892	BF60 VJN
DE1641	YX58 FOP	DE1665	YX09 AEU	VW1845	BF60 UUD	VW1869	BF60 UUW	VW1893	BF60 VJO
DE1642	YX58 FOT	DE1666	YX09 AEV	VW1846	BF60 UUC	VW1870	BF60 VHT	VW1894	BF60 VJP
DE1643	YX58 FOU	DE1667	YX09 AEW	VW1847	BF60 UUE	VW1871	BF60 VHX		

The Pound Lane entrance to **Willesden Bus Garage** on November 2nd, 2013.

WILLESDEN (AC)
287 High Road, Willesden, London NW10 2JY
Operated by: Metroline
Location: TQ21998470 [51.548275, -0.238189]
Nearest Tube Station: Dollis Hill (0.6 miles)
Nearest Bus Routes: 52/98/260/266/302/460 &
N98 - Willesden Bus Garage (Stop WN)
Bus Routes Serviced: 6/52/98/260/302/460 N52 &
N98

The exit from **Willesden Bus Garage** in Pound Lane on November 2nd, 2013 with Metroline Nos **VP566**, **VWH1409**, **VP523**, **VP513**, **VP541**, **VP539** & **VWH1417** parked in the yard.

The High Road entrance to **Willesden Bus Garage** on June 22nd, 2013 with staff on Metroline No. **VP511** effecting a crew change.

VEHICLE ALLOCATION							
VP473	LK03 GKU	VP513	LK04 CPZ	VP542	LK04 CVC	VP572	LK04 ELX	VW1396	LK62 DVF
VP475	LK03 GKX	VP514	LK04 CRF	VP543	LK04 CVD	VP573	LK04 EMF	VW1397	LK62 DVG
VP478	LK03 GLF	VP515	LK04 CRJ	VP544	LK04 CVE	VP574	LK04 EMJ	VW1398	LK62 DVH
VP482	LK03 GLZ	VP516	LK04 CRU	VP545	LK04 CVF	VP575	LK04 EMV	VW1399	LK62 DVJ
VP483	LK03 GME	VP517	LK04 CRV	VP546	LK04 CVG	VP576	LK04 EMX	VW1400	LK62 DVL
VP489	LK03 GMY	VP518	LK04 CRZ	VP547	LK04 CVH	VP577	LK04 ENE	VW1401	LK62 DVO
VP490	LK03 GMZ	VP519	LK04 CSF	VP548	LK04 CVJ	VP578	LK04 ENF	VW1402	LK62 DVP
VP491	LK03 GNF	VP520	LK04 CSU	VP549	LK04 CVL	VP579	LK04 ENH	VW1403	LK62 DVR
VP492	LK03 GNJ	VP521	LK04 CSV	VP550	LK04 CVM	VP580	LK04 ENJ	VW1404	LK62 DVU
VP493	LK03 GNN	VP522	LK04 CSX	VP551	LK04 CVN	VPL168	Y168 NLK	VW1405	LK13 BHW
VP494	LK03 GNP	VP523	LK04 CSY	VP552	LK04 CVP	VPL169	Y169 NLK	VW1406	LK13 BHX
VP495	LK53 LXM	VP524	LK04 CSZ	VP553	LK04 CVR	VPL171	Y171 NLK	VW1407	LK13 BHY
VP496	LK53 LXN	VP525	LK04 CTE	VP554	LK04 CVS	VPL173	Y195 NLK	VWH1360	LK62 DHX
VP497	LK53 LXO	VP526	LK04 CTF	VP555	LK04 CVT	VPL175	Y195 NLK	VWH1361	LK62 DHZ
VP498	LK53 LXP	VP527	LK04 CTU	VP556	LK04 CVU	VPL178	Y178 NLK	VWH1362	LK62 DJY
VP499	LK53 LXR	VP528	LK04 CTV	VP557	LK04 CVV	VPL180	Y197 NLK	VWH1363	LK62 DJZ
VP500	LK53 LXT	VP529	LK04 CTX	VP558	LK04 CVW	VPL181	Y181 NLK	VWH1364	LK62 DKE
VP501	LK53 LXU	VP530	LK04 CTZ	VP559	LK04 CVX	VPL183	Y183 NLK	VWH1408	LK62 DWA
VP502	LK53 LXV	VP531	LK04 CUA	VP560	LK04 EKU	VPL185	Y185 NLK	VWH1409	LK62 DWD
VP503	LK53 LXW	VP532	LK04 CUC	VP562	LK04 EKW	VPL186	Y186 NLK	VWH1410	LK62 DWE
VP504	LK53 LXX	VP533	LK04 CUG	VP563	LK04 EKX	VPL189	Y189 NLK	VWH1411	LK62 DWF
VP505	LK53 LXY	VP534	LK04 CUH	VP564	LK04 EKY	VPL191	Y191 NLK	VWH1412	LK62 DWJ
VP506	LK53 LXZ	VP535	LK04 CUJ	VP565	LK04 EKZ	VPL192	Y192 NLK	VWH1413	LK62 DWM
VP507	LK53 LYA	VP536	LK04 CUU	VP566	LK04 ELC	VPL193	Y193 NLK	VWH1414	LK62 DWO
VP508	LK53 LYC	VP537	LK04 CUW	VP567	LK04 ELH	VPL196	Y146 NLK	VWH1415	LK62 DWU
VP509	LK53 LYD	VP538	LK04 CUX	VP568	LK04 ELJ	VPL197	Y147 NLK	VWH1416	LK62 DWV
VP510	LK53 LYF	VP539	LK04 CUY	VP569	LK04 ELU	VPL198	Y148 NLK	VWH1417	LK62 DWY
VP511	LK53 LYG	VP540	LK04 CVA	VP570	LK04 ELV	VPL208	Y208 NLK	VWH1418	LK62 DXF
VP512	LK04 CPY	VP541	LK04 CVB	VP571	LK04 ELW	VW1395	LK62 DVC	VWH1419	LK62 DXG

Wood Green Bus Garage on September 17th, 2013.

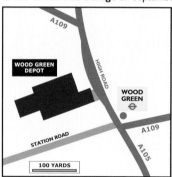

WOOD GREEN (WN)
Jolly Butchers Hill, High Road, Wood Green, London N22 7TZ
Operated by: Arriva London
Location: TQ30909045 [51.597956, -0.110871]
Nearest Tube Station: Wood Green (200 yards)
Nearest Bus Routes: 121/141/144/184/221/232/243/329/W3 & W4
Bus Routes Serviced: 29/141/144/184/221/382/617 & N29

The garage was opened as a horse tram depot in 1895 by the North Metropolitan Tramways & Omnibus Company. It was converted to electric working in 1904 and subsequently extended, becoming part of London Transport on July 1st, 1933. It was utilized as a trolleybus depot from May 8th, 1938 and solely as a bus garage from November 20th, 1961.

Arriva London Nos **T266** & **DW574** passing **Wood Green Bus Garage** on September 17th, 2013.

Arriva London No.**HV111** departing from **Wood Green Bus Garage** on September 17th, 2013.

VEHICLE ALLOCATION

DW465	LJ61 CCV	DW505	LJ62 BAA	HV 94	LJ13 FCP	PDL 82	LF52 URY	VLW 53	LF02 PSU
DW466	LJ61 CCX	DW506	LJ62 BBZ	HV 95	LJ13 FCU	PDL 83	LF52 URZ	VLW 54	WLT 554
DW467	LJ61 CCY	DW507	LJ62 BDF	HV 96	LJ13 FCV	PDL 84	LF52 USB	VLW 55	LF02 PSY
DW468	LJ61 CCZ	DW508	LJ62 BDO	HV 97	LJ13 FCX	PDL 86	LF52 USD	VLW 56	LF02 PSZ
DW469	LJ61 CDE	DW509	LJ13 CCE	HV 98	LJ13 FCY	PDL 91	LF52 URN	VLW 57	LF02 PTO
DW470	LJ61 CDF	DW510	LJ13 CCF	HV 99	LJ13 FCZ	PDL 92	LF52 URO	VLW 58	LF02 PTU
DW471	LJ61 CDK	DW511	LJ13 CCK	HV100	LJ13 FDA	PDL 93	LF52 URP	VLW 59	LF02 PTX
DW472	LJ61 CDN	DW512	LJ13 CCN	HV101	LJ13 FDC	PDL 94	LF52 URR	VLW 60	LF02 PTY
DW473	LJ61 CDO	DW513	LJ13 CCO	HV102	LJ13 FBY	VLW 21	LJ51 DGX	VLW 61	LF02 PVE
DW474	LJ61 CDU	DW514	LJ13 CCU	HV103	LJ13 FBZ	VLW 22	LJ51 DGY	VLW 62	LF02 PVJ
DW475	LJ61 CBX	DW515	LJ13 CCV	HV104	LJ13 FCA	VLW 23	LJ51 DGZ	VLW 63	LF02 PVK
DW476	LJ61 CBY	ENL30	LJ09 KPR	HV105	LJ13 FCC	VLW 24	LJ51 DHA	VLW 64	LF02 PVL
DW477	LJ61 CCA	ENL31	LJ09 KPT	HV106	LT63 UKJ	VLW 25	LJ51 DHC	VLW 65	LF02 PVN
DW478	LJ61 CCD	ENL32	LJ09 KPU	HV107	LJ13 FCE	VLW 26	LJ51 DHD	VLW 66	LF02 PVO
DW479	LJ61 CCE	ENL33	LJ09 KPX	HV108	LJ13 FCF	VLW 27	LJ51 DHE	VLW 67	LF52 UTC
DW480	LJ61 CCF	ENL34	LJ09 KPX	HV109	LJ13 FCG	VLW 28	LJ51 DHF	VLW 68	LF52 UTE
DW481	LJ61 CCK	ENL35	LJ09 KPY	HV110	LJ13 FCL	VLW 29	LJ51 DHG	VLW 69	LF52 USE
DW482	LJ61 CCN	ENL36	LJ09 KPZ	HV111	LJ13 FCM	VLW 30	LJ51 DHK	VLW 70	LF52 UTG
DW483	LJ61 CCO	ENL37	LJ09 KRD	HV112	LJ13 FBE	VLW 31	LJ51 DHL	VLW 71	LF52 UTH
DW484	LJ61 CCU	ENL38	LJ09 KRE	HV113	LJ13 FBF	VLW 32	VLT 32	VLW 72	WLT 372
DW485	LJ61 CAA	ENL39	LJ09 KRF	HV114	LJ13 FBG	VLW 33	LJ51 DHO	VLW 73	LF52 UTL
DW486	LJ61 CAE	ENL40	LJ09 KOX	HV115	LJ13 FBP	VLW 34	LJ51 DHP	VLW 74	LF52 UTM
DW487	LJ61 CAO	ENL41	LJ09 KPA	HV116	LJ13 FBL	VLW 35	LJ51 DHV	VLW 75	LF52 USM
DW488	LJ61 CAU	ENL42	LJ09 KPE	HV117	LJ13 FBN	VLW 36	LJ51 DHX	VLW 76	LF52 USN
DW489	LJ61 CAV	ENL43	LJ09 KPV	HV118	LJ13 FBO	VLW 37	LJ51 DHY	VLW 77	LF52 USO
DW490	LJ61 CAX	ENL44	LJ09 KPG	HV119	LJ13 FBU	VLW 38	LJ51 DHZ	VLW 78	LF52 USS
DW491	LJ61 CBF	ENL45	LJ09 KPK	HV120	LJ13 FBV	VLW 39	LJ51 DJD	VLW 79	LF52 UST
DW492	LJ61 CBO	ENL46	LJ09 KPL	HV121	LJ13 FBX	VLW 40	LJ51 DJE	VLW 80	LF52 USU
DW493	LJ61 CBU	ENL47	LJ09 KPN	HV122	LJ13 FAM	VLW 41	LJ51 OSK	VLW 81	LF52 USV
DW494	LJ61 CBV	ENL48	LJ09 KPO	HV123	LJ13 FAO	VLW 42	LF02 PKO	VLW 82	LF52 USW
DW495	LJ61 CKA	HV 84	LJ13 FDF	HV124	LJ13 FAU	VLW 43	LF02 PKU	VLW 83	LF52 USX
DW496	LJ61 CKC	HV 85	LJ13 FDG	HV125	LJ13 FBA	VLW 44	LF02 PKV	VLW 84	LF52 USY
DW497	LJ61 CKD	HV 86	LJ13 FDK	HV126	LJ13 FBB	VLW 45	LF02 PKX	VLW 85	LF52 UPV
DW498	LJ61 CKE	HV 87	LJ13 FDL	HV127	LJ13 FBC	VLW 46	LF02 PKY	VLW114	LJ03 MJV
DW499	LJ62 BKD	HV 88	LJ13 FDM	HV128	LJ13 FBD	VLW 47	LF02 PKZ	VLW115	LJ03 MGX
DW500	LJ62 BKG	HV 89	LJ13 FDN	HV129	LJ13 FEO	VLW 48	LF02 PLJ	VLW116	LJ03 MGY
DW501	LJ62 BKN	HV 90	LJ13 FDO	HV130	LJ13 FEP	VLW 49	LF02 PLN		
DW502	LJ62 BMO	HV 91	LJ13 FDP	HV131	LJ13 FET	VLW 50	LF02 PLO		
DW503	LJ62 BNA	HV 92	LJ13 FCN	PDL 80	LF52 UOR	VLW 51	WLT 751		
DW504	LJ62 BZV	HV 93	LJ13 FCO	PDL 81	LF52 UNV	VLW 52	LF02 PSO		

Arriva buses in the yard at **Edmonton Bus Garage** on August 20th, 2013, including Nos **DLA164**, **DLA122** & **DLA199**. The depot was opened in 1993 by London Suburban Bus to accommodate its buses being used on Route Nos 4 & 271. The company was taken over in 1995 and the depot closed. It was re-opened by Arriva County Bus in 1997 and continued in use with Arriva until formally closed on March 24th, 2012. In 2013 it was in use as a maintenance depot (See Page 108).

Single-deck Metroline buses Nos **DLD178**, **MM820** & **DSD209** parked alongside of the garage building at **Perivale (East) Bus Garage** on November 2nd, 2013. The road leads to a large storage area at the back of the depot (See Page 108).

STORAGE, MAINTENANCE & TOUR BUS GARAGES

This short section notes the four garages that at the end of 2013 were primarily engaged in maintenance or storage duties and not supplying buses for TFL routes. Also listed are the three garages utilized for the supply and maintenance of tour buses operating in London.

CN — BEDDINGTON FARM BUS GARAGE — ZONE 5

The entrance to **Beddington Farm Bus Garage** on September 21st, 2013.

100 YARDS

CROYDON DEPOT*
BEDDINGTON INDUSTRIAL ESTATE
BEDDINGTON FARM ROAD
BEDDINGTON FARM DEPOT
BEDDINGTON LANE
B272

BEDDINGTON FARM (CN)
Beddington Farm Road, Croydon, CR0 4XH
Operated by: Arriva London
Location: TQ30206633 [51.381022, -0.130496]
Nearest Tram Station: Therapia Lane (0.4 miles)
Nearest Bus Route: 463 – Beddington Farm Road
Primary use: Maintenance Depot only

*SEE PAGE 30

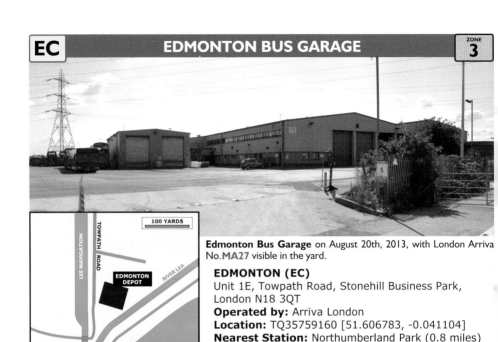

EC EDMONTON BUS GARAGE — ZONE 3

Edmonton Bus Garage on August 20th, 2013, with London Arriva No.**MA27** visible in the yard.

EDMONTON (EC)
Unit 1E, Towpath Road, Stonehill Business Park, London N18 3QT
Operated by: Arriva London
Location: TQ35759160 [51.606783, -0.041104]
Nearest Station: Northumberland Park (0.8 miles)
Nearest Bus Routes: 33 & 444 – Harbet Road/Cooks Ferry
Primary Use: Heavy maintenance and vehicle storage

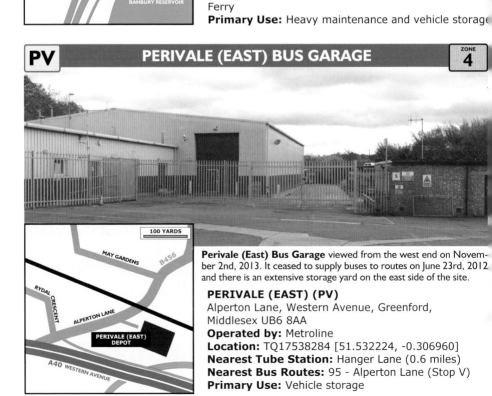

PV PERIVALE (EAST) BUS GARAGE — ZONE 4

Perivale (East) Bus Garage viewed from the west end on November 2nd, 2013. It ceased to supply buses to routes on June 23rd, 2012 and there is an extensive storage yard on the east side of the site.

PERIVALE (EAST) (PV)
Alperton Lane, Western Avenue, Greenford, Middlesex UB6 8AA
Operated by: Metroline
Location: TQ17538284 [51.532224, -0.306960]
Nearest Tube Station: Hanger Lane (0.6 miles)
Nearest Bus Routes: 95 - Alperton Lane (Stop V)
Primary Use: Vehicle storage

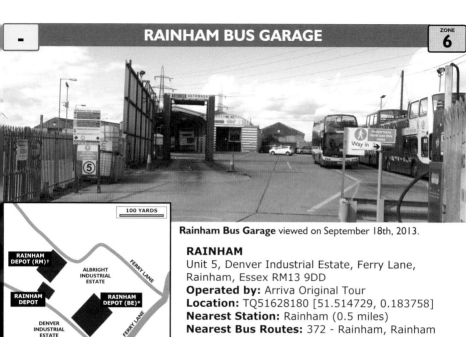

Rainham Bus Garage viewed on September 18th, 2013.

RAINHAM

Unit 5, Denver Industrial Estate, Ferry Lane, Rainham, Essex RM13 9DD
Operated by: Arriva Original Tour
Location: TQ51628180 [51.514729, 0.183758]
Nearest Station: Rainham (0.5 miles)
Nearest Bus Routes: 372 - Rainham, Rainham (London) (Stop B)
Primary Use: Maintenance and garaging of tour buses

*SEE PAGE 76 †SEE PAGE 77

NC   TWICKENHAM BUS GARAGE

ZONE 5

Twickenham Bus Garage on August 17th, 2013.

TWICKENHAM (NC)

The Skills Centre, Twickenham Trading Estate, Rugby Road, Twickenham TW1 1DQ
Operated by: London United
Location: TQ15767439 [51.456671, -0.335170]
Nearest Station: Twickenham (0.7 miles)
Nearest Bus Routes: 481 - Twickenham, Twickenham Trading Estate (Stop K)
Primary use: Maintenance Depot only

TWICKENHAM BUS GARAGE (NC) VIEWED FROM THE EAST

A general view of **Twickenham Bus Garage** (NC) on August 17th, 2013 showing the small storage yard on the east side of the site, with the garage building beyond. Entrance to the depot is via a gateway on the right of the picture (See Page 109).

LONDON UNITED BUSES Nos VA48 & VA49 AT TWICKENHAM

London United Nos **VA48 & VA49** in the yard alongside of the depot building at **Twickenham Bus Garage** (TF) on August 17th, 2013 (See Page 109).

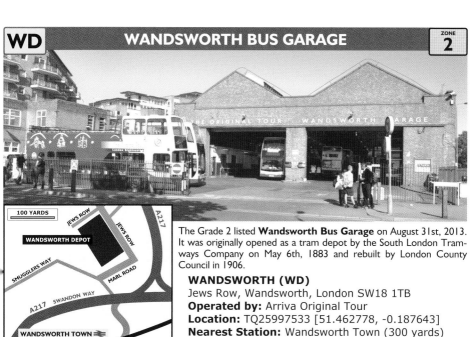

WD — WANDSWORTH BUS GARAGE — ZONE 2

The Grade 2 listed **Wandsworth Bus Garage** on August 31st, 2013. It was originally opened as a tram depot by the South London Tramways Company on May 6th, 1883 and rebuilt by London County Council in 1906.

WANDSWORTH (WD)
Jews Row, Wandsworth, London SW18 1TB
Operated by: Arriva Original Tour
Location: TQ25997533 [51.462778, -0.187643]
Nearest Station: Wandsworth Town (300 yards)
Nearest Bus Routes: 28/44/N28 & N44 - Wandsworth, Swandon Way (Stop TC)
Primary use: Garaging tour buses

- — WIMBLEDON BUS GARAGE — ZONE 3

Wimbledon Bus Garage on September 19th, 2013 with Big Bus Company Nos **DA206**, **D956** & **DM96** in the yard.

WIMBLEDON (-)
St Martins Way, Summerstown, London SW17 0AR
Operated by: Big Bus Company
Location: TQ26077206 [51.433921, -0.186564]
Nearest Station: Earlsfield (0.7 miles)
Nearest Bus Routes: 44/77/270 & N44 - Burntwood Lane (Stop SD)
Primary use: Garaging tour buses

First London's **Dagenham Bus Garage** on September 18th, 2013 when it was still operating Transport for London Routes Nos 165, 179, 252 and 365. The contract to run these expired nine days later, with Stagecoach taking them over, leaving Dagenham Depot with no TFL services and thus falling out of the criterion for featuring in this book.

INFORMATION UPDATE

Additional Operator in 2014: As and from May 31st, 2014 the contract for Route No.E10 has been awarded to **Tellings Golden Miller** (a subsidiary of Arriva) and this will involve the deployment of 8 new single-decker buses, probably operating out of their **Heathrow Bus Garage**.